Hiking
Maine

A Guide to the State's Greatest Hiking Adventures

Revised Edition

Greg Westrich

FALCONGUIDES

GUILFORD, CONNECTICUT
HELENA, MONTANA

FALCONGUIDES®

An imprint of Rowman & Littlefield
Falcon, FalconGuides, and Outfit Your Mind are registered trademarks of Rowman & Littlefield.

Distributed by NATIONAL BOOK NETWORK

Copyright © 2015 by Rowman & Littlefield
Photos by Greg Westrich
Maps by Alena Joy Pearce © Rowman & Littlefield

British Library Cataloguing-in-Publication Information available

Library of Congress Cataloging-in-Publication Data available

ISBN 978-0-7627-9304-4 (paperback)
ISBN 978-1-4930-1484-2 (ebook)

∞™ The paper used in this publication meets the minimum requirements of American National Standard for Information Sciences—Permanence of Paper for Printed Library Materials, ANSI/NISO Z39.48-1992.

Contents

The Hikes

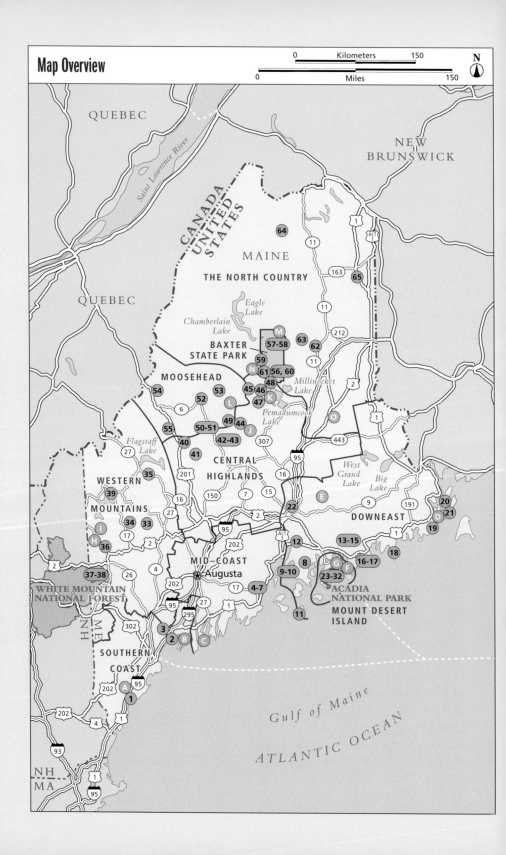

Acknowledgments

This guide would not be possible without the hard work and dedication of the people who work to protect Maine's natural places and build the trails we all love and use. Whether they are individuals like Chris Keene bushwhacking all around the Moosehead region looking for new trails to construct or organizations like the Downeast Coastal Conservancy, we owe them all our gratitude. I own more than a dozen Maine hiking guides and piles of maps. Those guides and maps have helped shape and inform my exploration of Maine; without them this guide would not be as good as it is.

Brian Swartz, and especially David Fitzpatrick, at the *Bangor Daily News* have been a great resource and help. Brian continues to buy and print my stories; David is a great friend and mentor. Thanks, guys.

I owe a special thanks to my wife, Ann, and my two children, Henry and Emma. Without their support and help, this guide would have never happened. They have supported me through all the ups and downs of this project, and my freelancing career in general. Their only payment has been a few hikes with me and getting their pictures in *Hiking Maine*.

Lady Slipper Orchid.

Looking toward Frenchman Bay from Dorr Mountain (hike 24).

Introduction

Maine is best known for its rockbound coast, granite peaks, and endless forest dotted with ponds large and small. The hikes in this guide include plenty of those, but there is much more to Maine. The state comprises half of New England and is the most forested state in the country. Maine is also the least densely populated state east of the Mississippi. That's a lot of wildlands to explore.

Maine's 230-mile coastline is so convoluted and irregular that if you pulled it out straight it would stretch more than 3,500 miles—more than the rest of the Atlantic coast in the United States. And except for extreme southern Maine, there are virtually no sand beaches. The longest stretch of undeveloped coastline in the East is between Cutler, Maine, and the Canadian border.

Mount Katahdin, Maine's highest peak, and Mount Desert Island are glacier-scoured granite plutons, leading many folks to believe the entire state is underlain by granite. Yet granite is the bedrock in less than a third of the state. The center of the state, for example, is a swath of black slate that is still commercially mined around Monson and creates numerous waterfalls and gorges. Granite and slate are both metamorphic rock. Except in the far north, most of Maine's bedrock is metamorphic. Maine's geologic history is tied to Europe's as much as North America's. When the supercontinent Laurasia broke up 180 million years ago, a piece of northern Europe was left behind, attached to North America. That chunk is Maine and Atlantic Canada. For our purposes, however, it was the last ice age that shaped Maine's famous landscape more than the bedrock beneath it.

The glaciers retreated about 12,000 years ago, leaving behind scarred bedrock covered with varying layers of debris. Where the debris was pushed into snake-like piles alongside the glaciers we now have eskers, often called whalesbacks. These narrow ridges tend to run north and south through the southern half of the state, often rising above low, wet areas. Where the debris dropped to the ground as the ice melted, we find erratics, ranging in size from small stones to house-sized boulders. In general the soils in Maine are poor and thin—12,000 years in a cool climate isn't long to build and lay down soil. Many trails have worn right through the soil down to the bedrock. The ice melted irregularly throughout the state; where large islands of ice melted more slowly, they created depressions in the landscape that formed the beds of many of the state's lakes and ponds.

One of the joys of hiking in Maine is reading the natural history of the woods and mountains as you walk along. There is also a human history that can be read in the landscape. Native Americans moved into what is now Maine almost as soon as the ice retreated. Their place names and trails are as much a part of Maine's mystique as its famous coast and granite mountains. Europeans began exploring and settling in Maine in the sixteenth century. The first attempt at a permanent British settlement in the New World wasn't in Virginia or Massachusetts; it was at Popham in southern

A moose feeds in Upper South Branch Pond with The Traveler in the background (hike 57).

Maine. By that time European fishermen had been trading with the natives for some time. They had established a number of seasonal stations on islands where workers processed fish and often traded with Indians. The French explorers, too, spent time sailing the coast, naming features and islands. For example, Mount Desert Island, home of Acadia National Park, was named by Champlain in 1604. On Sommes Sound, near Acadia Mountain, a waterfall drops straight into the sea. French ships stopped here to refill their water casks.

Even in the seemingly untouched North Woods, the effects of humans can be read on the landscape in big and little ways. Ecologists can walk a woods and tell you exactly what was there generations ago by observing the trees and understory. While most of us are not able to do that, it can still be fun to find a crumbling stone wall or foundation deep in the woods, miles from the nearest road or town. More dramatically, you can often find rusting bits of Maine's lumbering past. Up in the Allagash Country there is even an entire locomotive sitting in the woods.

This guide covers all Maine's landforms and regions: from towering sea cliffs topped with spruce to cobbled beaches; from granite mountains to crumbling, volcanic peaks; from bogs to high slate waterfalls. No hiking guide to Maine can be complete, but this guide should get you well under way to discovering all Maine has to offer.

Wildlife

Maine has the greatest concentration of bears of any state, but you are unlikely to see one on a hike. It may be because there's so much habitat for them to roam around in, or because bears are widely hunted in the state. Still, reasonable precautions should be taken, especially with food. Maybe you'll get lucky and see one at a distance.

Many people come to Maine to look for moose; they are rarely disappointed. You are much more likely to see a moose than a bear while hiking. The best places to see them are where their food is. In the summer look in areas with aquatic vegetation; in spring and fall look where there is good hardwood browse. In winter they tend to congregate on south-facing slopes with hardwoods near stands of thick softwoods. But moose do move around—especially bulls—and can be found almost anywhere, even high on rocky mountains. Moose are big animals and enjoy traveling on roads, so be sure to look around as you drive, especially down all twitch trails (aka skidder trails, a rough cut in the woods used to drag logs out to the road where they are loaded on trucks) and little logging roads that intersect your route.

Maine is home to coyotes. Not the small western ones that skulk about, but wolf-like coyotes that hunt deer. They are fairly common, but you are unlikely to see one of these beautiful animals. At night, though, you may be serenaded by their spine-tingling howls.

Male Northern Crescent butterfly.

By weight there are more salamanders in Maine than moose. Which is another way to say that most wildlife isn't big but small. You may not see a bear or moose on a hike, but you will—if you look around—see plenty of wildlife. Dozens of species of amphibians are out there for you to find. It's not uncommon to see a half dozen different kinds of frogs and toads on a hike. Maine also has several kinds of snakes—none poisonous—that often bask in the sun on warm trails.

Maine is also home to numerous weasels and rodents. You are unlikely to see one of the weasels, and it is quite a treat when you see a stoat or fisher. But you would be hard pressed to take a hike free of squirrels. They sit on downfall or in trees, commenting loudly on passing hikers. Beavers are common in Maine's lakes and streams. Their handiwork is easy to find, but seeing one of the shy rodents is less common. They are most active in the twilight of early morning and late evening. Be on the lookout for porcupines. During the day they can often be found sleeping in trees near where they've been feeding.

Maine is a magnet for birders because of the diverse habitats and the presence of northern species not found elsewhere in the United States. Birdsong is a constant presence on hikes, whether it's the chatter of a family of chickadees, the musical song of a hermit thrush, or the eerie wail of a loon. Your ears will find many more birds than your eyes.

Bugs

One theory holds that Maine is so sparsely populated because of the biting insects. They can be quite annoying—even ruin an otherwise great day of hiking. There are blackflies, checker flies, moose flies, no-see-ums, mosquitoes, and, recently, ticks. Blackflies are worst between Mother's Day and Father's Day, but are around all summer. They are only active during the day. Blackfly saliva numbs your skin, so you often aren't aware of all your bites until they start bleeding and itching. Over time their bites seem to cause less swelling and itching, as if the immune system learns to fight back. Even so, when they are at their worst, many Mainers wear a bug net over their head for protection.

Mosquitoes are active day and night, and are most common in cool, damp areas. Which means that unless there's snow on the ground, there is something out there wanting to bite you. Always carry bug dope. Having said that, you will have many bug-free hiking days, especially when it's breezy.

Plant Life

Tourists flock to New England in the fall for the foliage. And it's well worth the trip, but what many people—even native Mainers—miss are the spring colors. When the trees begin to leaf out, the mountainsides are awash in varying shades of green with reds and yellows thrown in. Maybe it's not as dramatic as in the fall, but beautiful just the same. Beneath the trees a profusion of wildflowers rush to bloom before the canopy closes and leaves them in the shade for the summer.

Fungus.

Through the summer, a succession of berries ripens for hikers to snack on. Especially prized are blueberries. Good blueberry spots are noted in this guide. The blueberries usually begin to ripen in mid- to late July; first in the southern part of the state and the lower elevations. When you're suffering through the blackflies early in the summer, remember them later as you are munching on trailside blueberries: Blackflies are an important blueberry pollinator.

In the fall, beneath the vibrant trees, there is an explosion of mushrooms. At least a thousand varieties of fungi are native to Maine. Most of the time they live unobserved within the soil, in rotting vegetation, and on tree roots. But in the fall they bloom: Fungi send up fruiting bodies that release spoors—like tiny seeds—into the air. We call these fruiting bodies mushrooms.

Weather and Seasons

You hear a lot of Mainers say that if you don't like the weather, wait five minutes and it'll change. Of course, that's an exaggeration, but not by much. On any given day the weather across the state can vary widely. In general it's cooler, milder, and breezier along the coast. The Maine coast is among the foggiest places on Earth; don't let that keep you off the trails. Hiking in the fog can be a wonderful experience. In winter, when most of the state is buried under deep snow, you can hike near the coast. You just have to be careful of ice; often the milder weather along the coast leaves trails sheened with ice instead of snow.

Many of the hikes in this book are inaccessible in winter; before you head out, check the individual trail description for access. Hiking in the winter—with or without snowshoes—can be extra work, but is often worth the effort. Maine in winter offers great solitude and beautiful landscapes.

Spring is mud season in Maine. Streams are swollen with snowmelt and trails are often muddy and wet. Swollen streams can be impossible or dangerous to cross; even into summer the water can be bone-chillingly cold. Very few stream crossings are bridged in Maine: The spring freshet would wash them away. When choosing a hike in spring, check the trail description for stream crossings. Still, spring hiking is wonderful. Wildflowers are beginning to emerge, the birds are singing, and there are no bugs yet. You just need to remember that snow lingers longer in the mountains and the north, pushing spring later into the year. For example, the mountains in Baxter State Park are often not open until well into June. Trails that are shaded or get winter use retain their snowpack even when the surrounding woods are clear and dry.

Summer more than triples the population of Maine. There are more summer homes here than in any other state. Most of the tourists and summer people congregate along the coast and in the towns. Most of the hikes never get crowded. Even in Acadia National Park—the second most visited in the country—you can find solitude on a hike most days. It rarely gets hotter than the mid-80s, but you still need to be prepared for hot, dry conditions in the summer. Many water sources, especially on

Killdeer nest at the edge of a field.

the granite landscapes, dry up by the middle of summer. If you're planning to supplement the water you bring on the hike, check the trail description to see if water is available.

Fall can be the best time for hiking: The summer crowds are gone, the weather is cooler, and after the first freeze the bugs are gone. And then there's the fall colors. Most years you can hike right up until around Thanksgiving without having to worry much about snow. It can and does snow as early as late September, though, so bring appropriate clothing and gear.

To be safe, no matter what the season or the weather when you start a hike, assume it will change. Always bring a jacket and raincoat, even on the warmest summer day. In spring and fall it's best to layer, so you can put on and take off layers as needed. Remember: It's best to start out cool; sweat is the enemy. Except in the summer, avoid cotton clothes. Cotton is comfortable, but when it gets wet or sweaty it can be cold, even dangerously so. Adding a few things to your pack just in case may make the climbs a little tougher, but in the long run will make your hikes safer and more comfortable. Maine's weather is not something to complain about; rather it's to be prepared for and then enjoyed in all its various manifestations. The bottom line is that in Maine every season and every kind of weather can make for great hiking.

How to Use This Guide

This guide is divided into nine regions. Each regional section begins with an introduction that gives you an overview of its history and geography. After this general overview, specific hikes within that region are described. You'll learn about what to see and look for on each hike.

To aid in quick decision making, each hike chapter begins with a hike summary. These short summaries give you a taste of the hiking adventure to follow. Next you'll find the quick, nitty-gritty details of the hike: where the trailhead is located, total hike length, approximate hiking time, difficulty rating, type of trail terrain, best hiking season, other trail users you may encounter, whether a fee is required, and trail contacts (for updates on trail conditions). The Finding the trailhead section gives you dependable directions from a nearby town right down to where you'll want to park your car. The hike description is the meat of the chapter, where you'll get a more detailed description of the trail. In Miles and Directions, mileage cues identify all turns and trail name changes, as well as points of interest.

Route maps show all the accessible roads and trails, points of interest, water, towns, landmarks, and geographical features along the hike. They also distinguish trails from roads. The selected route is highlighted, and directional arrows point the way.

Trail Finder

	Back-packers	Swimming	Waterfalls	Geology Lovers	Children	Peak Baggers	Great Views	Solitude	Birders
1. Carson Trail					•				•
2. Wolfe's Neck Woods State Park					•				•
3. Bradbury Mountain					•		•		
4. Mount Megunticook						•	•		
5. Maiden Cliff							•		
6. Fernald's Neck Preserve					•				
7. Ragged Mountain						•			
8. Blue Hill						•	•		
9. John B Mountain					•				
10. Holbrook Island Sanctuary State Park		•			•			•	•
11. Isle au Haut	•						•	•	•
12. Great Pond Mountain						•	•	•	
13. Black Mountain Bald						•	•		
14. Tunk Mountain						•	•		
15. Catherine Mountain					•				
16. Petit Manan		•		•	•				•
17. Pigeon Hill					•		•		
18. Great Wass Island					•				•
19. The Bold Coast	•			•	•		•		
20. Shackford Head State Park					•				
21. Quoddy Head					•				
22. Bangor City Forest and Orono Bog Boardwalk					•				

	Back-packers	Swimming	Waterfalls	Geology Lovers	Children	Peak Baggers	Great Views	Solitude	Birders
23. Cadillac Mountain			•	•		•	•		
24. Dorr Mountain						•	•		
25. Great Head		•			•		•		
26. Pemetic Mountain–North Bubble Loop						•	•		
27. Norumbega Mountain								•	
28. Beech Mountain					•	•			
29. Acadia and St. Sauveur Mountains						•	•		
30. Western Mountain						•	•	•	
31. Ship Harbor Nature Trail				•	•				•
32. Hadlock Falls and Bald Peak			•						
33. Mount Blue									•
34. Tumbledown Mountain						•	•		•
35. The Bigelows	•					•	•		
36. Puzzle Mountain				•		•		•	
37. East Royce Mountain						•	•		
38. Caribou Mountain			•		•	•			
39. Bald Mountain (Oquossoc)					•		•		
40. Moxie Falls			•		•				
41. Moxie Bald	•				•	•		•	
42. Borestone Mountain						•	•		
43. Little Wilson Falls			•	•	•	•	•		
44. Gulf Hagas			•	•					

	Back-packers	Swimming	Waterfalls	Geology Lovers	Children	Peak Baggers	Great Views	Solitude	Birders
45. Nesuntabunt Mountain					•	•	•	•	
46. Debsconeag Backcountry	•		•				•	•	
47. Turtle Ridge		•					•	•	
48. Debsconeag Ice Caves		•		•	•				
49. Laurie's Ledge							•		
50. Big Moose Mountain						•	•		
51. Little Moose Mountain	•				•				
52. Mount Kineo				•	•				
53. Little Spencer Mountain						•	•	•	
54. Boundary Bald						•	•	•	
55. Coburn Mountain						•	•	•	
56. Katahdin				•		•	•		
57. The Traveler				•	•	•	•	•	
58. Howe Brook Falls		•	•		•				
59. Doubletop Mountain						•	•		
60. South Turner Mountain						•	•		
61. Niagara Falls		•	•		•		•		
62. Mount Chase					•	•	•	•	
63. Shin Brook Falls			•						
64. Deboullie Mountain						•	•	•	
65. Quaggy Joe Mountain		•					•		

Map Legend

95	Interstate Highway		✕	Airport
211	US Highway		▬	Bench
176	State Highway		⬗	Boat Launch
	Local Road		⏜	Bridge
	Unpaved Road		▪	Building/Point of Interest
	Gravel Road		⛟	Campground
	Carriage Road		▲	Campsite
	Railroad		⊛	Capital
	Featured Trail		⌒	Cave
	Trail		†	Cemetery
	Ferry		🗼	Lighthouse
‖‖‖‖‖‖	Boardwalk/Steps		⚒	Mine
	Regional Border		🅿	Parking
	State Border		▲	Peak/Summit
	International Border		⊞	Picnic Area
	Small River or Creek		∥	Rapids
	Marsh/Swamp		⊞	Restrooms
	Body of Water		⬓	Scenic View/Viewpoint
	National Forest/Park		⟲	Spring
	National Wilderness/Preserve Area		▯	Tower
	State/County Park		○	Town
	Miscellaneous Area		①	Trailhead
			⋙	Waterfall

Southern Coast

The Southern Coast is a typical coastal plain: long sweeping beaches separated by prominent headlands backed by a relatively flat plain. This geography is typical of much of the Atlantic Coast. In New England, as the Appalachian Mountains bend toward the coast, the coastal plain narrows and almost disappears east of Casco Bay. The Casco Bay region transitions from the sandy beaches in the south to the rockbound coast of the rest of Maine. The transition has less to do with a change in bedrock and more to do with the direction of the

The Carson Trail winding through a pine-oak forest (hike 1).

bedding in relation to the coast. Along the Southern Coast, the bedrock is laid down parallel to the shoreline. At Casco Bay the coast begins to bend to the east, and the bedrock juts out into the ocean.

There are no major rivers in the region, but numerous small streams that flow through lowland woods and salt marshes on their short journeys to the sea. The Mousam River, for example, flows 26 miles from Mousam Lake to the river's mouth in Kennebunkport. Along the way it flows past farms and through woods and salt marsh. There are two dams on the short river, and still it remains surprisingly wild. A hike along its bank in the woods of the Kennebunk Plains (hike A) or an exploration of its mouth at Parsons Beach (see hike 1) can attest to that.

There are few mountains in the region, but a number of promontories have views, such as Mount Agamenticus and Bradbury Mountain (hike 3). Both of these are granite, even though there is little granite along the Southern Coast. There are several places along the Southern Coast where granite has been intruded into gaps in older, usually sedimentary, rock. It makes for some interesting formations; the shore on the east side of Wolfe's Neck (hike 2) is a good example.

The changes in sea level during and after the last ice age left their mark on the Southern Coast. During the ice age the sea level was much lower. But because the ice depressed the bedrock, right after the ice age, the coast was much farther inland than it is today. The ice melted—and raised the sea level—faster than the bedrock rebounded. There are places along the Southern Coast where sand beaches can be found miles inland.

Southern Maine is about 10 percent of the state's area, but has more than a third of its people. The Southern Coast is much more developed than any other part of Maine. Only in Southern Maine are sprawl and disappearing wildlands a serious concern. There are many local land trusts working to keep some of the land wild. Most of the protected tracts are small, with walking paths, not hiking trails. Similarly, the beaches and state parks along the Southern Coast are best suited for day use and recreation, not hiking. Even so, it is surprising how much wildness still exists along the Southern Coast, and how much hiking you can do.

1 Carson Trail

The Carson Trail is a self-guided nature trail that follows the Merriland River and Branch Brook. Along the way you get fine views of the extensive salt marsh along the Little River. Many shore and wading birds can be seen here. What birds are where changes as the land floods twice a day on the rising tide. The trail winds along the edge of the salt marsh in a forest of mature white pines and hemlocks. In late spring look for lady slippers in the woods.

Start: The Carson trailhead at the south end of the parking area
Distance: 1.3-mile lollipop
Hiking time: 1 to 2 hours
Difficulty: Easy
Best seasons: Apr to Oct
Trail surface: Graded woodland path
Land status: Rachel Carson National Wildlife Refuge
Nearest town: Wells

Other trail users: None
Water availability: None
Canine compatibility: Dogs must be on a leash at all times
Fees and permits: None
Maps: *DeLorme: The Maine Atlas and Gazetteer:* map 3; USGS Wells
Trail contact: Rachel Carson National Wildlife Refuge, (207) 646-9226; www.fws.gov/northeast/rachelcarson

Finding the trailhead: From exit 19 on I-95, drive east on ME 9 for 1.6 miles to US 1 in Wells. Turn left onto US 1, heading north, and drive 1.9 miles to Port Road (ME 9). Turn right onto ME 9; there is a sign for the Rachel Carson National Wildlife Refuge. (Do not follow the NWR signs to the Laudholm Division.) Drive 0.7 mile to the refuge entrance. Turn right into the refuge parking area at the large sign. The trailhead is at the south end of the parking area, at the information kiosk.
Trailhead GPS: N43 20.831' / W70 32.898'

The Hike

Kennebunk is at the heart of an arc of the Maine coast made up of sandy beaches, salt marshes, and prominent rounded heads. Between Kittery and Cape Elizabeth, many of the marshes are protected as part of the Rachel Carson National Wildlife Refuge. In Wells, at the refuge's headquarters, is the Carson Trail. This short, easy hike loops along the Merriland River and Branch Brook with views of the surrounding salt marshes and islands of forest. The trail is a self-guided nature trail that explains the importance of salt marsh habitat and the plants and animals that live there.

Along the trail are a number of overlooks. The views from the overlooks change dramatically as the tide ebbs and flows. At low tide the stream channels are low, mud-lined snakes winding through the salt grasses. You can find wading birds feeding there. Often families of ducks paddle along the channels, feeding. In the salt grass there are ponds that are higher than the streams; the water is isolated in bowls until the tide comes in and the water rises to them. These pools attract herons and snowy egrets.

The Little River winds its way through salt marsh to Crescent Surf Beach.

These southern Maine shores are as far north as egrets are found along the Atlantic coast.

The southernmost point on the hike is where the Merriland River and Branch Brook flow together to form the Little River. It really is a little river. From the overlook it is less than 0.5 mile to where the river empties into the ocean. You can see the river's mouth across the waving salt grass. Of course, the river's course is about as indirect as it can be, making the water's journey to the ocean nearly three times as long as it needs to be. Out across the expanse of salt marsh between the trail and Crescent Surf Beach, clouds of snowy egrets move back and forth—seemingly at random. It's not unusual to see osprey and eagles soaring above the salt marsh or winging with purpose to or from their nest.

If you spend all your time looking out across the salt marsh, you'll miss the beauty of the woods the trail passes through. The forest is mature evergreens, mostly white pine and hemlock. In late spring and early summer, look for lady slipper orchids and other wildflowers.

After completing the hike, you may want to visit one of the area's beaches. Try nearby Parsons Beach. To get there, drive east for 1.4 miles on ME 9. Turn right onto Parsons Beach Road. Beach access is at the end of the road. You can swim and play on the beach, as well as explore the mouth of the Mousam River. Much of the lower Mousam River is part of the wildlife refuge. From the mouth of the river, you get to see a salt marsh from the other side.

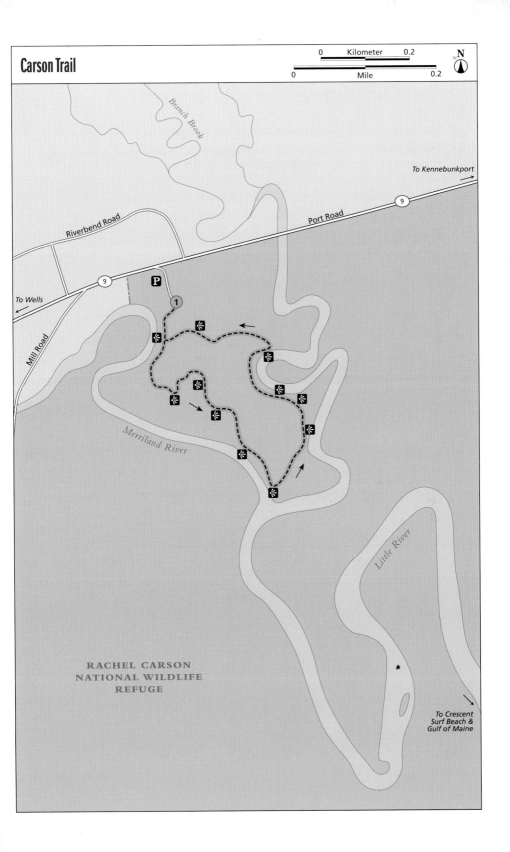

Miles and Directions

0.0 Start from the information kiosk at the south end of the parking area.

0.1 Stay right at the fork.

0.2 The trail follows along the Merriland River to the first overlook.

0.6 The trail follows the Merriland River to an overlook at the confluence with Branch Brook. From here the combined stream, the Little River, meanders to the ocean through a salt marsh.

0.7 The trail follows Branch Brook to an overlook of an extensive salt marsh.

1.0 Continue to follow Branch Brook, passing two overlooks, before turning inland.

1.2 Arrive back at the fork in the trail. Turn right to return to the trailhead.

1.3 Arrive back at the trailhead.

2 Wolfe's Neck Woods State Park

This easy hike loops along the shore of Casco Bay past Googins Island and its osprey nest. The shore of the bay is made up of interesting and varied bedrock that changes in character with the changing tide. The shore of the Harraseeket River—actually a long, narrow bay—is a high bluff with several rocky overlooks. The forest in between is oak-pine and hemlock; in each you will find many mature trees.

Start: The White Pines trailhead on the north side of the parking area, near the restrooms
Distance: 2.6-mile loop
Hiking time: 2 to 4 hours
Difficulty: Easy
Best seasons: May to Oct
Trail surface: Woodland path
Land status: Wolfe's Neck Woods State Park
Nearest town: Freeport
Other trail users: None

Water availability: Spigot next to restrooms near the trailhead
Canine compatibility: Dogs must be under control at all times
Fees and permits: State park entrance fee
Maps: *DeLorme: The Maine Atlas and Gazetteer:* map 6; USGS Freeport
Trail contact: Wolfe's Neck Woods State Park, (207) 865-4465; www.maine.gov/wolfesneckwoods

Finding the trailhead: From exit 22 on I-295, drive east on ME 125 for 0.5 mile into Freeport. Turn right onto US 1 and drive 0.2 mile to Bow Street. There is a very small sign at the intersection directing you toward Wolfe's Neck Woods State Park. Turn left onto Bow Street and drive 1.5 miles to a fork in the road. Bear right at the fork; there is a sign for the park at the fork. Drive 0.9 mile to Wolf Neck Road; there is a sign for the park at the intersection. Turn right onto Wolf Neck Road and drive 2.1 miles to the state park entrance. Turn left into Wolfe's Neck Woods State Park and drive 0.5 mile to the end of the road. The trailhead is on the north side of the parking area next to the restrooms.
Trailhead GPS: N43 49.339' / W70 04.988'

The Hike

For a mile or so, through Freeport, US 1 is a long string of shops, outlets, and restaurants. The sidewalks are crowded with window shoppers and kids eating ice cream cones. Traffic moves at a crawl, as pedestrians overflow the sidewalks or jaywalk between destinations. Anchoring all this chaos is the LL Bean store. Actually, calling it a store doesn't do it justice. It is a campus. Several retail buildings with spaces for demonstrations and presentations take up an entire block. Some summer days it feels like there are more people in the town of Freeport than in some of Maine's northern counties.

Down a side street, just minutes from the crowds in downtown Freeport, Wolfe's Neck Woods State Park offers quiet hiking along Casco Bay and the Harraseeket River. Wolfe's Neck was named for the family that first settled the area in 1733. The

The narrow channel between Googin's Island and Wolfe's Neck at high tide.

name is variously spelled: Wolfe, Wolf, Woolfe. For example, the state park and the road to the park spell the name differently.

The hike loops around the outside of the park, maximizing the amount of time you spend on the shore. The bedrock along the shore is mostly sedimentary rock that was folded and contorted by tectonic movement. During the folding, granite was injected into the gaps that were created. The result is a shoreline of rock with varied and interesting textures and colors. The same spot along the shore often looks quite different at high tide than at low tide because different rock is exposed.

Along the Casco Bay Trail, there are several places where steps lead you out onto the rocky shore. One of the first of these is opposite Googins Island. At low tide you can almost walk onto the island, a small lozenge of close-growing evergreens. The island contains one of Wolfe Neck Woods' osprey nests. You can sit on the shore and watch the osprey come and go, bringing fish for their nestlings. Between parental stops, you can sit and look out across Casco Bay while the chicks squawk to be fed again. You can't see Portland from the park—a line of islands between Yarmouth and Harpswell bisects the bay—but the view is varied and interesting.

Where the Casco Bay Trail becomes the Harraseeket Trail, the hike turns inland and crosses the wooded neck to the Harraseeket River. Along the way you pass several trails that can be used to make shorter loops. The trail passes through mature forest dominated by large hemlocks. Along the shore the forest is oak-pine with many large white pines. Just the small change in elevation and rockying of the soil changed the forest type.

The trail reaches the river atop a high bluff. The Harraseeket River is actually a long, narrow bay that two small streams empty into at its head. The topography here

IN ADDITION: LISTENING TO BLUE JAYS

In the summer, groups of blue jays move noisily through the woods, letting everyone know where they are and where possible dangers may exist. Their calls are varied and expressive. It's easy to imagine they actually speak a language to each other. Sometimes the only way to know that what you're hearing is a blue jay is by eliminating all other possibilities. They are not mimics like the starlings, although they sometimes do imitations: There is a group of blue jays in the woods near my house that likes to scare my family's chickens by imitating hawks.

One warm summer morning I was out hanging laundry on the line. The breeze in the trees and the birds nearby were just background sounds, until the blue jays broke through my domestic reverie. They were a couple of hundred feet away, up in the trees at the edge of the woods, calling especially loudly and frantically. I hung a shirt on the line, and then walked up the path through the high, brown grasses and goldenrod. Scraggly young apple trees blended into maples and popples where the path turned to the left. Looking up into the swaying tree-tops, I saw the jays, 40 feet up, swooping and jumping between two maple trees, making their ruckus. My eyes naturally followed the birds back and forth; there were maybe six or seven of them. After a moment I realized that there was a point at the center of their attention—the trunk of one of the trees. And there, hanging on, its dark tail straight down, was a large fisher.

The fisher hung there, moving its head back and forth as the jays swooped past. Its fur was dark, almost black, and it measured 3 feet from its black nose to the tip of its long, luxuriant tail. Like all weasels the fisher was long and lean, capable of moving in snake-like undulations. But unlike most weasels, it was as big as a raccoon, with long claws. Fishers will eat eggs and baby birds, but by the middle of summer the baby jays would've already fledged. This attack was more out of principle than necessity.

After a few minutes of staring straight up with my mouth open, I ran back to the house to get my wife and kids. As we returned up the path, the woods were quiet. The jays were gone, as was the fisher. We stood, looking up at the morning light dancing on the maple leaves. If I hadn't paid attention to the blue jays, I never would have seen the fisher. I returned to the clothesline and continued my ritual of hanging clothes to dry in the warm sun, having learned an important lesson. When the blue jays speak, listen. More generally, when hiking, the best way to see wildlife or find something surprising and unusual is to listen to the woods with all your senses.

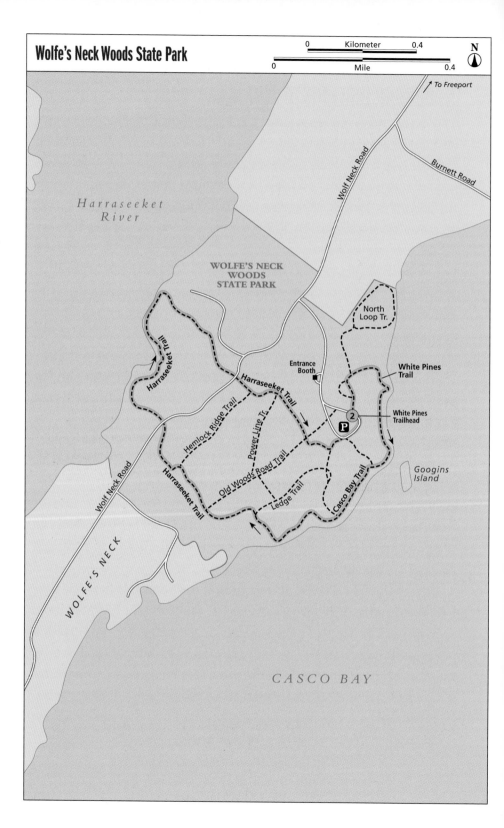

Wolfe's Neck Woods State Park

0   Kilometer   0.4
0   Mile   0.4

N

To Freeport

Wolf Neck Road

Burnett Road

Harraseeket River

WOLFE'S NECK WOODS STATE PARK

North Loop Tr.

Entrance Booth

Harraseeket Trail

White Pines Trail

Harraseeket Trail

White Pines Trailhead

Hemlock Ridge Trail

Power Line Tr.

P

2

Wolf Neck Road

Harraseeket Trail

Old Woods Road Trail

Googins Island

WOLFE'S NECK

Ledge Trail

Casco Bay Trail

CASCO BAY

is like that of the Mid-Coast: long, narrow peninsulas and islands with bays between them, a function of the folding of the sedimentary rock you saw along the Casco Bay Trail. Wolfe's Neck is one of the smaller peninsulas and is situated along the coast, rather than sticking out into the Gulf of Maine.

The trail follows along the Harraseeket River with several rocky overlooks, but no easy water access. Below the bluff you hike along, the shore is a tidal mudflat. Not great for exploring anyway. It is, though, a good place to find shorebirds feeding on the changing tide. The shore along the Harraseeket River is completely different from that along Casco Bay on the other side of Wolfe's Neck. The difference is a result of the folded bedding of the sedimentary bedrock. Along the river the bedding is soft sedimentary rock that has broken apart, creating high bluffs of loose and crumbly rock.

As you hike back from the river to the parking area, be sure to look for lady slipper orchids and blueberries. They can be found in late spring and midsummer, respectively, throughout the woods here, especially on the high, dry sections in the oak-pine forest.

Miles and Directions

0.0 Start from the White Pines trailhead at the north end of the parking area, next to the restrooms.

0.1 Pass the North Loop Trail.

0.2 The White Pines Trail reaches the shore of Casco Bay.

0.4 The White Pines Trail ends at the Casco Bay Trail. To the right is a short walk back to the parking area; to the left are steps down to the shore. Opposite the shore at this point, across a narrow channel, is Googins Island. On this small island is an osprey's nest. Continue straight ahead on the Casco Bay Trail.

0.5 Pass a trail on the right that leads back to the parking area.

0.7 Pass another trail that leads back to the parking area. There is shore access on the left.

0.9 The Casco Bay Trail ends at the Harrasseeket Trail. To the left are stairs down to the shore. This is the last shore access on Casco Bay. Turn right onto the Harrasseeket Trail.

1.1 Pass the Ledge Trail. This trail can be used to make the shortest loop back to the parking area.

1.2 Pass the Old Woods Road Trail. This trail, too, can be used to make a shorter loop back to the parking area.

1.3 Pass the Hemlock Ridge Trail. This trail can also be used to make a shorter loop back to the parking area.

1.6 The Harrasseeket Trail reaches a high bluff above the Harrasseeket River.

2.0 The trail follows along the shore of the river and then turns away, heading back toward the parking area.

2.6 Follow the Harrasseeket Trail back to the parking area, passing several trails along the way. The trail ends at the southeast corner of the parking area.

3 Bradbury Mountain

Bradbury Mountain State Park is crisscrossed with more than 20 miles of trails. Most of the trails are open to hikers, horses, mountain bikers, and cross-country skiers in the winter. The Summit Trail up to the open granite summit is one of the few hiker-only trails. The summit offers fine views east across the flat coastal plain to the ocean. The descent off the mountain follows two of the other hiker-only trails through mature forest that has grown up on former farm land.

Start: The Summit trailhead at the northwest corner of the parking area, near the playground
Distance: 1.2-mile loop
Hiking time: 1 to 2 hours
Difficulty: Easy
Best seasons: May to Oct; park open year-round
Trail surface: Woodland path
Land status: Bradbury Mountain State Park
Nearest town: Freeport

Other trail users: Many trails open to mountain biking and skiing in the winter
Water availability: Spigot near the trailhead
Canine compatibility: Dogs must be under control at all times
Fees and permits: State park entrance fee
Maps: DeLorme: The Maine Atlas and Gazetteer: maps 5 and 6; USGS Freeport
Trail contact: Bradbury Mountain State Park, (207) 688-4712; www.bradburymountain.com or http://maine.gov/bradburymountain.

Finding the trailhead: From exit 22 on I-295, drive north on ME 125 for 0.2 mile. Turn left onto Durham Road at the sign for Bradbury Mountain State Park. Drive 4.6 miles to ME 9 in Pownal Center. Turn right onto ME 9; there is a sign for the state park at the intersection. Drive 0.5 mile to the state park entrance. Turn left into Bradbury Mountain State Park. Past the entrance gate, turn right into the parking area. The trailhead is at the northwest corner of the parking area, near the playground.
Trailhead GPS: N43 54.014'/W70 10.793'

The Hike

In Britain there is an official definition of a mountain. To be called a mountain, a landform has to be more than 2,000 feet high or stand out from the surrounding country by more than 500 feet. In the United States there used to be a similar definition, but it has fallen out of use. It's almost too bad. If we still had to come up with other designations for less lofty landforms, we could use more descriptive names. Bradbury Mountain, for example, is only 485 feet high. Not a mountain by either definition. In Britain it would have to be called something else. "Hill" doesn't quite capture the exposed granite summit that juts east toward the coast. Maybe it could be called Bradbury Brow. That accurately captures the nature of the landform. It has a rocky summit that offers views in only one direction and slopes gently down on the other, western, side.

A young hiker looks out across the coastal plain from Bradbury Mountain's summit.

Whatever we call it, Bradbury Mountain is a short, steep climb to a fine view. The state park has about 20 miles of trails that snake around and over Bradbury Mountain. Most trails are open to hikers, horses, mountain bikers, and cross-country skiers in the winter. A few of the trails are hiker-only; this hike traverses three of the four hiker-only trails. Five trails converge on the summit of Bradbury Mountain; you ascend the Summit Trail, the only one that is hiker only. The descent is on the Bluff and Terrace Trails, which are also hiker only. After this short hike you may want to explore the South Ridge Trail, the other hiker-only trail with views to the south. Or you can hike along any of the multiuse trails that wander the woods of the state park. In general the west-side trails—that include Bradbury Mountain—are better suited for hiking than the east-side trails. Throughout the park, trail junctions are well marked and the official park map is accurate, so you can wander the trails without having to worry about getting lost.

The area around Bradbury Mountain has not always been the recreational mecca that it is today. As you hike, you pass several old stone walls that crisscross the wooded hillside—a reminder that this land was once cleared for pasture and farming. A further reminder can be found near the end of the hike along the Northern Loop Trail: an old stone cattle pound.

There is also the remains of a small feldspar quarry along the Northern Loop Trail. Feldspar is the most common mineral found in granite. Bradbury Mountain is mostly granite and related pegmatite. The feldspar crystals in pegmatite get fairly large and therefore quarryable. Small-scale mining operations like the one here were common

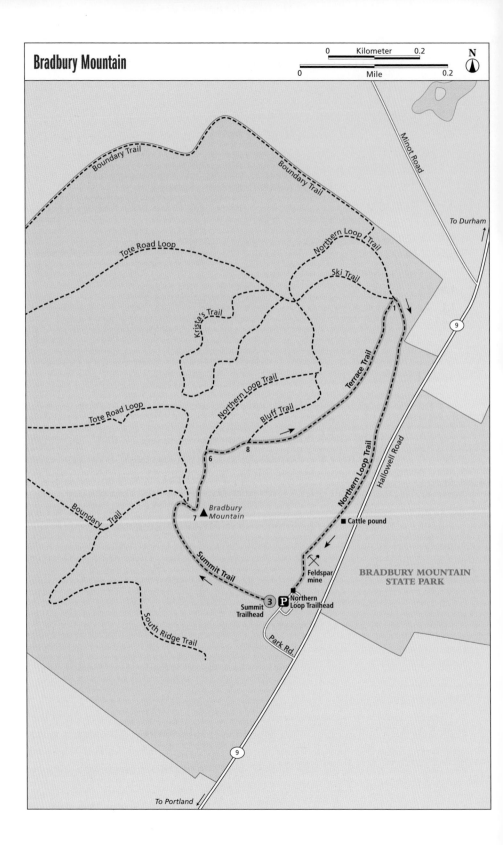

in southern Maine until the middle of the last century. The feldspar was ground up and used as an abrasive and in ceramics.

Miles and Directions

0.0 Start from the Summit trailhead at the northwest corner of the parking area, near the playground.

0.2 The hiker-only trail climbs steadily to the open summit with views south and east. Continue across the summit onto the multiuse Northern Loop Trail.

0.3 Arrive at Junction 7. Pass the Tote Road Trail and the Switchback Trail. Continue to Junction 6. Turn right onto the hiker-only Bluff Trail.

0.4 Arrive at Junction 8. Turn right onto the hiker-only Terrace Trail.

0.7 The Terrace Trail descends gently to end at the multiuse Northern Loop Trail at Junction 1. Turn right onto the Northern Loop Trail.

1.0 The trail passes an old stone cattle pound.

1.1 The trail passes an abandoned feldspar mine.

1.2 Arrive at the east end of the parking area.

Honorable Mentions

A Kennebunk Plains

The grasslands of the Kennebunk Plains are among the rarest and most endangered habitat type in Maine. The plain was formed about 14,000 years ago when streams flowing out of the receding glaciers left a landscape that won't support trees and is subject to frequent droughts and fires. For a time the Kennebunk Plains was used as a commercial blueberry barrens. Enough blueberry bushes survive to make a late summer hike a snacking opportunity. The Kennebunk Plains supports Maine's only population of northern blazing star, and the largest concentration of the wildflower anywhere in the world. The northern blazing star turns the plains purple in August. The trails through and around Kennebunk Plains are mostly what remains of the roads used by blueberry growers. The sandy trails are open to hikers and bikers. An easy 2-mile loop circles the grassland on the northern section of the preserve. You can extend the hike by including the outer loop, which goes through the forest along the Mousam River. To find the preserve, take exit 25 off I-95 in Kennebunk. Drive west on Alfred Road 1 mile into the village of West Kennebunk. Turn left at the Stop sign onto Mill Street. At the intersection there is a sign directing you to ME 99 and Sandford. Drive 0.7 mile on Mill Street, crossing the Mousam River, to ME 99. Turn right onto ME 99 and drive 2.1 miles to the Kennebunk Plains Preserve. The unmarked parking area is on the right side of the road. For more information contact The Kennebunk Plains Preserve, http://nature.org/maine/kennebunkplains.

B Harpswell

The Harpswell Heritage Land Trust and the town of Harpswell have twenty-four small preserves, many with trails. The town consists of Harpswell Neck and numerous small and large islands. The bedrock is almost entirely sedimentary layers stood on end with granite intrusions in the gaps created by the geological forces that upended the bedding. As a result Harpswell Neck and the islands around it are all long and narrow, jutting far out into the Gulf of Maine. Soils are thin, supporting evergreen forests down to the shore. Many of the inlets and reaches are so shallow that they become mudflats at low tide. The longest hike in Harpswell is the Cliff Trail, which begins behind the town hall and follows Strawberry Creek—a tidal inlet—to its head, then cuts across Long Reach Mountain to high cliffs overlooking Long Reach. The trail is an easy 2.2-mile loop. Across Long Reach is the Long Reach Preserve; its trails offer access to Long Reach and views of the 150-foot cliffs that the Cliff Trail tops. On Orrs Island the Devil's Back Preserve has an easy 1.3-mile loop trail that hugs the shore of Long Cove. All three hikes offer good wildlife viewing opportunities, especially for waterbirds, eagles, and osprey. To find the trailheads, ME 123 runs from

Brunswick south down Harpswell Neck. ME 24, which passes through Brunswick, extends down Sebascodegan, Orrs, and Baileys Islands. The Cliff Trail begins behind the Harpswell Town Hall on Mountain Road, 0.6 mile east of ME 123 and 0.2 mile west of ME 24. The Long Reach Preserve is on ME 24, 1.3 miles north of Mountain Road. The Devil's Back Preserve is on ME 24, 1.1 miles south of Mountain Road. For more information contact Harpswell Heritage Land Trust, (207) 721-1121; http://hhltmaine.org.

Mid-Coast

Maine's Mid-Coast is one of the most convoluted coastlines in the United States. Hundreds of miles of shoreline are packed into a compact arch of coast between the mouths of the Kennebec and Penobscot Rivers. The region is characterized by long, narrow peninsulas and islands bounded by equally narrow bays—often called rivers. This landscape is a result of the underlying bedrock. The Mid-Coast's bedrock is mostly deformed

Lake Megunticook is nestled in the valley between Mount Megunticook and Bald Mountain (hike 4).

sedimentary rock—especially shales—that have been folded and stacked on end, per-pendicular to the coastline. The dips in the bedding form the bays; the high points the peninsulas. The tectonic action that deformed and metamorphosed some of the Mid-Coast's bedrock also injected other minerals, such as granite, into the gaps. The result is a coastline that is interesting and varied.

There are a number of sand beaches—at Reid and Popham Beach State Parks, for example—where tidal action has sorted the beach debris and deposited large amounts of sand. Popham has the distinction of being the site of the earliest attempt by the British at a permanent settlement in North America. The settlement was abandoned when they realized how harsh the winters were. Later the Mid-Coast was settled by fiercely independent folks who named their towns not after where they came from or famous people, but after ideals like Freedom, Unity, Hope, Union, and Liberty. The ancestors of those settlers live quiet, rural lives inland from a coastline characterized by quaint towns that cater to well-heeled tourists.

Where the coastline bends north to form the western side of Penobscot Bay, the shore becomes less convoluted. Just as with the Southern Coast, this is because the bedrock is parallel to the coastline. Behind the coast from Rockland to Belfast are low, rugged mountains. Even though many of the coastal towns of Penobscot Bay were built around quarrying granite, these mountains are not granite. The only granite in the region is around Mount Waldo, northeast of the Camden Hills and much farther inland. The granite that made the Mid-Coast rich was quarried from the islands on the east side of Penobscot Bay. You can tell which islands are granite and which are not by looking at a map: The round islands are granite; the elongated or irregular islands are not.

The Camden Hills, and the other mountains of the region, are close to the coast, offering fine views from their rocky flanks and summits. Camden Hills State Park contains many of these mountains (hikes 5, 6, and C), but just as many are scattered south and west along the coast. The town of Camden owns a small ski area on the northeast flank of Ragged Mountain (hike 7) that is the only ski resort in the country with a view of the Atlantic coast.

4 Mount Megunticook

Mount Megunticook is the highest of the Camden Hills. The hike to Ocean Lookout on the Mount Megunticook Trail climbs over metamorphic sedimentary rock through a hardwood forest that comes alive with color in the fall. From Ocean Lookout the hike follows the Ridge Trail through a spruce forest to the wooded summit. On the return to the trailhead, you cross Adam's Lookout as you descend the mountain. There are several different trails up Mount Megunticook, and you can extend your hike to include them to reach other mountains such as Mount Battie and Maiden Cliff.

Start: The north end of the hiker's parking area

Distance: 3.7 miles out and back

Hiking time: 2 to 4 hours

Difficulty: Moderate

Best seasons: May 15 to Oct 15

Trail surface: Woodland path

Land status: Camden Hills State Park

Nearest town: Camden

Other trail users: None

Water availability: In the campground and a small stream at mile 1.0

Canine compatibility: Dogs must be on a leash at all times

Fees and permits: State park entrance fee

Maps: *DeLorme: The Maine Atlas and Gazetteer:* map 14; USGS Camden

Trail contact: Camden Hills State Park, (207) 236-3109; www.maine.gov/dacf/parks

Finding the trailhead: From the junction of US 1 and ME 52 (Mountain Road) in Camden, drive north on US 1 for 1.6 miles. Turn left into the Camden Hills State Park entrance. Before the entrance gate turn left into the hiker's parking area. The trailhead is 0.2 mile up the road in the campground. Pay your entrance fee at the gate and walk into the campground. Stay straight ahead through the campground. The trailhead is on the left; there is a sign for Mount Megunticook. **Trailhead GPS:** N44 13.934' / W69 03.170'

The Hike

Mount Megunticook, at 1,385 feet, is the highest of the Camden Hills. Its summit ridge runs northwest to southeast from Maiden Cliff to Ocean Lookout. This hike climbs to Ocean Lookout and on to the wooded summit. The mountain's name is a corruption of the Native American name for Camden Harbor and roughly means "big mountain harbor." There are several hiking routes up the mountain. This hike uses the shortest and most direct, although not the busiest. Many visitors to the Camden Hills drive to the top of Mount Battie, which is between Mount Megunticook and Camden. The road to its summit is clearly visible from Ocean Lookout. Two trails leave this road and climb Mount Megunticook. There is also an old carriage road that leaves ME 52 in Camden, 1.4 miles north of US 1. This trail is the least direct way to the summit, but is popular with local hikers. Maiden Cliff and Ocean Lookout are connected by the Ridge Trail. From the summit of Mount Megunticook to Maiden

Cliff is 2.1 miles along the Tablelands Trail. There are many ways to combine this hike with climbs of other mountains in the western park of Camden Hills State Park. Once you hike away from Ocean Lookout, you are unlikely to see another hiker, even on a sunny summer day.

The Camden Hills are knobs of very hard metamorphic rock. The tectonic action that resulted in the volcanic eruptions that created much of the Downeast coastal bedrock ground the sand and gravel on the continental shelf into very hard, weather-resistant rock. As you hike up the Mount Megunticook Trail, notice how many different colors and textures of rock there are. Unlike the rather uniform granites of Mount Desert Island, the bedrock on Mount Megunticook reflects the diversity of the rock that was metamorphosed into these hills. Their hardness allowed them to resist the grinding of the glaciers, leaving rounded, rocky mountains. Much of the bedrock is gray, but you can find areas that are clearly made of gravel—the different rocks and gravels that made up the rock still visible even though they are all fused together—and areas of purple rock.

Penobscot Bay from Ocean Lookout.

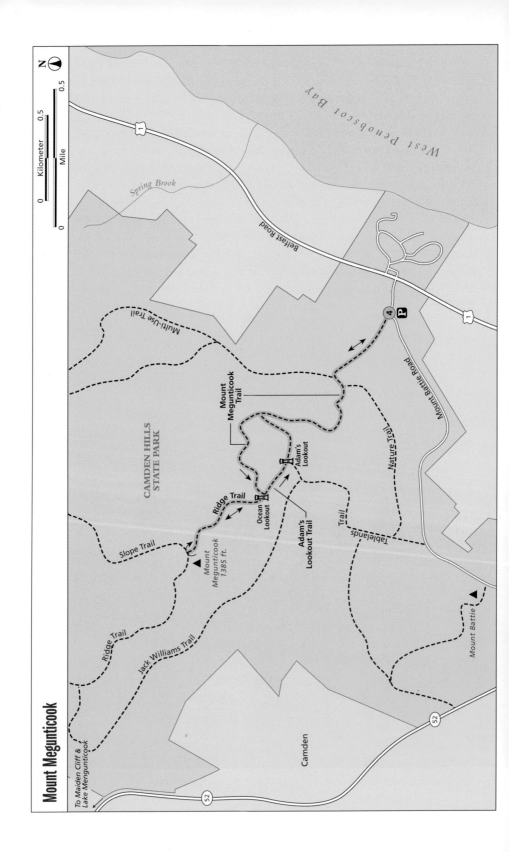

Mount Megunticook

N

Kilometer
0   0.5

Mile
0   0.5

West Penobscot Bay

Spring Brook

Belfast Road

Multi-Use Trail

CAMDEN HILLS
STATE PARK

Mount
Megunticook
Trail

Ridge Trail

Slope Trail

Mount
Megunticook
1385 ft.

Ocean
Lookout

Adam's
Lookout

Adam's
Lookout Trail

Tablelands
Trail

Nature Trail

Mount Battie Road

Ridge Trail

Jack Williams Trail

To Maiden Cliff &
Lake Menguticook

Camden

Mount Battie

4

P

The hike climbs through a hardwood forest that is alive with color in the fall, making it one of the best fall hikes in the state. Above Ocean Lookout, the Ridge Trail passes through a spruce forest. The hike to the summit is well worth the effort—even though there are no views to be had—just to walk through this quiet green woods. Along the way, be sure to look for lady slipper orchids and other wildflowers that like acidic soils.

From Ocean Lookout you can see the coast from Owl's Head to Castine. Penobscot Bay is dotted with islands; the two long, irregular islands of North Haven and Vinalhaven are in the foreground. Inland, the hills and mountains around Lake Megunticook march down the coast. Northern goshawks can often be seen soaring along the cliffs, above the forest below the lookout.

The hike follows the Ridge Trail down along the edge of the cliffs to the Adam's Lookout Trail. Continuing down would eventually take you across Mount Battie and on into Camden. This hike follows the Adam's Lookout Trail east to the Mount Megunticook Trail. The open area that the trail crosses is not really Adam's Lookout. An abandoned trail leaves the west end of this open area and follows the open rock to the actual lookout with views much the same as Ocean Lookout.

Miles and Directions

0.0 Begin at the north end of the hiker's parking area.

0.2 Walk up the park road into the campground, stopping to pay the entrance fee at the gate. Stay straight ahead through the campground to the Multi-Use Trail on the left.

0.3 Turn left onto the Mount Megunticook Trail.

0.9 Mount Megunticook Trail climbs, then turns east to junction with the Adam's Lookout Trail. Continue straight on the Mount Megunticook Trail.

1.4 The trail climbs on rock slabs beside a small stream, then turns south away from the stream. The trail comes out onto the open ledges known as Ocean Lookout, where the Mount Megunticook Trail ends at the Ridge Trail.

1.9 From Ocean Lookout to reach Mount Megunticook's summit, hike north on the Ridge Trail. The trail winds through a spruce forest. Just before the summit, which is marked with a large cairn, is the junction with the Slope Trail. (**Option:** You can hike another 2.1 miles from here to Maiden Cliff.) To continue the hike, retrace your steps back to Ocean Lookout.

2.4 Arrive back at Ocean Lookout.

2.5 Continue south on the Ridge Trail, descending along the cliff edge. Arrive at the junction with the Adam's Lookout Trail. Turn left onto Adam's Lookout Trail.

2.6 Arrive at Adam's Lookout.

2.8 Arrive back at the Mount Megunticook Trail. Turn right to retrace your steps back to the trailhead and hiker's parking area.

3.7 Arrive back at the hiker's parking area.

5 Maiden Cliff

The Maiden Cliff Trail climbs steeply up to the cliffs. Maiden Cliff offers fine views west across Lake Megunticook of the mountains to the west. To the south, across Camden, the islands of Penobscot Bay march to the horizon. The hike continues to the top of Millerite Ridge with views in every direction.

Start: From the Maiden Cliff trailhead at the north end of the parking area
Distance: 2.1-mile lollipop
Hiking time: About 2 hours
Difficulty: Moderate
Best seasons: May to Oct
Trail surface: Woodland path
Land status: Town of Camden parkland
Nearest town: Camden
Other trail users: None

Water availability: Small stream at miles 0.3 and 1.7
Canine compatibility: Dogs must be under control at all times
Fees and permits: None
Maps: *DeLorme: The Maine Atlas and Gazetteer:* map 14; USGS Lincolnville
Trail contact: Camden Hills State Park, (207) 236-3109; www.maine.gov/dacf/parks

Finding the trailhead: From the junction of US 1 and ME 52 (Mountain Street) in Camden, drive north on ME 52 for 2.9 miles. The trailhead parking is on the right just past the sign for the Lake Megunticook Beach and Maiden Cliff. The trailhead is at the north end of the parking area. **Trailhead GPS:** N44 14.839' / W69 05.272'

The Hike

Maiden Cliff is an escarpment overlooking Lake Megunticook with views out across Camden of Penobscot Bay. The cliff was named for 12-year-old Elenora French, who fell 300 feet from the cliff during an 1860s outing and was killed. As the group stopped to enjoy the view from the cliffs on their way to Mount Megunticook, the group leader wanted to find a boulder to roll off the cliff to demonstrate its height. As Elenora and the others waited, her hat blew off in the wind. She fell trying to retrieve it. A cross was erected on the spot in her memory. The cross was later destroyed by wind, but was replaced with the current steel one in 1992.

Maiden Cliff is on the north ridge of Mount Megunticook, known as Millerite Ridge. It was named for the religious sect that came to believe Jesus's Second Coming would be on October 22, 1844. As many as 100,000 believers, mostly from Upstate New York and New England, had sold or given away their belongings, left their crops unharvested and affairs unattended. On the date they believed the Second Coming would occur, Millerites around the country went to hilltops to await the Rapture. The Millerites from Mid-Coast Maine made their way up the north ridge of Mount Megunticook and waited on the open ridgetop. Jesus did not return that day, and the

Lake Megunticook from Maiden Cliff.

Millerites had to descend the next morning and try to put their lives back together. This event was big news in Camden and across the country, so the ridge came to bear their name.

The hike up to the cliff and the ridgetop begins across ME 52 from the public beach at the south end of Lake Megunticook. The trail climbs alongside a small brook that tumbles down the mountainside. Beyond the junction with the Ridge Trail, the Maiden Cliff Trail climbs north, switchbacking up to the cliffs. The cross is at the south end of the cliff, at the point with the most exposure. The cliff runs a distance to the north with a cleft in it. Rough trails run along the cliff top, through the stunted oak trees, allowing you to explore the cliff. Most cliffs in the Camden Hills, like Maiden Cliff, run north–south. From Maiden Cliff, Bald Mountain, across Lake Megunticook, appears to be just a rounded tree-covered hill. It is its east face that is bare rock. Similarly, Ragged Mountain, beyond Bald Mountain, shows a plain green face. Its eastern face is nearly vertical bare rock. All these mountains were shaped the same way by the glaciers of the last ice age.

The Scenic Trail climbs Millerite Ridge from Maiden Cliff, leaving the oaks and entering a maple forest. The open ridgetop offers views in every direction. To the east you can see the open ledge called Zeke's Lookout and the rolling green Camden Hills beyond. Look for blueberries along the trail in late summer.

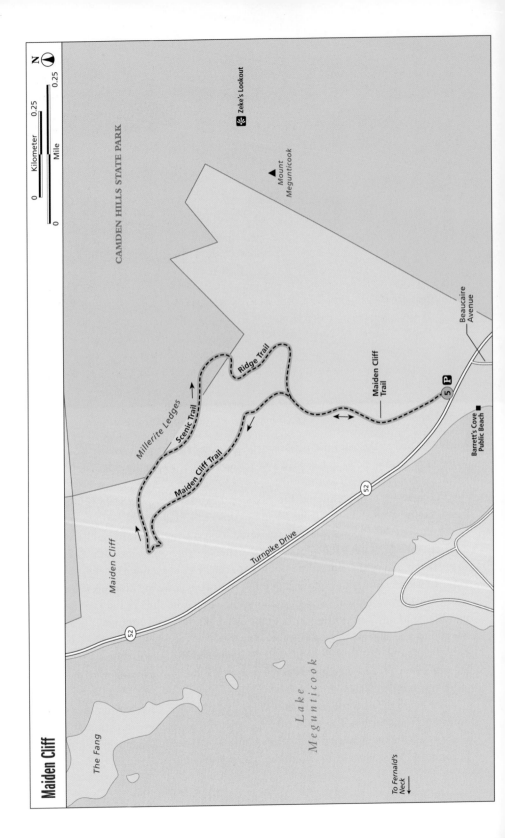

Maiden Cliff

The Fang

Lake
Megunticook

To Fernald's
Neck

52

Turnpike Drive

52

Maiden Cliff

Millerite Ledges

Scenic Trail

Ridge Trail

Maiden Cliff Trail

Maiden Cliff
Trail

CAMDEN HILLS STATE PARK

Zeke's Lookout

Mount
Megunticook

5 P

Barrett's Cove
Public Beach

Beaucaire
Avenue

N

Kilometer
0   0.25

Mile
0   0.25

The Scenic Trail drops off the rocky ridge to a flat area where it ends at the Ridge Trail. This trail follows the ridgetop southeast to the summit of Mount Megunticook. You can also use it to reach Zeke's Trail, which leads to Zeke's Lookout and farther east across the Camden Hills. The hike turns right, and after one last open view to the west, descends steeply down to the unnamed brook you followed at the beginning of the hike. The brook must be spring fed, because even high on the ridge it runs all summer. Just below the brook the Ridge Trail ends at the Maiden Cliff Trail.

Miles and Directions

0.0 Start from the Maiden Cliff trailhead at the north end of the parking area.

0.4 The trail climbs along a stream. After crossing the stream the trail climbs to the junction with the Ridge Trail. You will come down this trail at the end of the hike. Turn left and continue on the Maiden Cliff Trail.

0.9 The Maiden Cliff Trail switchbacks up the ridge and then around to junction with the Scenic Trail. Turn left and hike a short distance out to the top of Maiden Cliff, staying to the left.

1.0 Several unmarked trails wind along the top of the cliffs; they all connect back to the junction of the Maiden Cliff and Scenic Trails.

1.1 Arrive back at the junction. Go straight ahead, east, onto the Scenic Trail.

1.2 The Scenic Trail climbs steeply to the open top of Millerite Ridge with fine views west and south.

1.5 The Scenic Trail crosses the open ridge, then drops down into the woods to end at the Ridge Trail. If you go straight 1.5 miles on the Ridge Trail, you will reach Mount Megunticook; you can also use this trail to climb Zeke's Lookout, visible on the ridge to the east, in 1.3 miles. The hike turns right and follows the Ridge Trail west, dropping off the ridge.

1.7 After passing the stream, the Ridge Trail ends at the Maiden Cliff Trail. Turn left and descend to the trailhead.

2.1 Arrive back at the trailhead.

6 Fernald's Neck Preserve

The mostly flat hike around Fernald's Neck offers fine views of Lake Megunticook and opportunities for swimming. The lake is surrounded by mountains, most notably the Camden Hills to the east. Maiden Cliff rises dramatically across the lake from the hike, visible from several viewpoints. The hike is through a forest of mostly old-growth white and red pine and hemlock, and passes the huge boulder known as Balance Rock. Even though this is a popular preserve, you can still have real solitude as you hike through the woods.

Start: The Fernald's Neck trailhead at the south end of the parking area next to the information sign
Distance: 3.6-mile lollipop
Hiking time: 2 to 3 hours
Difficulty: Easy
Best seasons: May to Oct
Trail surface: Woodland path
Land status: Coastal Mountains Land Trust preserve

Nearest town: Camden
Other trail users: None
Water availability: Lake Megunticook
Canine compatibility: Dogs not allowed in Fernalds Neck Preserve
Fees and permits: None
Maps: DeLorme: The Maine Atlas and Gazetteer: map 14; USGS Lincolnville
Trail contact: Coastal Mountains Land Trust, (207) 236-7091; www.coastalmountains.org

Finding the trailhead: From the junction of US 1 and ME 52 (Mountain Street) in Camden, drive north on ME 52 for 4.9 miles, passing the Maiden Cliff trailhead and Youngstown Road. Turn left onto Fernald's Neck Road. Drive 0.5 mile and bear left at the fork, then drive 0.5 mile to the end of the road. The last 0.1 mile to the parking area is a very narrow lane. The trailhead is at the south end of the parking area next to the information sign.
Trailhead GPS: N44 15.634' / W69 06.578'

The Hike

Lake Megunticook is a long, sinuous lake that lies between Bald Mountain and Mount Megunticook. The lake curls around to the east behind the Camden Hills, becoming a series of ponds. Fernald's Neck sticks out into the southern end of the lake, almost bisecting it. The channel on the west side of the neck that connects the southern and northern ends of Lake Megunticook is more like a languid river than a lake. The hike around Fernald's Neck offers views of the surrounding mountains and various aspects of Lake Megunticook. On a breezy day the lake east of the neck can be choppy and dangerous, while the western side is a calm lagoon.

The hike begins at the end of Fernald's Neck Road in a meadow with views across the lake of Maiden Cliff on the north end of Mount Megunticook. There are several color-coded trails around the neck; this hike loops around the outside of Fernald's Neck and makes use of most of them. You can shorten or lengthen the hike to fit your needs. The trails are well blazed with trail maps at the intersections. The Blue Trail leads into the woods through a forest of old-growth white pine, hemlock, and red pine. The forest stays cool even on the hottest days. Since so little light reaches the ground, little grows beneath the trees; rust-colored needles and cones collect on the trail, hushing your footsteps. The trail is fairly level and mostly dry. There are a few low, mossy spots where the ground is spongy and mosquitoes hang in the air. On the west side of Fernald's Neck, the trail climbs a low, rocky rise that supports blueberries, lichen, and other sun-loving plants. The lake's channel is only 100 feet wide here, the green wall of Bald Mountain rising across the water. The Blue Trail ducks back into the forest and skirts around the Great Bog. Sunlight streams beneath the tall

Bog boards through towering pines on the Blue Trail.

evergreens; the rocky ground supports more diverse plants along the bog. Birds and frogs noisily spend their day feeding or defending their territory. This is a good spot to carefully look for both species of bitterns, wading birds that freeze with their necks extended in imitation of the dry cattails they hide in. The male American bittern has a call that sounds more like a bullfrog than a bird.

The Orange Trail is a lollipop that loops the rest of the way around Great Bog and toward the southern end of Fernald's Neck. Along the Orange Trail the trees aren't so large, more are spruce, and there is more dead wood beneath the trees. The forest is much less open, but is home to more wildflowers. On the east side of the neck, the trail comes out onto a slab of bedrock that angles down into the lake. Mountain View, as the spot is called, offers fine views across the lake of Maiden Cliff and the Camden Hills. This is a popular spot for hikers to take a dip in Lake Megunticook to cool off. Boulders stick up out of the lake, offering swimmers spots to sit and relax.

Back on the Blue Trail, the hike heads north to the Yellow Trail. This short trail leads out to another popular swimming spot on the rocky shore. Just behind the shore, along the trail, is Balance Rock. The rock is a roughly round boulder the size of a small cabin that sits on the exposed bedrock. It is possible, if you have some rock climbing skills, to climb atop Balance Rock and stand among the treetops.

Fernald's Neck is popular, but it is surprising how much solitude you still get on this hike. You are unlikely to see anyone else except at Mountain View and Balance Rock.

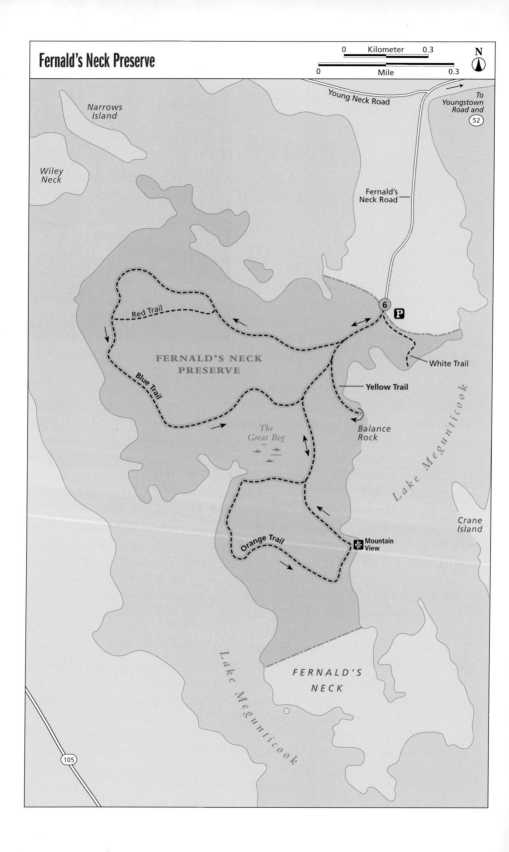

Fernald's Neck Preserve

0   Kilometer   0.3

0   Mile   0.3

N

Young Neck Road

To Youngstown Road and 52

Narrows Island

Wiley Neck

Fernald's Neck Road

6   P

Red Trail

FERNALD'S NECK PRESERVE

White Trail

Blue Trail

Yellow Trail

Lake Megunticook

The Great Bog

Balance Rock

Crane Island

Orange Trail

Mountain View

Lake Megunticook

FERNALD'S NECK

105

Lake Megunticook

Miles and Directions

0.0 Start from the Fernald's Neck trailhead on the Blue Trail next to the information sign.

0.2 The trail passes the White Trail, which gives access to Lake Megunticook, and enters the woods. The Blue Trail forks; go right.

0.4 Pass the Red Trail, staying on the Blue Trail.

0.8 Pass the other end of the Red Trail, staying on the Blue Trail.

1.5 After crossing an open area with views west across a narrow arm of Lake Megunticook, the trail turns inland and goes around the Great Bog. Arrive at the junction with the Orange Trail. Turn right onto the Orange Trail.

1.8 The Orange Trail is a lollipop that loops around the southern end of the preserve. Take the right fork to begin the loop.

2.5 The Orange Trail descends to Lake Megunticook, coming out onto bare rock on the shore. This is Mountain View. Maiden Cliff and the Camden Hills are visible across the lake. The trail goes back into the woods at the north end of the rock. (This is different from the maps posted around the preserve, which show Mountain View at the end of a short side trail.)

2.7 Arrive back at the fork on the Orange Trail; turn right to return to the Blue Trail.

2.9 Arrive back at the Blue Trail; turn right to continue the hike.

3.0 Turn right onto the Yellow Trail to Balance Rock.

3.2 Balance Rock is a round, cabin-size boulder sitting on a dome of bedrock just into the woods from the shore of Lake Megunticook. Return back to the Blue Trail to return to the trailhead.

3.4 Arrive back at the Blue Trail. Turn right to return to the trailhead.

3.6 On the Blue Trail, turn right at the fork and arrive back at the trailhead.

7 Ragged Mountain

The hike up Ragged Mountain on the Georges Highland Path is part of a network of trails from the headwaters of the St. George's River in Montville to its mouth in Thomaston. The trail up Ragged Mountain, through oak-pine forest, crosses several old stone walls before climbing the mountain's south ridge. From the south ridge, covered with stunted oak trees and blueberries, you have fine views of the surrounding country and Penobscot Bay. The hike ends at the top of the cliffs on Ragged Mountain's west face that give it its name. The summit of the mountain is on the spruce-covered ridge to the north.

Start: From the Georges Highland Path trailhead at the north end of the parking area
Distance: 4.8 miles out and back
Hiking time: 3 to 4 hours
Difficulty: Moderate
Best seasons: May to Oct
Trail surface: Woodland path
Land status: Georges River Land Trust preserve
Nearest town: Rockport

Other trail users: None
Water availability: None
Canine compatibility: Dogs must be under control at all times
Fees and permits: None
Maps: *DeLorme: The Maine Atlas and Gazetteer:* map 14; USGS West Rockport
Trail contact: Georges River Land Trust, (207) 594-5166; www.georgesriver.org

Finding the trailhead: From the junction of US 1 and ME 90 in Rockport, take ME 90 and drive 2.8 miles to the junction of ME 90 and ME 17. Turn right onto ME 17. Drive 1.8 miles to the Georges Highland Path trailhead parking on the right at the sign. The trailhead is at the north end of the parking area.
Trailhead GPS: N44 12.125' / W69 09.543'

The Hike

The trail up Ragged Mountain is part of the larger Georges Highland Path. The Path is not one continuous trail, but a series of short trails from the headwaters of the St. George's River in Montville to the mouth of the river in Thomaston. There are 45 miles of trails in this network, with more in the works. The longest stretch of trail is over Ragged Mountain. From the trailhead you can also hike west up Spruce Mountain with fine views of Ragged Mountain and Penobscot Bay. Across Ragged Mountain to the east is the trail up Bald Mountain with its bare, rocky ledges.

In between, the hike up Ragged Mountain begins in an oak-pine forest that was once a farm. Stone walls cross the trail in several places. The last wall incorporates a natural rock ledge that the trail climbs. The trail crosses a small stream, then turns south along the jumbled rocks at the base of Ragged Mountain's nearly vertical west face. As the trail approaches Mirror Lake, it turns east and climbs steeply. Once up

Looking north from the cliffs on Ragged Mountain.

on the ridge, the trail switchbacks and comes to an open ledge with the first views of the hike.

The trail continues to climb with views through oak trees that are stunted and twisted in Dr. Seuss shapes. This open, rocky forest allows enough light to reach the ground for blueberries to thrive, especially along the several ledges the trail crosses. At just over 1,000 feet of elevation, you get your first open view of the Camden Hills and Penobscot Bay to the east. The trail then ducks back into the trees and climbs to the top of the cliffs.

Atop the cliffs you have fine views in every direction. There is a tower on the highest point. This is not Ragged Mountain's summit, but is the end of the hike. The summit is on the spruce-covered ridge to the north. The Georges Highland Path continues around the summit and descends to the north. A mile from the cliffs, the trail forks: The west fork drops down to Gilette Road, a side road off ME 17 north of the trailhead; the east fork descends to Barnestown Road north of Camden Snow Bowl. Across the road is the beginning of the trail up Bald Mountain.

From the cliffs on Ragged Mountain, you cannot see Camden Snow Bowl, the town-owned ski area on the mountain's east face. There is a rough trail that begins around the east side of the tower and descends the ski slopes of Camden Snow Bowl. This trail is part of a network of mountain biking trails on the mountain. The best

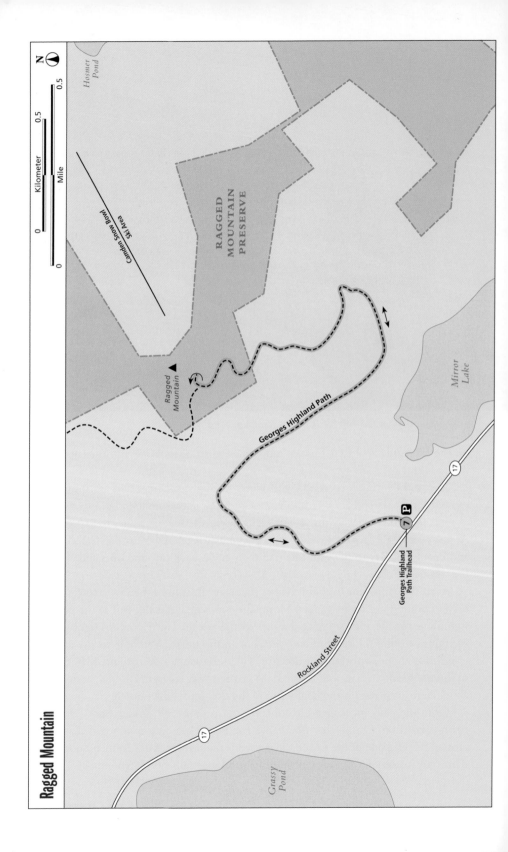

Ragged Mountain

views on the mountain, though, are those from our hike up Ragged Mountain's west side. Camden Snow Bowl is the only ski resort in the United States within view of the Atlantic Ocean.

Miles and Directions

0.0 Start at the Georges Highland Path trailhead at the north end of the parking area.

1.7 The trail heads straight toward Ragged Mountain, then turns south and skirts along its flank. As it nears Mirror Lake, the trail turns east and climbs. Above a switchback the trail comes to an open area with views to the west and south.

2.4 The trail climbs through an open oak forest of stunted trees with intermittent views, arriving at the top of the ridge with views in every direction but east. The summit of Ragged Mountain is along the spruce-covered ridge to the north. An unmarked trail goes around to the east with views in that direction of Bald Mountain and the Camden Hills. To complete the hike, return the way you came.

4.8 Arrive back at the trailhead.

Honorable Mention

○ Josephine Newman Sanctuary

Maine Audubon's Josephine Newman Sanctuary in Georgetown is on a peninsula between the two arms of Robinhood Cove among the complex array of islands, bays, and rivers at the mouth of the Kennebec River. The sanctuary has 2.5 miles of hiking trails that connect with The Nature Conservancy's Berry Woods Preserve and its trails. The hike around the sanctuary passes a steep-sided valley with a waterfall at its head, a rocky headland crossed by an old stone wall, access to the cove's shore on a rocky spit of land, a reversing falls, and woods of mature trees. Most visitors to Georgetown head straight for the beaches at Reid State Park and miss these quiet woods. To get to the trailhead, from the junction of US 1 and ME 127 in Woolrich, drive south on ME 127 for 9.3 miles to the village of Georgetown. Staying on ME 127, drive down the hill and cross the first bridge over Robinhood Cove. The sanctuary's narrow drive is just across the bridge on the right. There is a small sign for the sanctuary at the turn. If you cross a second bridge, you've gone too far. For more information contact Maine Audubon, (207) 781-2330; maineaudubon.org.

Downeast

The Downeast coast is the quintessential rockbound coast—mile after mile of rugged shoreline, the spruce forest crowding down to the sea, and in the distance, mountains with bare summits. The Downeast coast is not as convoluted as the Mid-Coast, especially east of Cutler, but there is an abundance of islands in the bays and far out in the Gulf of Maine. Some of the islands are accessible by car, others by ferry, but most only by boat. Isle au Haut (hike 11), for example, is several miles off Stonington, and reachable only by the mail ferry from that town. Stonington itself is on Deer Isle, connected to the mainland by a high, arching suspension bridge over Eggemoggin Reach. Around these two islands are hundreds of smaller islands, many showing visible signs of granite quarrying.

Hikers pass beneath the cliffs on John B Mountain (hike 9).

AGASSIZ OUTCROP

In 1864 Louis Agassiz—the swiss-born Harvard scientist—visited Maine to study its islands and coast. He was working to extend his theories about ice age glaciation to North America. His work was instrumental in showing how glaciers and ice ages had shaped the landscape, earning him the title, "Father of Glaciation." During his visit to Maine, he noted that "between Bangor and Mount Desert the usual evidence of glaciation is very extensive." He was especially impressed by the polished bedrock with scratches running roughly north–south. Today one of those exposed slabs of bedrock in Ellsworth Falls on the shoulder of US 1A is known as the Agassiz Outcrop. Even though it's now a National Historic Landmark, there is no sign to let folks driving past know its significance. The outcrop is located on the west side of US 1A just south of the junction with ME 179 in front of the parking lot for The Falls diner.

You will find less granite Downeast than you might expect. The inland mountains—Blue Hill (hike 8), in the Great Pond Preserve (hike 12), and around Donnell Pond and Tunk Lake (hikes 13, 14, and 15)—are parts of three different granite plutons. In fact, much of the low, lake country of inland Downeast is underlain by granite bedrock. The bedrock on the shore, however, is mostly various volcanic and metamorphic rocks laid down over a series of events around 400 million years ago. Some of the Downeast islands are granite, especially in Penobscot and Blue Hill Bays, but also Great Wass Island (hike 18). The variety of bedrock along the coast makes for interesting and varied hiking. Even areas of coastline only a few miles apart can be very different.

There are few sand beaches Downeast, but many gravel and cobble beaches, some hidden beneath towering headlands. The difference between high and low tides are among the largest in the world. The farther east you go as the Gulf of Maine narrows between Maine and Nova Scotia, the more dramatic the tide. Differences can range as much as 25 feet. As you might expect, a hike along the coast can be dramatically different depending on the tide. Wide cobble beaches disappear beneath the rising tide all along the Downeast coast, and expansive mudflats are exposed on the falling tide. Where the shore is most rocky and irregular, the rising and falling tides can create unnatural sounds, like ghostly voices conversing just beyond hearing.

The variability of the coast and the abundance of remote islands make Downeast a magnet for shorebirds, seabirds, seals, and whales. The birds and the aquatic mammals tend to follow seasonal patterns, following the fish and making use of nesting sites on many islands. But on most coastal hikes on most days, you have a good chance of seeing wildlife.

Behind the rocky shore is not all coastal spruce forest; there are a wide variety of forest and habitat types, including a type of raised peat bog found nowhere else in the world. Farther inland there are few towns, but extensive forest with chains of lakes and rivers. Much of the land is low and swampy, making for few hiking opportunities. The best way to explore inland Downeast is by canoe. The country is as wild and remote as any in the United States. ME 9—known as The Airline—crosses this wildland, passing a number of mountains including Bald Bluff Mountain (hike E). The higher, drier areas of inland Downeast are famous for commercial wild blueberry barrens. Every year between 75 and 90 million pounds of blueberries are harvested in Maine. Much of the harvesting is still done by hand with blueberry rakes. There is a small commercial blueberry operation in the Bog Brook Cove Preserve (hike D) that you can visit.

8 Blue Hill

Blue Hill is a monadnock—an isolated granite mountain—in the town of Blue Hill near Blue Hill Bay. Ledges near the summit offer sweeping views of Blue Hill Bay, Mount Desert Island, Penobscot Bay, and the Camden Hills. The trails are well marked and easy to follow.

Start: Osgood trailhead on Mountain Road
Distance: 1.8-mile lollipop
Hiking time: 1 to 2 hours
Difficulty: Moderate
Best seasons: Year-round; in winter the snow is usually packed down on the trail
Trail surface: Woodland path and bare granite
Land status: Blue Hill Heritage Trust
Nearest town: Blue Hill

Other trail users: None
Water availability: None
Canine compatibility: Dogs must be under control at all times
Fees and permits: No fees or permits required
Maps: *DeLorme: The Maine Atlas and Gazetteer:* map 15; USGS Blue Hill
Trail contact: Blue Hill Heritage Trust, (207) 374-5118; bluehillheritagetrust.org

Finding the trailhead: From the town of Blue Hill, drive north for 0.9 mile on ME 15. Turn right onto Mountain Road. Trailhead parking is 0.5 mile on the right. The trailhead is across the road from the parking. To find the trailhead from the north: From US 1 in Orland, turn south onto ME 15 toward Blue Hill. Drive 11.8 miles, then turn left onto Mountain Road. The trailhead parking is 0.5 mile on the right.
Trailhead GPS: N44 25.697' / W68 35.408'

The Hike

Blue Hill is a monadnock that rises behind the town of Blue Hill at the head of Blue Hill Bay. A monadnock is an isolated granite mountain, named for the mountain in southern New Hampshire. Like Mount Desert Island, Blue Hill is a granite pluton. Many of the islands in the Blue Hill and Penobscot Bays are as well. It's easy—even just from looking at a map—to tell which ones are granite: They tend to be round. Many of these islands were quarried for their granite. The town of Blue Hill shipped local granite for such building projects as the Brooklyn Bridge and the New York Stock Exchange. The area, because of its abundant forests and good water for mills, was first a shipbuilding center. The town was founded by veterans of the French and Indian War who settled at nearby Blue Hill Falls—a reversing tidal falls—because of its potential as a power source. The timber and shipbuilding booms ended after the Civil War, just in time for the granite boom. In the late 1800s there was also a copper mining boom.

With all this extractive industry over the years, you might think the region would be worse for wear. But, in fact, today the area is mostly a quiet tourist mecca. Up close some of the islands look like they were shaved, but from Blue Hill, with its sweeping views, there's no indication of past mining or timbering.

Mount Desert Island across Blue Hill Bay in early April.

The Osgood Trail climbs up to a shoulder on the mountain, then slabs around to the north through mixed forest. Once around the north side of the mountain, the trail climbs up onto the summit on exposed granite. Along the way are good views to the north and west.

The summit offers only limited views—and those are blocked by the tower just below the summit. The Hayes Trail drops down and around the summit to open ledges with sweeping views to the south and east. Beyond Long Island, across Blue Hill Bay, rise the mountains of Mount Desert Island, and to the east lie the endless line of islands and irregular shoreline that is the Downeast coast.

The trail drops down the front of the cliffs among twisted and stunted birches—an open forest that glows yellow much of the year. Below the cliffs the Hayes Trail meets the South Face Trail, which skirts around to the west below the mountaintop. The South Face Trail passes through an open, grassy hillside that colors with summer wildflowers, then drops down into the woods and ends at the Osgood Trail.

The trails on Blue Hill are popular with winter hikers and snowshoers. As a result the snow gets packed down and is easy to walk on. This is a good hike to try out winter hiking for the first time. When the snow is deep, it is recommended that you descend by the road rather than the Hayes Trail, avoiding the steepest section of the hike.

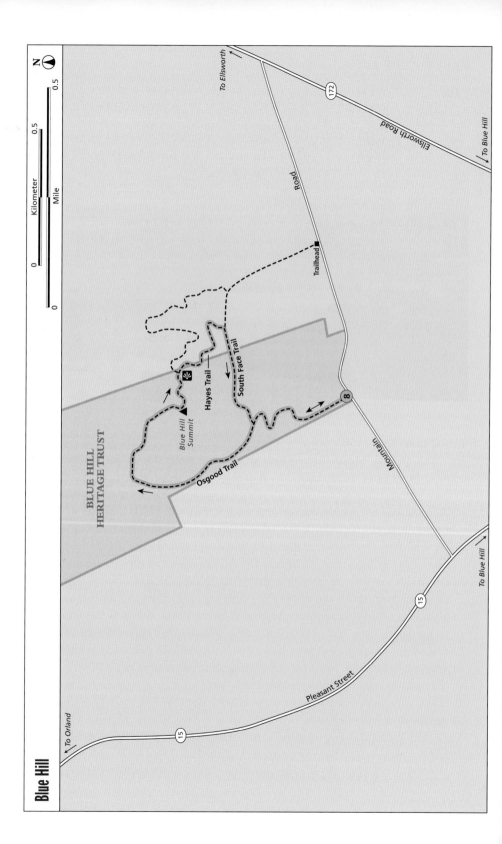

Blue Hill

Miles and Directions

0.0   Start at the Osgood trailhead across Mountain Road from the parking lot. There is an information kiosk with maps and other information. The Osgood Trail climbs gently, following an old road, then climbs more steeply.

0.3   The South Face Trail comes in from the right. Continue straight ahead. The trail climbs gently, slabbing around to the back of the mountain. Once behind Blue Hill the trail climbs steeply to the flat summit area. There are views to the north.

0.9   Arrive at the summit, with limited views to the south. There are better views on the ledges farther along the hike. Descend off the summit.

1.0   The radio tower service road continues straight. Turn right onto the Hayes Trail.

1.1   The trail emerges onto ledges with open views of the town of Blue Hill below and Blue Hill Bay. In the distance the mountains of Mount Desert Island are visible. The trail drops steeply off the ledges, switchbacking down along the cliffs.

1.3   The South Face Trail comes in from the right. The Hayes Trail goes left, down to Mountain Road and a different trailhead. Turn right onto the South Face Trail. The trail crosses an open area. Where the trail reenters the woods, it drops down to the Osgood Trail.

1.5   The South Face Trail ends at the Osgood Trail. Turn left to descend back to the trailhead.

1.8   Arrive back at the trailhead.

9 John B Mountain

John B Mountain is only 250 feet high and the hike is only 1.1 miles, but there is a lot to see in that small package. The mountain has an interesting geologic history and offers fine views of Penobscot Bay, Eggemoggin Reach, and the islands that fill those waters.

Start: John B Mountain trailhead
Distance: 1.1-mile loop
Hiking time: About 1 hour
Difficulty: Easy
Best seasons: Apr to Nov
Trail surface: Woodland trail
Land status: Blue Hill Heritage Trust
Nearest town: Brooksville
Other trail users: None

Water availability: None
Canine compatibility: Dogs must be on a leash at all times
Fees and permits: No fees or permits required
Maps: DeLorme: The Maine Atlas and Gazetteer: map 15; USGS Cape Rosier
Trail contact: Blue Hill Heritage Trust, (207) 374-5118; bluehillheritagetrust.org

Finding the trailhead: From the north: Drive south on ME 175 from US 1 in Orland for 17.9 miles, through several turns. At the T intersection turn right onto ME 176 and drive 6.1 miles. Turn right onto Breezemere Road and drive 0.8 mile. The parking is a small turnout on the right in front of the trailhead.
Trailhead GPS: N44 20.700' / W68 45.603'

The Hike

The hike begins by following an old woods road around the west side of John B Mountain through an open forest of towering hardwoods. This first section is a good place to find spring wildflowers in May and early June before the trees fully leaf out. When the trail leaves the woods road, it winds along the base of cliffs then climbs gradually up the mountain from the north through thick moss and evergreens. Across the mountain's top, the forest is drier and more open with more lichen than moss. It is interesting that such a low mountain—John B is only 250 feet high—would have so many forest types, but what is most interesting about this mountain is its geologic history.

A half million years ago the ancient ocean of Iapetus was being squashed between North America and Europe as they slowly collided. A line of volcanoes developed to relieve some of the pressure—just as the Pacific Ring of Fire volcanoes do today. The bedrock around John B Mountain is the remains of one of those volcanoes. On Cape Rosier, around Castine, and on many of the islands along Eggemoggin Reach, gray bedrock composed of compacted ash and other volcanic rock can be found.

Geologically, this area has more in common with the Bold Coast than with nearby Mount Desert Island or the coastal mountains in this region. The granite in those areas takes on a rounded appearance—like rising bread dough—as it weathers. The rock is also rough to the touch and has visible grain. The volcanic rock on and around John B Mountain is either gray rock with no visible grain made of compacted ash that tends to fracture in a way that leaves long, smooth faces, or tan rock that resembles granite but crumbles into gravel and doesn't take on that rounded look as it weathers.

John B Mountain is composed of that tan, metamorphic rock known as rhyolite. As you hike along the base of the cliffs on the trail, then hike over the top of those cliffs and climb the mountain's summit, notice that the rock is hard but crumbly. Its hardness enabled it to resist erosion better than the softer rock around it—which allowed John B Mountain to emerge over time as that gray, compacted ash eroded away. John B Mountain's rock is hard enough that on the tops of the cliffs and atop the summit you can find long scratches in the bedrock made by glaciers.

Don't spend the whole hike looking down. The views from John B Mountain are unique. John B Mountain sits on a small peninsula between Buck and Orcutt Harbors in the town of Brooksville. The town is nearly an island bounded on the west and north by the tidal estuary called the Bagaduce River and on the south by Eggemoggin Reach. From John B Mountain you can see all this island-filled water around you. Across Penobscot Bay to the west, dark on the horizon, are the Camden Hills.

After enjoying the geology beneath your feet and the views of the surounding waters, you complete the hike by descending steeply down the mountain's east side.

Looking west from near the summit of John B Mountain.

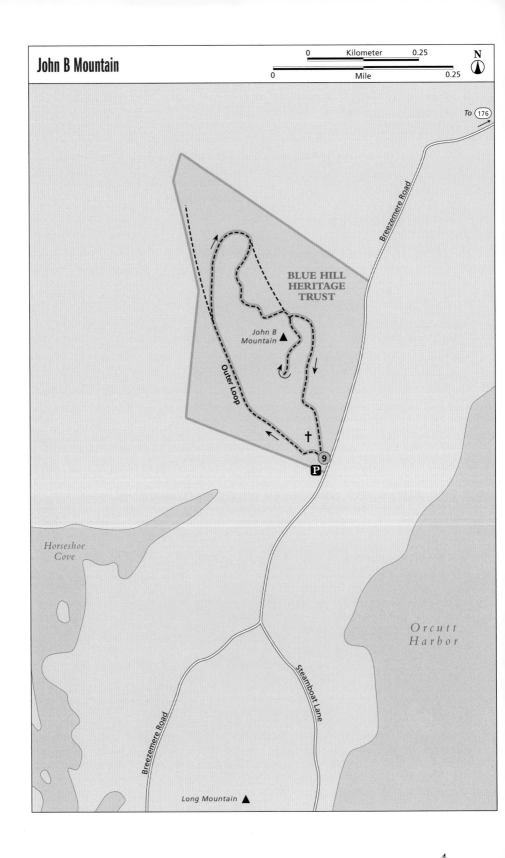

John B Mountain

0 Kilometer 0.25
0 Mile 0.25

N

To 176

Breezemere Road

BLUE HILL
HERITAGE
TRUST

John B
Mountain

Outer Loop

9
P

Horseshoe
Cove

Orcutt
Harbor

Breezemere Road

Steamboat Lane

Long Mountain

You quickly drop down into the hardwoods, leaving the moss and spruce behind. The trail ends by passing an old cemetery—evidence that John B Mountain's story did not end with the last ice age, but is ongoing.

Miles and Directions

0.0 Start at the Outer Loop trailhead behind the fence. The trail to the right is the return trail.

0.3 Turn right to stay on the Outer Loop. The trail to the left leaves the preserve property; the trail straight ahead ends at the property line.

0.4 The trail winds along the foot of a cliff, then climbs to a trail junction. Turn right at the junction of the Outer Loop to hike over the cliffs.

0.6 The trail winds along the tops of the cliffs, then climbs to the east and rejoins the Outer Loop Trail.

0.7 Turn right onto the side trail that leads to the summit.

0.8 The trail crosses the unmarked summit, then a short loop trail goes out to a cliff top with views.

0.9 Arrive back at the Outer Loop Trail. Turn right to descend the mountain and return to the trailhead just beyond the small cemetery.

1.1 Arrive back at the trailhead.

10 Holbrook Island Sanctuary State Park

Holbrook Island Sanctuary includes the island and land on Cape Rosier—where the hikes are. There are eight short hikes in the park. The three combined here are all off Back Road. Each offers a short hike through a different habitat. The Mountain Loop circles around and then climbs a rocky hill with some views. The Backshore Trail goes through old estate fields to a rocky beach and a homesite. The Goose Falls Trail follows the rocky shoreline with views of and across Penobscot Bay.

Start: Mountain Loop Trailhead
Distance: 4.1 miles: a lollipop and 2 out and backs
Hiking time: 2 to 4 hours
Difficulty: Easy
Seasons: May to October
Trail surface: Woodland path
Land status: Holbrook Island Sanctuary State Park
Nearest Town: Blue Hill

Other users: None
Water availability: None
Canine compatibility: Dogs must be on a leash less than 4 feet long
Fees and permits: None
Maps: *DeLorme: The Maine Atlas and Gazetteer:* map 15; USGS Cape Rosier
Trail contact: Holbrook Island Sanctuary State Park, (207) 362-4012; www.maine.gov/parks

Finding the trailhead: From US 1 in Orland, take ME 175 south toward Castine. Drive 7.8 miles, then turn left, staying on ME 175. Drive 7 miles, then turn right at the sign for Holbrook Island Sanctuary, staying on ME 175. Drive 1.1 miles, crossing Bagaduce Reversing Falls. Turn right onto ME 176. Drive 5.7 miles, then turn right onto Back Road at the state park sign. The trailhead is on the left in 0.8 mile.
Trailhead GPS: N44 21.275' / W68 48.512'

The Hike

Like Baxter State Park, Holbrook Island Sanctuary was donated to the state with the stipulation that the park remain undeveloped. In 1971 Anita Harris gave the state 1,230 acres on Cape Rozier for the park so that it would be left in the wild state she remembered from her childhood. As a result the park seems more remote and wild than it otherwise would. There are nine short hikes in the park either accessed from Back Road or Cape Rozier Road. The Back Road hikes offer a wide variety of habitats in several short walks: from a freshwater pond surrounded by forest to the rocky coast and mudflats. Three of the hikes are combined here; they're connected with short drives or you could add 1.8 miles to your hike by walking from trail to trail.

Backwoods Mountain is the highest point on Cape Rozier. The Mountain Loop Trail circles around it and offers a side trail to the rocky summit. The woods around the mountain are mostly spruce and fir with pine and birch. The woods are quiet and

Holbrook Island across a narrow channel from the beach at the end of the Backshore Trail.

cool year-round. The climb to the summit follows a rock spine and offers limited views of the surrounding estuaries and bays.

The Backshore Trail begins at the ruins of an old homesite, among broken foundations on Indian Bar Road. It drops down along an old road to a grassy meadow and an old cemetery. The trail forks, leading to a rocky beach with views past Holbrook, Ram, and Nautilus Islands of Castine. The steeples of the Congregational church and the Maine Maritime Academy rise above the trees behind the busy portside. The other fork of the trail leads to a small, open hardwood forest atop a small hill where the Hutchins estate once stood. Several foundations are still there—for the main house, garage, and other outbuildings.

Just outside the park, where Back Road becomes Goose Falls Road, is a one-lane steel bridge across Goose Falls. The falls is a reversing tidal falls, meaning it changes character and even direction of water flow depending on the level of the tide. It is one of several reversing falls in the area. Cape Rozier is part of the eastern side of Penobscot Bay, famous for its numerous islands and complex waterways. Where these waterways connect with each other, there is often a choke point where the tide determines the amount and direction of the flow. In the case of Goose Falls, at low tide the water flows out of Goose Pond, dropping 10 feet over rough rocks. At high tide the falls disappears entirely, and the water flows into the pond.

Holbrook Island Sanctuary State Park

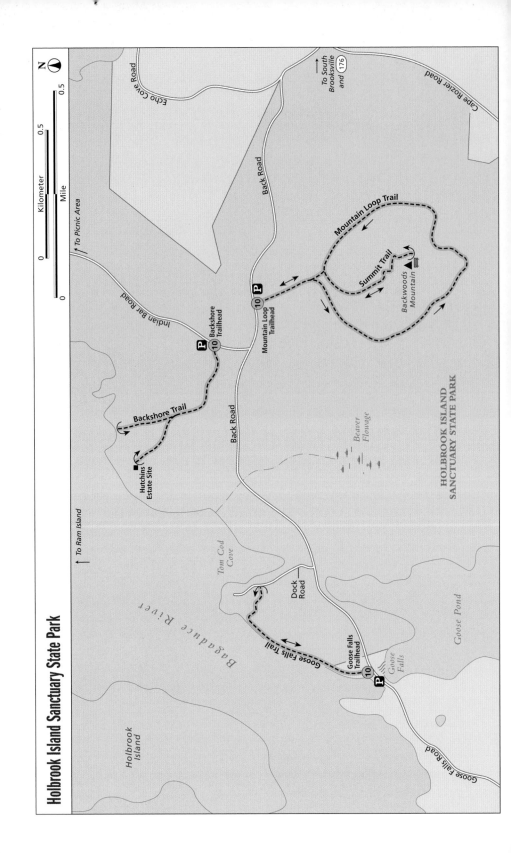

Goose Falls on a falling tide.

The Goose Falls Trail follows along the edge of the bay from Goose Falls along the narrow channel between Cape Rozier and Holbrook Island. There are views across Penobscot Bay of distant islands and the Camden Hills. Farther along the hike you can see Castine peeking out between islands across the Bagaduce River—which looks more like a bay than a river. There are several spots along the hike where you can get down onto the rocky shore and explore the flats and pools at low tide, or just enjoy the views.

The state park has a picnic area near a gravel beach at the end of Indian Bar Road. At Indian Bar you have a choice of two beaches separated by a boggy meadow.

Miles and Directions

0.0   Start from Mountain Loop Trailhead next to the trail sign.

0.1   Reach the actual loop trail. Turn right and hike through mixed softwood forest around the mountain.

1.3   Junction with the Summit Trail. Turn left and climb to the summit.

1.5   After a short, steep climb up a rocky slope, the trail arrives at a bench where you can sit and enjoy the view. The view to the west and north is partially blocked by trees.

1.6   The trail crosses the unmarked summit of Backwoods Mountain and then ends at a spot with limited views to the east. To continue the hike, retrace the Summit trail to the loop trail.

1.9 Arrive back at Mountain Loop Trail. Turn left and pass the Summit Trail on the right.

2.0 Return to the trail that leads out to the trailhead. Turn right.

2.1 Arrive back at the trailhead. To reach the Backshore Trail, drive 0.2 mile west on Back Road. Turn right on the road that leads to the park headquarters and picnic area. The Backshore Trailhead is 0.1 mile down the road on the left, at the south end of the parking area between two old foundations. Start out on this second leg of the hike.

2.2 The trail passes several more foundations and a meadow, then reaches an intersection. Turn right.

2.3 The trail, an old lane, passes a small cemetery and then comes to a fork. The right-hand fork drops down to the shore with a view of Castine in 0.1 mile. The left-hand fork climbs a small hill to an open woodland in 0.1 mile that is the Hutchins estate site. After hiking both forks, return to the trailhead the way you came.

3.1 Arrive back at the trailhead. To reach the Goose Falls Trailhead, drive back to Back Road and turn right. Drive 0.6 mile and park across the steel bridge over Goose Falls. The Goose Falls Trailhead is 100 yards east, back up Back Road on the left just past a house. Follow the trail as it parallels the shore with several easy access points to the shore and views.

3.6 The trail turns inland and ends at Dock Road. To complete the hike, return the way you came.

4.1 Arrive back at the trailhead.

11 Isle au Haut

This hike around Western Head on Isle au Haut covers some of the most rugged country on the island. The trails are lightly maintained and often little more than route suggestions, giving the hike a real wilderness feel. Around Western Head the hike crosses several different bedrock types. On the eastern side of Western Head are cliffs more than 100 feet high that the trail passes over. Beyond the cliffs the hike climbs Duck Harbor Mountains's long, spruce-covered ridge. Numerous knobs of bedrock jut out of the forest, offering the best views on the island.

Start: Duck Harbor boat dock
Distance: 5.2-mile loop
Hiking time: 4 to 6 hours
Difficulty: Moderate
Best seasons: May to Oct
Trail surface: Woodland path, woods road, and exposed bedrock
Land status: Acadia National Park
Nearest towns: Isle au Haut Village (limited services) and Stonington
Other trail users: None
Water availability: Water pump 0.1 mile north on Western Head Road from the junction with Duck Harbor Mountain Trail

Canine compatibility: Dogs must be on a leash at all times
Fees and permits: No fees or permits for day use on Isle au Haut; fee for camping on the island. You will have to take the mail boat to Isle au Haut.
Maps: *DeLorme: The Maine Atlas and Gazetteer:* map 9; USGS Isle au Haut East and Isle au Haut West
Trail contacts: Acadia National Park, (207) 288-3338; www.nps.gov/acad/index.htm. Isle au Haut Boat Services, (207) 367-5193; www .isleauhaut.com

Finding the trailhead: The Isle au Haut mail boat leaves from the dock in Stonington. You will need to take the boat to Duck Harbor, about a 1-hour ride. The trail begins at the head of the dock at the information kiosk. There is generally a ranger there to meet the boat who can answer your questions.
Trailhead GPS: N44 01.705' / W68 39.164'

The Hike

Isle au Haut is connected to Mount Desert Island by more than the fact that both are part of Acadia National Park. Both islands were named by the French explorer Champlain in 1604. Both islands had been used by the Penobscots for generations before that. Isle au Haut was first settled by Henry Barter, who gained title to the island in 1792. It was his ancestors who donated 60 percent of the island to Acadia National Park. By that time the isolated fishing village on the island had evolved into a much smaller fishing community and a community of summer folks. The improvements in transportation in the late 1800s that allowed fishermen to live on

A hiker looks out to sea from Western Head on a foggy afternoon.

the mainland and fish the waters off Isle au Haut also gave seasonal visitors access
to the island.

Geologically, like Mount Desert Island, Isle au Haut is a granite pluton—a plug of
granite pushed to the surface through existing sedimentary and volcanic bedrock. But
unlike Mount Desert Island, you can find several types of bedrock on Isle au Haut—
especially on the west side of the island and Western Head, where this hike goes. The
beaches are mostly granite boulders and cobbles, but you'll walk across volcanic rock
that ranges from purple to tiger-striped, and even white.

There are 18 miles of trails in the national park on Isle au Haut and several miles
of trails outside the park. There is a spine of granite that runs the length of the island,
higher toward the north, but the only mountaintop that is not tree covered and
offers views is Duck Harbor Mountain near Western Head. The trails on the island
are much rougher and less maintained than those in the rest of Acadia National Park.
This, and the lack of crowds, gives Isle au Haut a real wilderness feel.

The hike starts at Duck Harbor where the mail boat drops visitors off near the
island's five-lean-to campground. The trail leads from the dock to the head of Duck
Harbor where there is a privy and a nearby water pump (the water tastes very rusty
and is brown in color). You turn right and follow Western Head Road—a two-track
closed to traffic—to Western Head Trail. This trail winds through forest with several

openings full of dead and fallen trees. These trees were killed by insects and blown over by winter storms.

The hike follows the trail down the west side of Western Head and back up the east side past numerous small coves, across rocky beaches, and around heads of variously colored and textured bedrock. As you hike up the east side of Western Head, the coves become larger and the cliffs higher. Just before turning inland the trail goes across the top of cliffs more than 100 feet high. Notice that the bedrock here is broken into square-edged blocks, not the rounded boulders you find on Mount Desert Island.

Beyond Squeaker Cove the hike climbs Duck Harbor Mountain. The trail over the mountain is little more than a series of blazes and cairns to suggest a route hikers can use to scramble up and over the many humps along the summit ridge. This trail is not well suited to small children or dogs—but it offers the best views on Isle au Haut. From the rocky, spruce-covered spine of Duck Harbor Mountain, you can see the entire southern half of the island and out across Penobscot Bay to the west and Blue Hill Bay and Mount Desert Island to the east.

On most days you can have the hike to yourself. According to the Park Service, which limits the number of visitors to the island, Isle au Haut gets around 7,000 visitors a year. Park rangers say that on a busy day, as many as fifty people take the mail boat to the island. Fifty hikers spread out over 18 miles of trails gives each group a lot of space.

Miles and Directions

0.0 Start from the trail at the head of the dock at Duck Harbor.

0.1 The trail follows along the south shore of Duck Harbor, ending at Western Head Road. There is a privy at the intersection; the water pump is 0.1 mile north on Western Head Road at the head of the harbor. Turn right and walk south on Western Head Road.

0.2 Pass the Duck Harbor Mountain Trail. You will return on this trail.

0.6 Turn right onto the Western Head Trail.

1.0 The trail descends gently through spruce to the rocky shore. You can walk out onto the rocks to an overlook.

1.1 The trail drops onto and crosses a cobbled beach.

2.3 The trail follows the shore either on rock, across cobbled beaches, or in the spruce behind the shore. The Western Head Trail ends at a junction with two other trails. Turn right onto the Western Ear Trail.

2.4 The Western Ear Trail ends at a cobbled beach on the very narrow channel between Western Head and Western Ear. Return to the junction to continue the hike.

2.5 At the junction turn right onto the Cliff Trail.

2.6 The trail skirts a boggy area and emerges back on the coast at a narrow cove that forces the incoming tide into good-size waves.

3.0 The trail crosses cliffs more than 100 feet high.

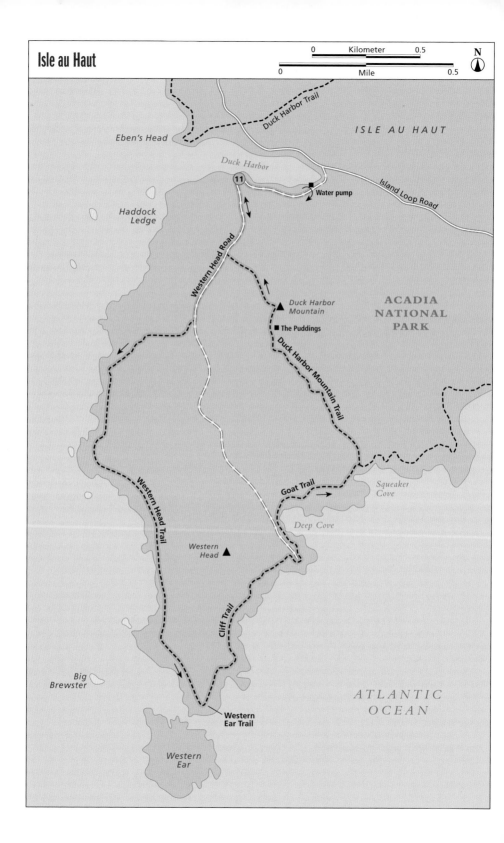

Isle au Haut

Kilometer 0 — 0.5

Mile 0 — 0.5

N

Eben's Head

Duck Harbor Trail

ISLE AU HAUT

Duck Harbor

11

Water pump

Island Loop Road

Haddock Ledge

Western Head Road

Duck Harbor Mountain

The Puddings

ACADIA NATIONAL PARK

Duck Harbor Mountain Trail

Western Head Trail

Goat Trail

Squeaker Cove

Deep Cove

Western Head

Cliff Trail

Big Brewster

Western Ear Trail

ATLANTIC OCEAN

Western Ear

3.1 The trail circles around the cove with the high cliffs and ends at Western Head Road. Turn left onto the road.

3.3 Turn right onto the Goat Trail. (***Option:*** If you wish to avoid the rocky climbs on Duck Harbor Mountain Trail, you can follow Western Head Road back instead.)

3.5 The Goat Trail loops around Deep Cove and then Squeaker Cove. Behind Squeaker Cove turn left onto the Duck Harbor Mountain Trail.

4.4 The Duck Harbor Mountain Trail climbs up bare rock to the first of several rocky crags along the summit ridge of Duck Harbor Mountain. You can see the coast on both sides of Western Head. The trail along the summit ridge involves climbing with some exposure. This trail is not suited for dogs or small children. The trail crosses the unmarked summit with fine views in every direction.

5.0 The trail descends off Duck Harbor Mountain and ends at Western Head Road. Turn right onto the road to return to the trailhead.

5.1 Arrive back at the junction with the trail to the dock. Turn left onto the trail to return to the trailhead. Remember, the water pump is 0.1 mile north on Western Head Road from this junction.

5.2 Arrive back at the trailhead.

12 Great Pond Mountain

Great Pond Mountain is one of the easiest granite peaks to climb in Maine. The trail climbs very gently up exposed bedrock with many views to the south. Near the summit the trail crosses a huge expanse of granite. From here you have fine views from east to west, including Mount Desert Island, Blue Hill and Penobscot Bays, and the Camden Hills. The actual summit is in the woods behind this open area; a short trail loops through the woods to the semi-open summit.

Start: From the signed Stuart Gross Path trailhead on the north side of the road
Distance: 2.4 miles out and back
Hiking time: 1 to 2 hours
Difficulty: Easy
Best seasons: June to Oct
Trail surface: Woodland path and bare bedrock
Land status: Great Pond Mountain Wildlands
Nearest town: Orland

Other trail users: Hunting allowed in the wildlands
Water availability: None
Canine compatibility: Dogs must be on a leash at all times
Fees and permits: No fees or permits required
Maps: *DeLorme: The Maine Atlas and Gazetteer:* map 23; USGS Orland
Trail contact: Great Pond Mountain Conservation Trust, (207) 469-6929; greatpondtrust.org.

Finding the trailhead: From the junction of Hatchery Road and US 1 in Orland, take Hatchery Road north. The junction is 2.5 miles south of the junction of US 1 and ME 176 and 1.7 miles north of the junction of US 1 and ME 15. Drive north on Hatchery Road 2.5 miles to the Stuart Gross Path trailhead. You will pass through the Craig Brook National Fish Hatchery, where the pavement ends, and pass the Dead River trailhead. The Stuart Gross trailhead is on the left just before a red gate across the road. There is a small sign at the trailhead and a shoulder for parking on the right.
Trailhead GPS: N44 35.751' / W68 40.860'

The Hike

The climb up Great Pond Mountain is almost entirely on exposed bedrock. As the trail nears the summit, it crosses a huge expanse of bare rock that slopes to the south. From a distance the bedrock appears to be granite; upon closer inspection the grains in the rock look too big and irregular for the rock to be granite. Most granite in Maine is made up of either equal-size grains or only two sizes of grains. The bedrock on Great Pond Mountain is made of grains of many sizes, including some that are very large. But, in fact, it is granite. Great Pond Mountain is part of one of the largest granite plutons in Maine, known as the Lucerne Formation. The pluton was named for the town along US 1A between Ellsworth and Bangor. It extends from south of Great Pond Mountain to near Blue Hill north all the way to Great Pond in northeastern Hancock County. The pluton is bounded on the west by a fault and on the east by

The mountains of Acadia National Park are visible on the horizon from the granite ledges near the summit.

the Union River, and measures 260 square miles. It is somewhat younger than much of the bedrock around it. Geologists can see where it intruded over other bedrock, sometimes creating dikes within those older bedrocks. Nearby Blue Hill is a granite monadnock whose granite abuts and predates the Lucerne Formation.

If you look at a map of Maine, you'll notice west of the Union River there are a number of narrow lakes—including Branch, Green, and Phillips Lakes and Toddy and Patten Ponds—that run roughly east–west and are surrounded by low, rocky mountains. This is the heart of the Lucerne Formation. From Great Pond Mountain you can see several of these lakes and ponds, but because the views from the summit are restricted to the north you cannot see the other mountains that are part of the pluton. And, of course, you can see two other famous areas of granite to the southeast and southwest: Mount Desert Island and Blue Hill.

Mountain Trail, the path to the summit of Great Pond Mountain, is an old woods road. The wide trail is worn down to the bedrock for almost its entire length. The climb is remarkably gentle; you hardly seem to climb at all until the very end. Along the way you pass wider open areas with views to the south. The open areas are bounded by blueberry bushes that blend into the scraggly forest that is struggling to survive on the thin soil laid down over the granite bedrock.

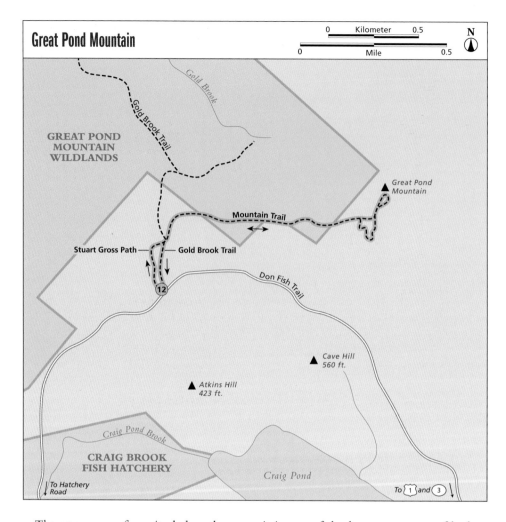

The open area of granite below the summit is one of the largest expanses of bed-rock you can hike across in Maine. In the early fall raptors use the thermals generated by all the exposed rock to get lift on their migration. On cool fall days you can lie on the rock, looking out to Mount Desert Island and Blue Hill and Penobscot Bays, soaking up the warmth held in the rock. By late afternoon the birds often congregate in the trees surrounding the open rock. As the sun moves lower in the sky, it heats the rock less and the thermals become weaker. The raptors roost for the night and then catch a thermal in the morning as the rock heats up to begin the next leg of their journey south.

After returning from the summit, you may want to stop at the Craig Brook National Fish Hatchery. (You drove through the hatchery on your way to the trail-head.) There is a visitor center and staff willing to answer your questions. Behind the visitor center a lawn slopes down to Almoosook Lake, which is a good place to relax, swim, or eat lunch. There are also trails on the hatchery's land between Almoosook Lake and Craig Pond.

Miles and Directions

0.0 Start from the Stuart Gross Path trailhead on the north side of the road.

0.2 The trail climbs steadily through a hardwood forest of mostly oak and beech to an intersection marked by two blue arrows. Turn right at the intersection and descend to the marked intersection with the Gold Brook Trail. Go straight onto the Mountain Trail.

0.6 The entirely unblazed Mountain Trail climbs gently, almost entirely on bare bedrock, to the first overlook with views to the south and west.

1.0 The trail climbs, then begins to slab around the mountain to the south. Turn left and climb to the open bedrock expanse that extends above and below where you come out onto it.

1.1 Climb the open bedrock. At the top a well-defined trail enters the woods. This is a loop trail that leads to the summit of Great Pond Mountain.

1.2 There is a sign on the semi-open summit. Continue on the loop trail back to the open bedrock.

1.3 Before heading down the mountain, you should explore the open bedrock expanse to take in all the views it affords. After that, return on the Mountain Trail toward the trailhead.

2.3 Arrive back at the junction with the Gold Brook Trail. You could retrace your steps to the trailhead on the Stuart Gross Path; for this hike turn left and follow the Gold Brook Trail, which is shorter. The Gold Brook Trail descends, quickly becoming more of an eroded streambed than a trail.

2.4 The trail ends at the road within sight of the Stuart Gross Path trailhead.

13 Black Mountain Bald

Black Mountain Bald is the eastern summit of Black Mountain. The summit is a large granite dome that offers fine views of the surrounding mountains and coast. The hike climbs the mountain from the south, up a rocky ridge through spruce forest and across granite bedrock. The open areas abound in blueberries. The trail descends a steep-sided notch, passing Wizard Pond, before the final climb to the summit.

Start: From the Big Chief trailhead, 100 feet up the road beyond the trailhead parking
Distance: 2.5-mile lollipop
Hiking time: About 2 hours
Difficulty: Moderate
Best seasons: May to Nov
Trail surface: Woodland trail and open granite ledges
Land status: Donnell Pond Public Reserved Land
Nearest town: Sullivan

Other trail users: Hunting allowed on Maine Public Reserved Lands
Water availability: No reliable water
Canine compatibility: Dogs must be under control at all times
Fees and permits: No fees or permits required
Maps: DeLorme: The Maine Atlas and Gazetteer: map 24; USGS Tunk Lake
Trail contact: Donnell Pond Public Reserved Land, (207) 941-4412; www.maine.gov/dacf/parks

Finding the trailhead: On US 1 east of Ellsworth, cross the Hancock Bridge. Drive 4.4 miles farther, then turn left onto ME 183, which is also known as Tunk Lake Road. Drive 4.3 miles; just beyond the Sunrise Trail, turn left onto Schoodic Beach Road at the Donnell Pond Public Reserved Land sign. Drive 0.3 mile to where the road forks. Bear right, uphill, onto Black Mountain Road. Drive slowly: This road can be rough and uneven in places. Drive 2.2 miles on Black Mountain Road; the trailhead parking is on the right, 100 feet before the trailhead. There is an information sign at the back of the parking area and two signs at the trailhead.
Trailhead GPS: N44 34.647' / W68 06.294'

The Hike

Black Mountain rises between Donnell Pond and Tunk Lake in the heart of the Donnell Pond Public Reserved Land. The mountain has two distinct summits separated by a deep valley. The western summit, Black Mountain, is spruce covered and gives the mountain its name. From a distance the thick, dark evergreens make the mountain appear black, especially in contrast with Schoodic Nubble to the west and Black Mountain Bald, the mountain's eastern summit, which have open, granite summits. The southern and western flanks of the horseshoe-shaped mountain are steep, with cliffs in places. The northern flank slopes more gently, creating a wide valley between Black Mountain and Caribou Mountain. The Caribou Mountain Trail loops around this wilderness valley.

There are several trails up Black Mountain and Black Mountain Bald. Black Mountain Cliffs Trail leaves from Schoodic Beach on Donnell Pond and climbs

The Big Chief Trail in fog.

steeply along a stream through open maple and beech. Once atop the ridge the trail turns east, skirts along the top of the cliffs, and ends on the low south end of Black Mountain. The Black Mountain Trail begins at the parking area at the end of Schoodic Beach Road. It climbs gradually through second-growth hardwoods along an old, swampy woods road for the first mile, then steeply up a slope of granite and grass overhung with twisting birch trees. Beyond Black Mountain Cliffs Trail, the trail follows along the north–south summit ridge of Black Mountain under the spruce. There are no views from Black Mountain, just spruce, moss, and quiet solitude. A trail connects Black Mountain with Black Mountain Bald, dropping down from a rock precipice into the wooded valley. The eastern end of this trail is part of the loop hike on Black Mountain Bald.

This hike follows the Big Chief Trail up the mountain—the most direct route. This trail is named for the commercial camps situated between Tunk Lake and Little Tunk Pond not far from the trailhead. The first 0.3 mile climbs through mixed forest to the ridgetop. Atop the ridge the trail winds between areas of exposed bedrock edged by spruce and blueberries. This trail is one of the better blueberry hikes in the region. Along this section are views that preview the 360-degree view from the summit. The trail drops off this open ridge into a narrow valley, passing near but not within sight of Wizard Pond. Please stay on the trail and avoid bushwhacking to the pond and damaging the fragile plants that grow in the spongy

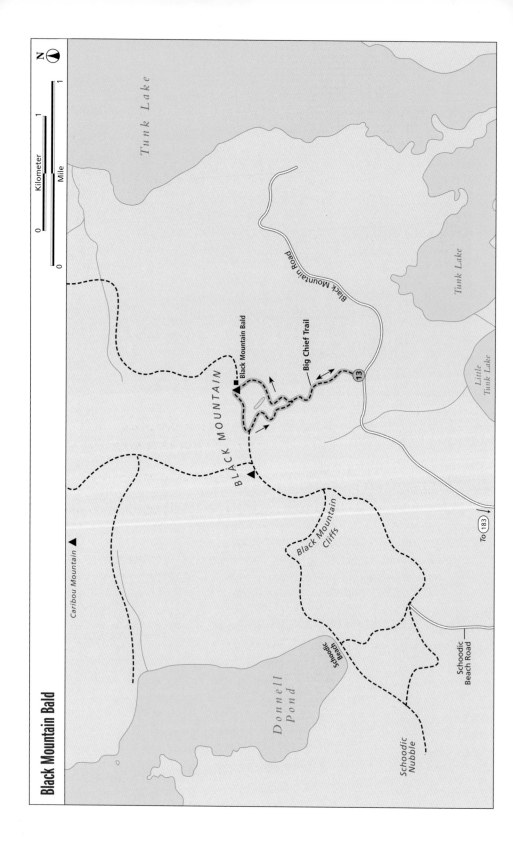

Black Mountain Bald

ground around the pond. You will get a good look at the pond from a cliff top on the return hike.

The summit of Black Mountain Bald is like a granite cake. The trail switchbacks along a layer, then climbs up to the next layer several times before topping out. The summit offers fine views in every direction. The already described Caribou Mountain Trail begins here and drops down off the summit to the north. To continue our hike, follow the trail to the west that connects Black Mountain Bald to Black Mountain and the Black Mountain Cliffs across its summit.

> Along the shore of Wizard Pond is a forest of old-growth red spruce. These trees have never been logged because of the steep, inaccessible terrain. Many of the spruce are more than 250 years old, including one that has been dated to 1692.

The trail drops down into the woods and skirts around to the north and west of Wizard Pond. Before the trail begins to climb Black Mountain in earnest, there is a junction with a trail that leaves to the east, connecting to Big Chief Trail. It is along this trail that there is an overlook with a view of Wizard Pond. Most people who climb Black Mountain Bald hike up Big Chief Trail and return the same way. By using these other trails on the return, you get to see another part of the mountain and enjoy some solitude as well.

Miles and Directions

0.0 Start at the Big Chief trailhead, 100 feet up the road beyond the parking area.

0.3 The trail climbs up to a cliff then skirts around to the south of it. Above the cliff the trail comes to the hike's first overlook.

0.6 On the open ridgetop the trail junctions with a trail that cuts over to the Black Mountain Trail. Turn right and stay on the Big Chief Trail.

0.8 The trail crosses the ridge, then drops down into a steep-sided valley. Wizard Pond is to the north of the trail in the valley. After stepping across the pond's outlet stream, the trail begins the switchback up Black Mountain Bald.

1.1 Reach Black Mountain Bald's summit. Three trails converge on the open summit: the Big Chief Trail you just ascended, the Caribou Mountain Trail that drops off the summit to the northeast, and the Black Mountain Cutoff Trail that descends into the notch between Black Mountain Bald and Black Mountain to the west. After taking in the expansive views from the summit, hike down the trail to the west.

1.5 Near the bottom of the valley, the trail junctions with the trail that cuts over to Big Chief Trail. Turn left onto this trail.

1.6 Out on the open ridge again, there is a 200-foot-long side trail that descends to an overlook atop a cliff that drops down into Wizard Pond.

1.9 Arrive back at the Big Chief Trail. Turn right to hike back to the trailhead.

2.5 Arrive back at the trailhead.

14 Tunk Mountain

Tunk Mountain lies north of Tunk Lake, surrounded by a group of ponds. The hike to the summit passes Salmon and Mud Ponds. The return hike passes Little Long Pond. The trail climbs, steeply at times, to the open, south-facing ledges on Tunk Mountain's summit ridge, then over the ridge to a cliff top on the mountain's north side. The trail does not actually cross the peak, which is at the west end of the summit ridge. The hike offers fine views in every direction from the summit ridge: south and east along the coast, west toward Blue Hill and the Camden Hills, and north across the endless lowlands of the Penobscot Valley and the Downeast forest.

Start: From the Tunk Mountain trailhead at the west end of the parking area
Distance: 4.7 miles out and back
Hiking time: 3 to 4 hours
Difficulty: Moderate
Best seasons: April to Nov
Trail surface: Woodland path and bare rock
Land status: Donnell Pond Public Reserved Land
Nearest town: Franklin

Other trail users: Hunting allowed on Maine Public Reserved Lands; many of the ponds along this hike are popular fishing spots.
Water availability: Salmon and Mud Ponds
Canine compatibility: Dogs must be under control at all times
Fees and permits: No fees or permits required
Maps: *DeLorme: The Maine Atlas and Gazetteer:* map 24; USGS Tunk Mountain
Trail contact: Donnell Pond Public Reserved Land, 941-4412; www.maine.gov/dacf/parks

Finding the trailhead: From Ellsworth drive north (okay, so you're actually driving east) on US 1 for 4.7 miles. Turn left onto ME 182 toward Franklin. Drive 14.3 miles through Franklin and past Fox Pond. As the road climbs away from Fox Pond, there is a sign for the Tunk Mountain trailhead. Turn left into the trailhead parking area. The trail begins at the west end of the parking area next to the information kiosk.
Trailhead GPS: N44 37.515' / W68 05.335'

The Hike

Tunk Mountain is the highest and most northerly of the group of mountains around Donnell Pond at the head of Frenchman Bay. There has only been a good trail to the summit since 2012 when the state completed its development of the area. The mountain was donated to the state—and made part of the Donnell Pond Reserved Land—by Harold Pierce's children in 1994. Before the new trail was completed, the hike mostly entailed following spray-painted arrows straight up the rocky mountainside.

The hike begins at the gravel parking lot complete with an information kiosk and outhouse. The first section of the trail winds through a mixed hardwood forest, crossing several small streams and winding among boulders. One boulder is nearly as big as a house and can be easily climbed from the back.

Looking east from Monument Overlook across frozen ponds.

Just before and just after Salmon Pond, the trail passes the loop trail to Little Long Pond that is part of the return hike. Of the three ponds on this hike, Salmon Pond is the least interesting. The other two, Little Long Pond and Mud Pond, both have cliffs that drop down into them and offer views of Tunk Mountain. Beyond Salmon Pond the trail climbs a dry, rocky ridge and then drops down to Mud Pond. The name seems a misnomer: The shore of the pond is mostly rock—in several places actual cliffs. You can hear the outlet stream dropping from the east end of the pond down over rocks on its way to Little Long Pond. At the west end of Mud pond, two small streams drop into the pond, clattering over rocks.

The trail climbs up alongside one of the streams. The ascent varies from rock scrambles to gentle climbs among spruce and fir. The trail crosses and recrosses the stream, then climbs away from it and pops out onto a ledge with views south and east. Across the Hidden Pond Valley rises Catherine and Caribou Mountains. Behind them are Black Mountain and Schoodic Nubble, with a tower on its summit; beyond and between these mountains you can catch glimpses of Mount Desert Island.

Higher, where the trail breaks out onto the open summit ridge, there are fine views south, east, and west. Off in the distance you can see Blue Hill all by itself along the irregular coastline. The trail cuts across the wooded summit ridge to the top of a cliff on the mountain's north side. From here there is an endless vista of the flat

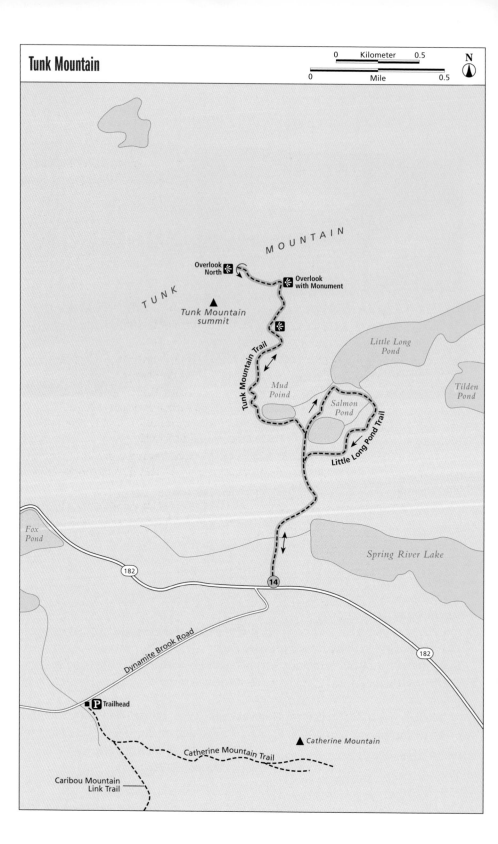

Tunk Mountain

Scale:
0 — Kilometer — 0.5
0 — Mile — 0.5

N

MOUNTAIN

TUNK

Overlook North

Overlook with Monument

▲ Tunk Mountain summit

Tunk Mountain Trail

Little Long Pond

Tilden Pond

Mud Poind

Salmon Pond

Little Long Pond Trail

Fox Pond

182

14

Spring River Lake

182

Dynamite Brook Road

P Trailhead

Catherine Mountain Trail

▲ Catherine Mountain

Caribou Mountain Link Trail

Penobscot Valley dotted with ponds and low mountains. In the foreground is one of Maine's many wind farms, its nineteen turbines silently generating electricity.

The trail never crosses the actual summit of Tunk Mountain. You can bushwhack west from the trail, past huge boulders, along the ridgetop to the summit. There is a small tower and building at the summit for collecting scientific data. The views from the summit are not as good as those from the vistas along the trail.

On you way back from the mountain, turn left onto the Little Long Pond Trail just before reaching Salmon Pond. The trail skirts around the pond and then follows the outlet stream from Mud Pond as it tumbles over and around rocks and boulders on its way to Little Long Pond. At Little Long Pond the trail follows atop a cliff on the pond's south side, then turns back toward Salmon Pond. It adds almost a mile to your hike, but is worth the extra walking.

Miles and Directions

0.0   Start at the west end of the parking lot next to the information kiosk. Walk down the steps and into the woods. The trail begins as an old road and quickly narrows to a trail that winds through wet areas on bog boards and among large boulders.

0.5   Reach an unmarked trail on the right on a rise just before Salmon Pond. This is the end of the loop to Little Long Pond. Go straight, dropping down to Salmon Pond.

0.6   Reach the marked junction with the other end of the loop to Little Long Pond. Go straight, climbing away from Salmon Pond. The trail goes over a rise, then drops down to the east end of Mud Pond. The trail skirts around Mud Pond and crosses two small streams that flow into it. At the second stream the trail begins to climb Tunk Mountain.

1.4   The trail comes to an area of exposed rock that offers fine views south and east. Above this point be sure to follow the blue blazes and ignore the arrows spray-painted on the rock.

1.7   A short side trail leads to another viewpoint with a monument to Harold Pierce, whose family donated this land to the state. Beyond the viewpoint the trail climbs and then comes out onto the open face of the mountain with fine views south and west. The trail turns to the north and passes over the summit ridge.

1.9   The trail ends at the top of a cliff with fine views north. Return back down the mountain the way you came.

3.1   Arrive back at the Little Long Pond Trail. Turn left to take this loop back. (**Option:** Going straight back to the trailhead from here will make the hike 0.9 mile shorter.) The Little Long Pond Trail skirts the edge of Salmon Pond, then cuts over to Mud Pond's outlet stream, which it follows downhill to Little Long Pond.

3.3   Reach Little Long Pond. The trail makes a sharp right just before the pond and climbs to follow atop a cliff on the edge of the pond. Do not follow the trail along the edge of the pond. It is a dead end that gives access for anglers.

3.9   Arrive back at the Tunk Mountain Trail. Turn left to return to the trailhead.

4.7   Arrive back at the trailhead.

15 Catherine Mountain

Catherine Mountain is the easternmost of the group of mountains in Donnell Pond Public Reserved Land. South-facing cliffs along the summit ridge offer views east across Tunk Lake and south and west of Black Mountain, Schoodic Nubble, and Caribou Mountain. Those mountains block any view of Mount Desert Island. Even so, Catherine Mountain offers fine views for not a lot of climbing.

Start: From the Caribou Mountain Link trailhead just before the bridge across Dynamite Brook
Distance: 2.3 miles out and back
Hiking time: 2 to 3 hours
Difficulty: Moderate
Best seasons: May to Nov
Trail surface: Woodland path
Land status: Donnell Pond Public Reserved Land
Nearest towns: Franklin and Cherryfield

Other trail users: Hunting allowed on Maine Public Reserved Lands
Water availability: Dynamite Brook crosses the road just beyond the trailhead
Canine compatibility: Dogs must be under control at all times
Fees and permits: No fees or permits required
Maps: *DeLorme: The Maine Atlas and Gazetteer:* map 24; USGS Tunk Lake
Trail contact: Donnell Pond Public Reserved Land, (207) 941-4412; www.maine.gov/dacf/parks

Finding the trailhead: From Ellsworth drive east on US 1 for 4.7 miles. Turn left onto ME 182 and drive 14.3 miles through Franklin and past Fox Pond. On the hill past Fox Pond, turn right onto Dynamite Brook Road at the blue Public Reserved Land sign. The trailhead parking is 0.7 mile up the road on the left. The trailhead is 0.1 mile farther down the road, just before the road crosses Dynamite Brook.
Trailhead GPS: N44 37.114' / W68 06.193'

The Hike

The trail begins on what appears to be an old woods road along Dynamite Brook, passing over a wet area on bog boards and then climbing through a mixed forest. The Caribou Mountain Link Trail climbs the shoulder of Caribou Mountain, skirting around the bog that is the source of Dynamite Brook, and ends at the Caribou Mountain Trail near the summit of Caribou Mountain. The Caribou Mountain Trail begins on the summit of Black Mountain Bald, passes through the Rainbow Pond valley, climbs Caribou Mountain, and then ends atop Black Mountain. Caribou Mountain's wooded summit has no views, and those from the open ridge that the trail climbs to the mountain's top are about the same as from Catherine Mountain. The pleasure of that trail is in its remoteness and the likelihood of seeing wildlife.

The Catherine Mountain Trail is less steep than the first 0.2 mile on the Caribou Mountain Link Trail of this hike, but quickly climbs out of the maple and beech and

The mountains of Mount Desert Island peeking out from behind Black Mountain.

into spruce. This is a pattern that is repeated on many hikes in Maine. As you climb, the soils tend to be thinner and the exposure to the elements increases. As a result the forest changes from hardwoods that need richer, better-drained soils to softwoods that can tough out the worst conditions. Similarly, the understory changes as well: In poor soils you'll find blueberries and similar shrubs that hug the ground and often turn vibrant red in the fall. In the forests that are almost exclusively spruce, you'll often have an understory that is little more than saplings and moss. The conditions on Catherine Mountain, at only 940 feet, are not that harsh, so a profusion of trees and undergrowth cover the mountaintop where the bedrock is not exposed.

Rather than pass directly over the mountain's wooded summit, the trail follows the open ledges along the mountain's south shoulder. Catherine Mountain is a mile-long ridge that runs roughly east–west. The trail ascends the gentle west end of the mountain. The east end and south side, in particular, are much steeper and have open granite expanses and rough cliffs. In this way the hike offers off and on views as you hike the length of the top of the mountain.

Across Catherine Mountain the trail descends to ME 182, ending outside the Public Reserved Land at a muddy turnaround. The descent off the mountain is steep and has no views, and you would also end your hike several miles from your car. On the steep eastern flank of the mountain, there are several areas of broken rock—evidence of a mining operation. Your best bet is to stop at the cliff tops shortly after the trail begins to descend, enjoy the views, and return back to your car across the mountaintop. On the way back take the side trail on the left that skirts along the cliff tops—you'll get the best views of the hike. There are also several patches of blueberries in the area the trail passes through. Late summer hikers can snack as they walk.

Miles and Directions

0.0 Start at the trailhead of the Caribou Mountain Link Trail 0.1 mile west of the trailhead parking. The trailhead is just before the bridge across Dynamite Brook.

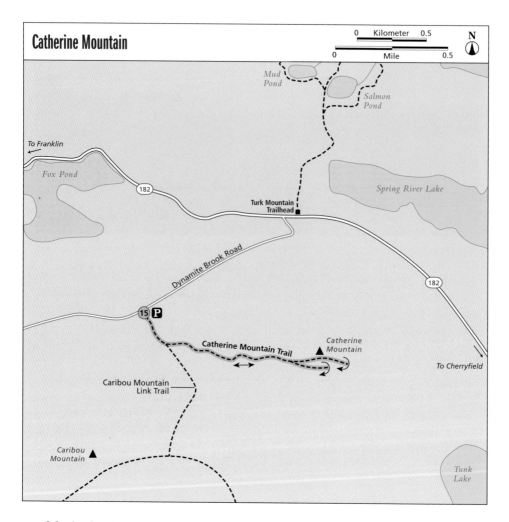

Catherine Mountain

0.2 At a junction is a sign giving the distance to the Caribou Mountain Trail. That trail is 0.7 mile farther to the right beyond the junction. Take the Catherine Mountain Trail to the left. The section of the trail just completed is the steepest on the hike.

0.9 The trail comes out onto a large granite slab, then continues up and across the slab. Near the top is a large stone sculpture.

1.0 An unmarked trail goes to the right. Continue straight ahead.

1.15 The Catherine Mountain Trail continues to descend down to ME 182. Stop here at the top of a cliff with fine views to the south and east.

1.3 Arrive back at the junction with the unmarked trail. Turn left onto the trail and emerge onto a cliff top. The trail bends to the right and goes through low bushes.

1.4 Arrive back at the main trail at the bottom of the open area where the sculpture is. Walk straight across the bottom of the granite to begin hiking back to the trailhead.

2.3 Arrive back at the trailhead.

16 Petit Manan

The Petit Manan hike follows the Hollingsworth Trail. The hike passes through blueberry barrens, rocky jack pine forest, a cedar bog, and along cobbled beaches. The trail offers the more adventurous hiker access to several miles of wild beach and two ponds frequented by migrating waterfowl and other birds.

Start: From the Hollingsworth trailhead across the road from the parking lot
Distance: 1.9-mile lollipop
Hiking time: About 1 hour; varies greatly depending on whether or not you swim or hike farther down the shore
Difficulty: Easy
Best seasons: Apr to Oct
Trail surface: Woodland path, bare granite, and beach cobbles
Land status: Petit Manan National Wildlife Refuge

Nearest towns: Steuben and Milbridge
Other trail users: None
Water availability: None
Canine compatibility: Dogs must be on a leash less than 10 feet long
Fees and permits: No fees or permits required
Maps: *DeLorme: The Maine Atlas and Gazetteer:* map 17; USGS Petit Manan Point
Trail contact: Petit Manan National Wildlife Refuge, Water Street, Milbridge, (207) 546-2124; www.fws.gov

Finding the trailhead: Drive east on US 1 out of Ellsworth; 14.8 miles past the Hancock Bridge, cross into Washington County and enter the town of Steuben. Drive 4.5 miles and turn right onto Pigeon Hill Road. Just before the turn there is a small sign for Petit Manan National Wildlife Refuge. Follow the road for 6.5 miles to the trailhead; parking is on the right, and the trail is on the left.
Trailhead GPS: N44 26.007' / W67 53.841'

The Hike

The Petit Manan National Wildlife Refuge complex contains thirty-eight islands on the Maine coast from Brunswick to Calais and three coastal areas between Gouldsboro and Milbridge. In all the refuge is nearly 7,000 acres. It was established in 1972 to protect colonial seabird nesting habitat, especially nesting sites for terns. As a result most of the islands are closed to visitors during the summer when the birds are nesting or young are present. The coastal areas are open, but access is limited.

Of the three mainland parcels, Petit Manan Point is the largest, a finger of rocky land that juts out between Gouldsboro and Pigeon Hill Bays, surrounded by many small and large islands. The 2,166-acre unit has two hiking trails. The first leaves from the information kiosk and winds through blueberry barrens, mixed woodlands, and along salt marshes to Birch Point and Carrying Place Cove on the west side of the point. The other trail, the Hollingsworth, winds over the peninsula's rocky spine, through scrub pine and a cedar bog to the west side. The

Along the Hollingsworth Trail.

Hollingsworth Trail offers access to Petit Manan Point and the two ponds there. These ponds, especially Big Pond, are magnets for migrating waterfowl. According to the US Fish & Wildlife Service, as many as 4,000 birds can be found there on a fall day. The smaller pond, behind Wood Pond Point, is usually a reliable place to find shorebirds.

The Hollingsworth Trail begins at an interpretive sign with background on the trail's namesake. There are several signs along the trail with information on the natural and human history of the area. The trail passes through a blueberry barren where you can find meadow birds and butterflies in the summer. After entering the woods, the trail follows the rocky spine down the peninsula. On this granite spine mostly jack pines grow, surrounded by dense shrubs and blueberries. These coastal jack pines are stunted, rarely more than 20 feet tall, with sinuous spreading branches. Porcupines strip the bark off to eat in the winter, leaving the yellow wood exposed. Many of the trees along this hike have scars from porcupine feeding. As you hike along, look for porcupines sleeping in a ball up in the trees.

Where the trail drops down off the exposed granite, it enters boggy areas where cedars and birch grow. The ground is covered with sphagnum moss and many low plants, including carnivorous pitcher plants. The cedar bog that the trail crosses on a winding boardwalk is the only cool, shady section of the trail, worth lingering in on a hot, sunny day.

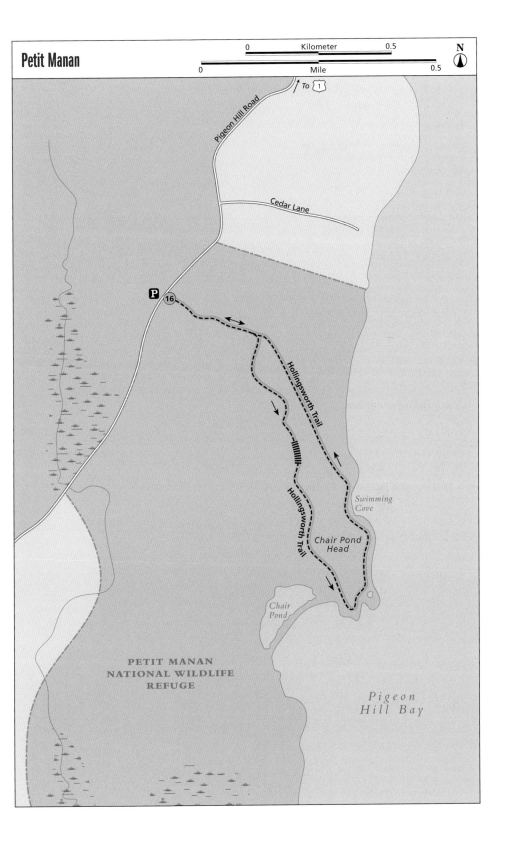

After hiking through an area of mixed woods with many good-size birch trees, you'll arrive at Chair Pond Point. A short side trail leads to the beach, behind which is Chair Pond. You can hike down along the cobbled beach to Wood Pond Point, visible down the shore, or even continue to Big Pond to see the waterfowl and gulls that congregate there during migration. Just remember that even though the walking is flat, it isn't easy. Walking on the cobbled beach can be very tiring. It's often easier to cross the mudflats at low tide, but that can be messy. You should assume it will take an hour to walk to Wood Pond Point and back. Add at least another hour to hike to Big Pond.

Visible to the southeast is Petit Manan Island and its lighthouse. The island, a part of the wildlife refuge, is an important tern nesting site. The island also hosts several species of alcids, including puffins. The inland waters along Petit Manan Point are, therefore, a good place to spot these birds as well as seals and sometimes dolphins.

The return hike is much like the hike out to the shore. Before turning inland the trail passes a small cove with a beach of softball-size cobbles. At or near high tide, this can be a refreshing spot for a swim. You just have to remember that even in August the water is only 65°F.

Miles and Directions

0.0 Start at the Hollingsworth trailhead across the road from the parking lot. The first 500 feet of the trail are gravel, until the path enters the woods.

0.2 Trail junction. The return trail comes in from the left. The hike continues straight ahead.

0.5 The trail dips down into a low, wooded area and follows bog boards through an area of cedars and sphagnum moss.

0.9 The trail breaks out of the woods. There is a short side trail to a cobbled beach with Chair Pond behind it. You can follow the shoreline for several miles to the tip of Petit Manan Point and Big Pond. Even though the walk is not far, walking on the uneven rocks is time-consuming and tiring.

1.0 The trail reaches Chair Pond Point. From here you can see down the peninsula to Wood Pond Point. Out in the bay you can see Petit Manan Island and its lighthouse. Beyond the point the trail reenters the woods and follows along the shore of Petit Manan Bay.

1.2 A short side trail goes out to a cobbled beach. This small cove is a great place for a swim when the tide is in. Be aware that the water is very cold even on hot summer days.

1.7 Return to the trail junction. Turn right to return to the trailhead.

1.9 Arrive back at the trailhead.

17 Pigeon Hill

This rocky hike climbs gently through dark forest, breaking out occasionally to offer previews of the view from the summit. Along the way the trail passes the site of a nineteenth-century silver mine. The summit of Pigeon Hill offers views of the coast from Mount Desert Island to Pleasant Bay.

Start: From the Pigeon Hill Preserve trailhead next to the information kiosk
Distance: 1.5-mile figure 8
Hiking time: About 1 hour
Difficulty: Easy
Best seasons: Apr to Oct
Trail surface: Woodland trail
Land status: Downeast Coastal Conservancy preserve
Nearest towns: Steuben and Milbridge

Other trail users: None
Water availability: None
Canine compatibility: Dogs must be under control at all times
Fees and permits: No fees or permits required
Maps: *DeLorme: The Maine Atlas and Gazetteer:* map 17; USGS Petit Manan Point
Trail contact: Downeast Coastal Conservancy, (207) 255-4500; www.downeastcostalconser vancy.org.

Finding the trailhead: Drive east on US 1 out of Ellsworth; 14.8 miles past the Hancock Bridge, cross into Washington County and enter the town of Steuben. Drive 4.5 miles and turn right onto Pigeon Hill Road. Just before the turn there is a small sign for Petit Manan National Wildlife Refuge. Follow the road for 4.5 miles to the Pigeon Hill Preserve parking lot on the right. There is a sign with trail information visible from the road. The trail comes out of the back of the parking lot.
Trailhead GPS: N44 27.275' / W67 53.014'

The Hike

There has been a trail to the summit of Pigeon Hill for more than a century. It is one of the highest points on the coast between Mount Desert Island and the Canadian border. For this reason, in 1857 Pigeon Hill was used as one of the survey points for the Eastern Oblique Arc. The original trail to the summit is known as the Historic Trail. The hike follows it down from near the summit back to the trailhead. On the way up, 160 feet from the trailhead, the trail leaves the Historic Trail to follow the Silver Mine Trail.

More history awaits you along the Silver Mine Trail. Some time after the Civil War, a silver mine was started on the eastern shoulder of Pigeon Hill. The ore was of low quality, and a full mining operation never took place. Today along the trail, heaps of broken rocks and a watering hole are still in evidence. The Downeast Coastal Conservancy, which owns the hill and maintains the trails, has placed a small sign on a tree near the old mine site with the little information that is known about the mine.

Of course, most folks who have climbed Pigeon Hill knew nothing of this history. They climbed to the summit for the view. Just before the summit there is an overlook

Fall colors along the Ledge Woods Trail.

with a sign to help you identify the islands and bays visible to the east. From the summit you can clearly see Cadillac Mountain on Mount Desert Island to the west; the mountains around Donnell Pond and Tunk Lake to the northwest; Petit Manan Point and Petit Manan Island with its lighthouse to the south; and the islands, bays, and heads of the Downeast coast to the east.

As you descend the open ledges on the southwest side of Pigeon Hill, you have a choice. You can follow the Summit Loop Trail, which slabs around the hill to the Historic Trail; this route is 0.3 mile shorter than the described hike. This hike follows the Ledge Woods Trail, which was constructed in 2013 and drops down off the hill to the south. The rocky trail passes through a mixed forest of maples and evergreens. The dry descent then gives way to a forest full of moss. The trail loops back to the north and climbs gently along semi-open ledges to the Summit Loop Trail. The open areas all along the trail are full of blueberry bushes. Just before the junction with the Summit Loop Trail, the trail passes through a group of very large boulders.

Miles and Directions

0.0 Start at the trailhead next to the information kiosk. In 160 feet come to the junction with the Silver Mine Trail. Turn right and follow the yellow blazes.

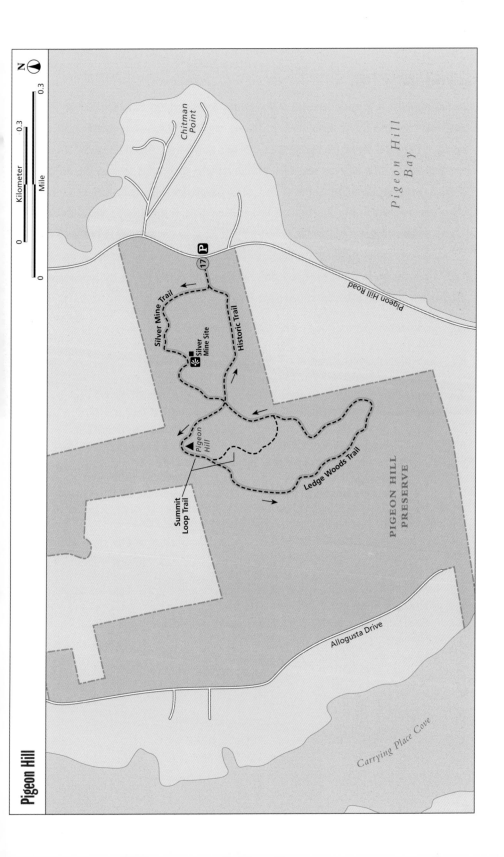

Pigeon Hill

EPPING BASE LINE

The Eastern Oblique Arc was surveyed in the mid-nineteenth century to tie together all the coastal surveys from Calais, Maine, to New Orleans, creating a database for better nautical charts. In Downeast Maine the Epping Base Line was visible from Pigeon Hill where it was measured in 1857. In all there were nine granite monuments erected to mark the survey points in the Epping Base Line section of the Eastern Oblique Arc. Today the Epping Base Line is in a commercial blueberry barren northeast of Cherryfield. It is the only baseline on the entire arc that still exists; the marble monument that stood on the west end of the line is in the Maine state museum in Augusta. Local residents have located a number of the granite markers that were placed along the base line, and the granite bases for the two monuments at either end of the base line are still in place.

0.1 Short side trail to an overlook. The overlook is atop a low cliff in the woods with no real views.

0.2 Reach another overlook. There is a stone bench to sit on with a view east of the coast and islands. The trail turns back into the woods beyond this point.

0.3 To the left of the trail are the remains of a silver mine. There is a small sign on a tree explaining that it was a small test mine that was dug after the Civil War.

0.4 Turn right onto the Historic Trail. Almost immediately bear right onto the Summit Loop Trail.

0.5 The trail climbs to an overlook with a sign showing what you are seeing to the east, along the coast. The trail climbs more gently for another 250 feet to the mostly open summit. You have clear views to the south of Petit Manan Point and to the east of the coast and islands. To the west, across Dyer Bay and Schoodic Peninsula, are the mountains of Acadia National Park on Mount Desert Island. To descend from the summit, follow the yellow-blazed Summit Loop Trail.

0.6 Continue over the summit on the Summit Loop Trail, then turn right onto the Ledge Woods Trail. *(Option:* You can make the hike a shorter, 1.2-mile loop by bearing left and staying on the Summit Loop Trail.)

1.2 The Ledge Woods Trail descends off the south face of Pigeon Hill, then loops around and returns up the hill to end at the Summit Loop Trail. Turn right to return to the trailhead.

1.3 Junction with the Historic Trail. Turn right and follow the blue-blazed Historic Trail back to the trailhead.

1.5 Arrive back at the trailhead.

18 Great Wass Island

Great Wass Island juts farther out into the Gulf of Maine than any other island you can drive to, making for excellent wildlife viewing opportunities. The hike out Little Cape Point Trail passes in and out of several ecosystems before reaching Cape Cove. The hike up the coast to Mud Hole Trail can be strenuous unless you take time to stop and watch for sea life. The hike back to the trailhead on Mud Hole Trail is not as varied as the hike out, but passes through at least two distinct forest types.

Start: From the Mud Hole and Little Cape Point trailhead at the back of the parking lot
Distance: 4.6-mile loop
Hiking time: 3 to 5 hours
Difficulty: Moderate
Best seasons: May to Oct; winter months can be good for seeing seabirds and overwintering waterfowl
Trail surface: Woodland trail, bare granite, and cobbled beach
Land status: Nature Conservancy preserve

Nearest town: Jonesport
Other trail users: None
Water availability: Small stream 0.3 mile into the hike
Canine compatibility: Dogs not allowed in any Nature Conservancy preserves
Fees and permits: No fees or permits required
Maps: DeLorme: The Maine Atlas and Gazetteer: map 17; USGS Great Wass Island
Trail contact: The Nature Conservancy, (207) 729-5181; www.nature.org/maine

Finding the trailhead: From US 1 in Columbia, turn south onto ME 187 at Wild Blueberry Land. Drive 10.6 miles into Jonesport. Turn right onto Bridge Street at the sign for Beals Island. Cross the bridge onto Beals Island, then turn left at the Stop sign onto Bay View Drive. Drive 1.2 miles, crossing the causeway onto Great Wass Island. Turn right onto Great Wass Island Road; there is no street sign at this intersection, but there is a small Nature Conservancy sign. After 1.8 miles the pavement ends. Continue driving for another 0.7 mile. The trailhead parking is on the left.
Trailhead GPS: N44 28.862' / W67 35.667'

The Hike

Great Wass Island is the largest of a group of nearly fifty islands off the coast at Jonesport. Of all the islands on the Downeast coast accessible by car, Great Wass sticks farthest out into the Gulf of Maine. As a result it offers exceptional opportunities to see marine mammals and seabirds. Along the route of this hike, you may see seals up close, and dolphins and even whales in the distance. You may get lucky and see a pelagic bird—seabirds that spend almost their entire lives at sea. During spring and fall migrations, many songbirds stop on Great Wass for a rest and to refuel. Hikers willing to brave the snow and winter weather can find all manner of sea ducks and other waterfowl that spend the winter along Great Wass's protected coastline.

The hike follows the Little Cape Point Trail 1.6 miles from the parking lot to the shore at Cape Cove. This leg of the hike climbs over the rocky spine of the island. The open jack pine forest offers hikers a blueberry snack in late summer and views of the open heath south of the trail surrounded by a dense spruce forest. Often eagles or osprey can be seen silently soaring above the island. Long before the ocean comes into view, you can smell it on the breeze. In early summer the breeze often carries what sounds like people in the distance having a good time. In fact, it is seals barking.

At high tide the sea comes right up on the bedrock close to the trees where the Little Cape Point Trail ends. When the tide is out, there is a wide cobble beach with boulders jutting out of it. At low tide the cove itself becomes a mudflat that attracts shorebirds. Children enjoy exploring the pools and spines of rock that jut out of the cove. There are crabs hiding under the seaweed, small fish and other creatures in the pools. Seals sometimes congregate on the small islands off the shore here, and rarely whales can be seen passing by beyond the island.

You can turn right here and hike several miles out toward the southern tip of the island. Just remember that hiking on the variously sized cobbles is more tiring than

The rugged coast in Cape Cove.

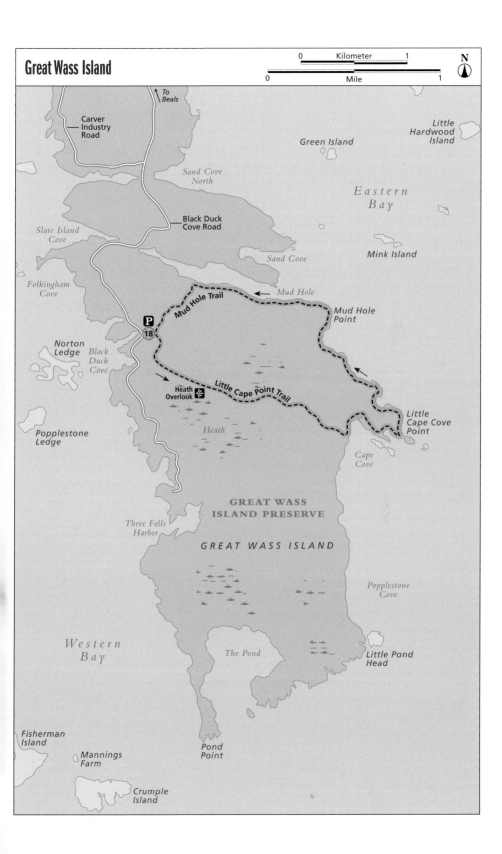

Great Wass Island

0 — Kilometer — 1
0 — Mile — 1

N

To
Beals

Carver
Industry
Road

Green Island

Little
Hardwood
Island

Sand Cove
North

Black Duck
Cove Road

Eastern
Bay

Slate Island
Cove

Sand Cove

Mink Island

Folkingham
Cove

Mud Hole

Mud Hole Trail

Mud Hole
Point

P

18

Norton
Ledge

Black
Duck
Cove

Little Cape Point Trail

Heath
Overlook

Little
Cape Cove
Point

Poppplestone
Ledge

Heath

Cape
Cove

GREAT WASS
ISLAND PRESERVE

Three Falls
Harbor

GREAT WASS ISLAND

Poppplestone
Cove

Western
Bay

The Pond

Little Pond
Head

Fisherman
Island

Mannings
Farm

Pond
Point

Crumple
Island

you would expect. Even though you can see more than a mile down the coast, expect the walk to take quite a while.

The hike goes around the back of the cove and out Little Cove Point. The trail stays on the rocks mostly, but occasionally turns into the spruce forest to get around spots where the rocks are too steep to pass. Keep watching for seabirds and seals as you hike along. The best way to see something interesting is to sit in one place and keep your eyes and ears open. The best place to see seals or dolphins up close is where the hike reaches Mud Hole Trail. From a perch on the high rocks, you can scan Mud Hole Channel between Great Wass and Steel Harbor Island. At times the seals will come within a few feet of the shore and pop their heads up, as if they were as interested in you as you in them. Ducks, especially in winter, congregate in this area and at the mouth of Mud Hole.

The hike follows the shore of Mud Hole through a spruce forest. It's a unique experience to walk through the forest with the sounds of gulls wheeling overhead and the scent of saltwater drifting in through the trees. Sea breezes and frequent fog keep the forest damp and mossy. When the trail turns south away from Mud Hole and climbs the spine of the island, the damp spruce and moss are once again replaced with blueberries and jack pine.

Miles and Directions

0.0 Start from the trailhead at the back of the parking lot, next to the information kiosk. In 250 feet see the Little Cape Point Trail straight ahead; the Mud Hole Trail is to the left. Go straight onto the Little Cape Point Trail; the hike returns on the Mud Hole Trail.

0.3 The trail crosses a small but reliable stream.

0.6 The trail emerges onto a spine of granite with views south across the heath in the center of the island.

1.6 The Little Cape Point Trail ends at Cape Cove.

2.1 Continue to the north around Cape Cove, following blue blazes on the rocks. The trail climbs along some cliffs and around a smaller cove, then reaches Little Cape Point.

3.3 The trail mostly follows the rocky shore, occasionally cutting into the spruce woods behind the shore, then reaches the Mud Hole Trail. The high rocks here are a good place to watch for wildlife: seals, dolphins, and sea ducks mostly.

3.4 The Mud Hole Trail follows the shore in the trees, then turns inland to follow the shore along Mud Hole.

4.1 The trail turns south away from Mud Hole and begins to climb gently over the spine of the island.

4.55 Arrive back at the first trail junction. Turn right to return to the trailhead.

4.6 Arrive back at the trailhead.

19 The Bold Coast

This iconic Maine hike is long for a day hike, but the terrain is relatively flat and never dull. You can also camp along the coast near Fairy Head and make the hike an easy two-day trip. The trail passes atop some of the highest sea cliffs in New England, and visits several miles of rocky coast and two cobbled beaches. You also hike through mossy spruce forest and meadows of rose bushes and tall grass.

Start: From the Bold Coast trailhead near the entrance into the parking area
Distance: 9.5-mile lollipop
Hiking time: 5 to 7 hours
Difficulty: Strenuous due to length
Best seasons: May to Oct
Trail surface: Woodland path and rocky headland
Land status: Cutler Public Reserved Land
Nearest towns: Cutler (no services) and Machias
Other trail users: None

Water availability: Seasonal streams; the only reliable water is from Black Point Brook where it empties into the ocean at mile 6.5. There is no water near any of the three campsites.
Canine compatibility: Dogs must be under control at all times
Fees and permits: No fees or permits required to hike or camp; permit required for a campfire
Maps: DeLorme: The Maine Atlas and Gazetteer: map 27; USGS Cutler
Trail contact: Cutler Public Reserved Land, (207) 941-4412; www.maine.gov/dacf/parks

Finding the trailhead: From the junction of US 1 and ME 191 in East Machias, drive south on ME 191 for 13.1 miles to the village of Cutler. Continue another 4 miles on ME 191. The trailhead parking is on the right; there is a brown sign for the trail just before the turn and a blue Cutler Public Reserved Land sign at the parking area.
Trailhead GPS: N44 41.919' / W67 09.473'

The Hike

The Bold Coast is one of Maine's most written about hikes. It has been featured in everything from local newspapers like the *Ellsworth American* to *USA Today*, and magazines as diverse as *Yankee* and *Backpacker*. But don't let all the publicity scare you off; the Bold Coast is worth all the attention it gets, and except for right around Pulpit Rock on the coast, you are unlikely to meet another hiker. If you choose to camp at one of the three campsites near Fairy Head, you will likely have the coast to yourself.

Most people who visit the Bold Coast hike from the parking lot directly to Pulpit Rock along the Coastal Trail and miss most of the Bold Coast. Our hike takes the Inland Trail to Fairy Head through spruce forest inhabited by rare—in the United States—black-backed woodpeckers; along the marshy fringes of Schooner Brook where blueberries abound on the higher, rocky areas; and past a valley flooded by a pond full of calling frogs and ducks. Beyond the pond the trail climbs a rocky hill

Looking west along the Bold Coast.

through birch and maple, then mostly spruce, with several viewpoints atop rocky outcroppings. From the final viewpoint you look across a mile of spruce forest to Fairy Head and the waters westward. You will probably smell the sea on the breeze long before you get to this overlook—a reminder of how moisture insinuates itself into these woods, keeping them cool and damp.

Fairy Head, the western end of the Bold Coast, is across the Little River from Little River Island and its lighthouse. The foghorn sounds every 10 seconds or so, and is a constant companion on the entire hike. You will likely also feel, as much as hear, the diesel thrum of passing lobster boats. From Fairy Head the hike follows along the rocky shore within reach of the sea. The cliffs at this end of the hike are much lower than at the eastern end. The rock here is mostly dark gray with little grain. This is not Maine's famous granite; it is rock of volcanic origin. Much of the Downeast coast is rock from volcanic activity more than 400 million years ago. There are even several places along the hike where you can find hexagonal basalt columns, formed when hot magma forced its way up through existing rock and then cooled.

The three campsites along this section are all very rustic with either views of the coast or close proximity to it. You can fall asleep listening to the almost human sounds of the moving tide surging into and draining out of the irregular rocks. Just remember that there are no privies or water at any of the campsites. But there will be a sky full of bright stars undiminished by ground clutter.

After the third campsite the trail turns inland through a mossy spruce forest. Look for irises near the rocks at the forest edge. As you hike east, the cliffs tend to get higher and access to the coast less common. When the trail turns inland to cross Long Point, it almost seems like you've left the coast. But when the trail winds back to the shore, you stand atop the highest cliff yet. The trail edges atop the cliff more than 100 feet above the water. The trail crosses two cobbled beaches, meadows overgrown with tall grasses and wild roses, and several more exposed cliffs before reaching the highest cliffs of all at Pulpit Rock. A short side trail goes out onto Pulpit Rock, where you can sit atop the bare rock and look down more than 150 feet into the water on both sides.

From Pulpit Rock it is a stroll through the spruce forest back to the trailhead. Remember to look for the elusive black-backed woodpeckers peeling bark off standing dead trees. Unlike other Maine woodpeckers, they tend to go quietly about their business. Quickly, you'll leave the smell of the sea and the sound of the surf behind, replaced by the stillness of the cool, dark spruce forest.

Miles and Directions

0.0 Begin at the Bold Coast trailhead on the Coastal Trail.

0.4 Turn right onto the Inland Trail.

1.8 The Inland Trail follows the edge of the marshes along Schooner Brook, sometimes with views of this wetland. The trail crosses rocky outcroppings, wet low areas, and several forest types. After one especially overgrown low spot, the trail climbs a rocky hill to the junction with the Black Point Brook Cutoff trail. (**Option:** To make the hike a shorter 4.7 miles, take this trail 0.8 mile to Black Point Cove and the Coastal Trail.) To continue the hike, stay on the Inland Trail.

2.4 Beyond the Black Point Brook Cutoff trail, the Inland Trail leaves Schooner Brook and arrives at an overlook of the pond at the head of Black Point Brook. This pond all but disappears in dry summers.

3.0 A side trail goes 0.1 mile to the top of a rocky outcropping with limited views.

3.3 Another side trail goes 100 yards to the top of a large rock with very limited views.

3.5 The trail descends from the two side trails and becomes an old woods road. The woods road continues straight ahead to the village of Cutler. The Inland Trail turns left and climbs a knoll.

3.7 Atop the knoll a very short side trail leads to an overlook with fine views to the west across Fariy Head toward Western Head. The lighthouse of Little River Island is clearly visible. You will hear its foghorn sound every 10 seconds or so for quite a while, if you haven't noticed it already.

4.4 The trail descends from the overlook into a spruce forest, switchbacking down toward Fairy Head. The trail comes out onto the rocky shoreline near Fairy Head. There is a sign that lets you know that the Inland Trail has ended and you are now on the Coastal Trail.

4.5 A short side trail leads inland to the first campsite.

4.6 A short trail climbs a headland, atop which is the second campsite.

4.8 Wooden stairs lead up to the third campsite.

5.7 From Fairy Head to the third campsite, the trail follows right on the rocky shore, from between 20 and 50 feet above the high tide line. After the third campsite the trail turns inland and climbs along higher cliffs through mossy spruce. It then turns farther inland and cuts across Long Point. The trail descends off Long Point and arrives at a set of wooden stairs that leads down to Long Point Cove's cobbled beach.

6.5 The trail turns inland again and climbs a small rocky hill. Beyond the hill the trail returns to the coast atop the highest cliffs so far. It then goes through a meadow behind Sandy Point Cove that is wet in the spring and overgrown with tall grasses and wild roses in the summer. The trail climbs across Black Point and then descends a set of stairs to Black Point Cove. Black Point Brook flows into the cobbled beach and disappears under the rocks, reemerging near the high tide line. Black Point Cove is the last time the hike will access the shore.

The Bold Coast east of Fairy Head.

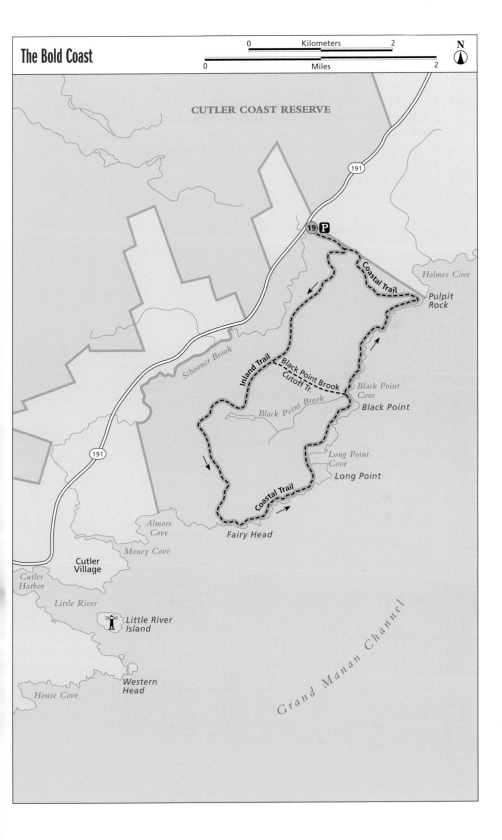

The Bold Coast

0   Kilometers   2

0   Miles   2

N

CUTLER COAST RESERVE

191

19 P

Holmes Cove

Coastal Trail

Pulpit Rock

Schooner Brook

Inland Trail

Black Point Brook Cutoff Tr.

Black Point Brook

Black Point Cove

Black Point

191

Long Point Cove

Long Point

Coastal Trail

Almore Cove

Fairy Head

Money Cove

Cutler Village

Cutler Harbor

Little River

Little River Island

Western Head

House Cove

Grand Manan Channel

6.6 The trail turns inland from the back of Black Point Cove and junctions with the Black Point Brook Cutoff. The Coastal Trail turns to the right and climbs a high, open head with fine views and blueberries.

8.0 The Coastal Trail follows the coastline atop high cliffs and around small heads. There are several small, deep coves that the trail passes. None have safe access. After passing across the highest cliffs on the hike, the trail reaches a junction with a side trail that goes 0.1 mile out onto Pulpit Rock, with exposure on both sides more than 100 feet above the water.

9.1 At the junction with the side trail out to the rock, the Coastal Trail turns inland for good, arriving back at the junction with the Inland Trail. Continue straight ahead on the Coastal Trail.

9.5 Arrive back at the trailhead.

20 Shackford Head

Shackford Head juts out into Cobscook Bay on the west side of Eastport. The hike passes through mixed forests over crumbling rhyolite bedrock. The cliffs along the shore are as high as 140 feet. The hike descends to Ship Point where you can stand on rocks just above the water with views of Cobscook Bay and the high cliffs you just hiked across. Even though this is an area of working waterfront, the hike offers surprising solitude and opportunities for spotting wildlife.

Start: From the Shackford Head trailhead at the west end of the parking area
Distance: 2.9-mile lollipop
Hiking time: 2 to 3 hours
Difficulty: Easy
Best seasons: May to Oct. Unlike many Maine state parks, Shackford Head is not gated in the winter.
Trail surface: Woodland path
Land status: Shackford Head State Park
Nearest town: Eastport

Other trail users: None
Water availability: None
Canine compatibility: Dogs must be under control at all times
Fees and permits: Self-service fee station at the trailhead
Maps: DeLorme: The Maine Atlas and Gazetteer: map 27; USGS Eastport
Trail contact: Shackford Head State Park, (207) 941-4014; www.maine.gov/dacf/parks

Finding the trailhead: From the junction of US 1 and ME 190 in Perry, take ME 190 south toward Eastport. Drive 6.6 miles, then turn right onto Deep Cove Road. There is a small sign at the intersection for Shackford Head State Park. Drive 0.8 mile, then turn left onto the park's short gravel road. At the entrance is a state park sign; the turn is just before the Maine State Marine Technology School. On the side of a building, in huge letters, it says: Boat School. The trailhead is at the west end of the parking area.
Trailhead GPS: N44 54.336' / W67 00.775'

The Hike

Shackford Head is a small peninsula sticking out into Cobscook Bay on the west side of Eastport, bounded by Deep and Broad Coves. Deep Cove is home to the Maine State Marine Technology School and a floating salmon farm. Broad Cove is where several Civil War–era naval vessels were burned on the tidal mudflats to recover the iron in the ships. Across the cove is Eastport's commercial port. All this is a reminder that the Downeast coast is and has always been a working coast. The deep thrum of marine diesels accompanies you on this hike as a reminder. What is surprising is how wild and beautiful Shackford Head is amid all this human activity.

The Schooner Trail passes through a relatively dry mixed hardwood forest. Even though Shackford Head is 5 miles the way the crow flies from Quoddy Head and the Bold Coast, the forest here is more like those found on the mountains of the

Looking northwest from Ship Point to the cliffs on Shackford Head.

Central Highlands. Maple and beech abound here, not the moss-covered spruce of the coastal forests. The understory, too, is bunchberry and other forest wildflowers. The trail passes several unmarked side trails out to low cliffs with views across Cobscook Bay. The rock you stand on is rhyolite, which also gives the hike a very different feel from those along the Bold Coast.

The trail climbs over rocky hills to high, rounded cliffs. Cobscook Bay arches across your view. The shape of Cobscook Bay and those smaller bays off it is a function of warping of the volcanic bedrock. Along much of Maine's coast, especially Mount Desert Island, it was the glaciers of the last ice age that shaped the coast; here the glaciers simply ground away everything down to the deformed bedrock, exposing a northwest to southeast arc. The low areas backfilled with seawater as the oceans rose, creating the present complex of bays and peninsulas.

As the trail continues toward Ship Point the cliffs get even higher, more than 130 feet. The rounded tops of the cliffs are loose, gravel-like rhyolite fragments covered with alpine shrubs and blueberry bushes. To the south Lubec is visible as a church steeple surrounded by buildings on a small hill across the bay. The trail turns inland behind where the highest cliffs arch around to the west side of Ship Point. At a five-point intersection, you can take a trail out Ship Point. At its tip, just below the trail, is a small arch of rock—a reminder of how differently rhyolite weathers from granite.

Notice too that along the shore the jumble of rocks tends to be sharp-edged with lots of straight lines. The rhyolite tends to fracture rather than wear down. Most Downeast beaches are cobbles of various sizes; here there is just a jumble of sharp rocks.

Another side trail leads up to an overlook with a bench. To the east, across Broad Cove, the commercial port thrums and clangs. Around you songbirds sing and butterflies flit from flower to flower. You have a commanding view across Ship Point of the eastern end of Cobscook Bay. On your return to the trailhead, there is a side trail down to the shore along Broad Cove. Here the beach is cobbles; at low tide the water retreats far out into the bay. This expanse of mudflats is the reason the Civil War ships were burned here. They could be sailed in on a high tide and burned when the water retreated. Later the iron could be collected from the mudflats, several tons from each ship. Back at the parking area there are several signs explaining in more details about the five ships burned here.

Miles and Directions

0.0 Start at the Shackford Head trailhead at the west side of the parking area. The self-service fee collection tube is at the trailhead. In about 500 feet the trail turns right just beyond the trailhead, then junctions with the Schooner Trail. Turn right onto the Schooner Trail.

0.2 An unmarked side trail leads out to the top of a cliff over the beach.

0.6 The trail follows along Cobscook Bay with numerous unmarked side trails to the shore or overlooks, then climbs to a junction with the Deep Cove Trail. Continue straight ahead on the Schooner Trail.

1.0 The trail comes out on an open rocky area with fine views of Cobscook Bay. The trail splits here: You can stay high and walk through the woods or drop down the rock face and hike along the cliff tops. The distance is the same, but the lower trail is more strenuous with better views.

1.2 The lower and higher Schooner Trail rejoin above a small cove.

1.3 The trail comes out on a cliff top 130 feet above the shore with views of Cobscook Bay and the islands and peninsulas around and in it. Lubec is visible to the south. Ship Point, where the hike goes next, is around the cliffs to the southeast.

1.5 The Schooner Trail turns inland and ends at a five-way trail junction. Turn right and descend on the Ship Point Trail.

1.6 The end of the Ship Point Trail is a loop. Stay to the right to complete the loop.

1.7 Ship Point with fine views in every direction. Note the small stone arch on the west side of the point below the trail.

2.0 To return to the five-way junction, stay to the right on the Ship Point Trail. Turn right again at the five-way junction onto the Shackford Head Overlook Trail.

2.1 Shackford Head overlook.

2.2 Return to the five-way junction again and turn right onto the Shackford Head Trail toward the trailhead.

2.4 Turn right onto the Broad Cove Trail.

2.5 The trail ends at the rocky beach. Retrace your steps back to the Shackford Head Trail to return to the trailhead.

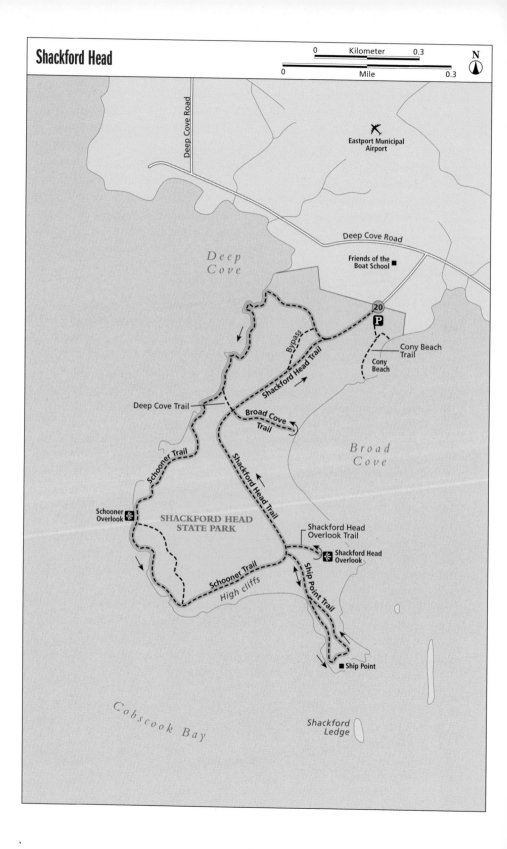

Shackford Head

Kilometer
0   0.3

Mile
0   0.3

N

Deep Cove Road

Eastport Municipal
Airport

Deep Cove Road

Friends of the
Boat School

Deep
Cove

20
P

Bypass

Shackford Head Trail

Cony Beach
Trail

Cony
Beach

Deep Cove Trail

Broad Cove
Trail

Broad
Cove

Schooner Trail

Shackford Head Trail

Schooner
Overlook

SHACKFORD HEAD
STATE PARK

Shackford Head
Overlook Trail

Shackford Head
Overlook

Schooner Trail

High cliffs

Ship Point Trail

Ship Point

Cobscook Bay

Shackford
Ledge

2.6 Turn right onto the Shackford Head Trail.

2.8 The trail comes to an unmarked fork. Take the right fork over the boardwalk. Across the boardwalk an unmarked trail to the right leads to Cony Beach. To complete the hike, go left and reenter the woods on the Shackford Head Trail.

2.9 Arrive back at the trailhead.

IN ADDITION: PEMBROKE REVERSING FALLS

There are numerous reversing falls in Downeast and Mid-Coast Maine. Some, like Goose Falls near Holbrook Island Sanctuary State Park, are where a stream flows into the ocean. At low tide there is a waterfall; at high tide the seawater rises above the falls and flows up the stream. In between, the waters can be chaotic, as if the outgoing fresh water and incoming seawater can't come to an agreement. Over time, so much salt water has flowed upstream into the pond behind Goose Falls that it has become brackish enough to support only sea animals and plants. Many reversing falls are of this type, including Blue Hill Falls on ME 175 south of Blue Hill, Bagaduce Falls on ME 175 in Brooksville, and the small falls on upper Robinhood Cove in the Josephine Newman Sanctuary (hike C).

Others, like Sullivan Falls on the Taunton River in Hancock, are found at a point where a bay narrows and bedrock is near the surface. At low tide Sullivan Falls looks like a regular waterfall even though it's on a narrow bay, not a river. At high tide the falls is like riffles in the bay.

The largest reversing falls in Maine is Cobscook Reversing Falls in Pembroke. The falls are at a pinch point between Cobscook Bay and Whiting and Dennys Bays. The difference between high and low tides here is 24 feet. The huge difference between high and low tide adds to the power of Cobscook Reversing Falls. On a rising tide, as seawater is racing into Dennys and Whiting Bays, the falls are visible between Mahar Point and Falls Island, and another spot to the west into Dennys Bay where standing waves speak to the power involved. The water moves so forcefully around and over the ledges that it creates a whirlpool, reputed to be the largest in the world. On the falling tide the falls reverse and push toward Cobscook Bay.

At Mahar Point there is a short trail along the shore to view the falls and a large grassy meadow for picnics. To truly appreciate Cobscook Reversing Falls, you need to spend enough time there to see the almost instantaneous switch of the flow. To get there from US 1 in Pembroke, turn east onto Old County Road, which is 0.3 mile south of ME 214. Drive 0.3 mile, then turn right onto Leighton Point Road. Drive 3.4 miles, then turn right onto Clarkside Road. There are no street signs at this intersection. Drive 1.3 miles to the end of Clarkside Road. Turn left onto Reversing Falls Road. Drive 1.6 miles to the end of the road. There are no signs at the falls or along this route directing you to the falls.

21 Quoddy Head

The Quoddy Head light sits on the easternmost point of the United States. The hike begins along the south shore of Quoddy Head, a small, round peninsula that is nearly an island. The Shore Trail, at the beginning of the Coastal Trail, passes atop some of the highest cliffs on the coast of Maine. The farther west you hike, the lower the cliffs, offering access to the rocky shore. Before turning inland the hike passes a side trail that leads to the sandy beach along the Carrying Place. The return hike on the Thompson Trail passes a raised peat bog that has a boardwalk through it.

Start: From the information sign on the shore side of the parking lot
Distance: 3.6-mile loops
Hiking time: 2 to 4 hours
Difficulty: Easy
Best seasons: May 15 to Oct 15
Trail surface: Woodland trail
Land status: Quoddy Head State Park
Nearest town: Lubec
Other trail users: None

Water availability: None
Canine compatibility: Dogs must be on a leash 4 feet or shorter
Fees and permits: No fees or permits required; state park open 9 a.m. to sunset daily
Maps: *DeLorme: The Maine Atlas and Gazetteer:* map 27; USGS Lubec
Trail contact: Quoddy Head State Park, (207) 733-0911; www.maine.gov/dacf/parks

Finding the trailhead: From the junction of US 1 and ME 189 in Whiting, take ME 189 east toward Lubec. Drive 10 miles and turn right onto South Lubec Road. There is a large sign for the state park just before the turn. Drive 4.6 miles to the end of South Lubec Road. At the road's end there are two state park roads: Straight ahead is the parking for the lighthouse, to the right is the picnic area. The trailhead parking is 0.2 mile down the right-hand road. The hike begins at the information sign on the shore side of the parking area. The Inland trailhead is at the west end of the parking area; that is where the hike ends.
Trailhead GPS: N44 48.831' / W66 57.126'

The Hike

Quoddy Head, the easternmost point in the United States, is a small oval peninsula connected to the mainland by a narrow, sandy neck known as the Carrying Place. At low tide this isthmus becomes a mile-wide mudflat that attracts hundreds of seabirds. At high tide it is a sandy beach accessible from the hike. Much of the near-island peninsula is part of the state park. At the eastern tip is the famous barberpole-striped West Quoddy Head Lighthouse. The lighthouse was first built in 1808, commissioned by President Jefferson. It is open to visitors and also contains a gift shop and art gallery. Beginning at the lighthouse is the 1-mile Coast Guard Trail that follows along Lubec Channel. Although not part of this hike, it is worth taking the time to explore.

The hike begins on the Coastal Trail west of the lighthouse on the south shore of Quoddy Head, which sticks out into Lubec Channel between Maine and Campobello Island in New Brunswick. To the south, across Grand Manan Channel, are the towering cliffs of Grand Manan Island. The channel is deep, and whales sometimes can be seen in the distance feeding or passing through. This coastline also attracts large numbers of inshore and pelagic seabirds. As you hike along the coast, be sure to scan the water nearby and farther out. The name Quoddy Head means "fertile and beautiful place" in Passamaquoddy. I suspect the fertility is in the sea, not the spruce- and bog-covered land. In addition to seabirds and whales, you may see dolphins and seals, especially near Sail Rock at the beginning of the hike.

The cliffs along the shore, particularly around Gulliver's Hole, are among the highest in Maine. The rock of the cliffs is a gray gabbro—a volcanic rock that was forced up into the cracks in existing rock. Because the gabbro was harder than the rock it intruded into, when the softer rock was worn away by the tide and weather, high cliffs of smooth gray rock were left. Farther west on the hike, when the tide is less than full, you can see the way the volcanic rock is arranged in bedding that is

Quoddy Head light at the easternmost point in the United States.

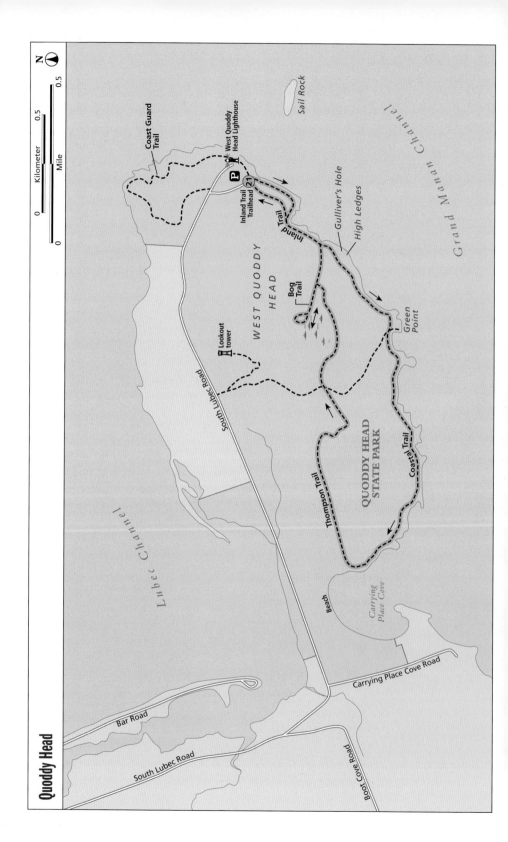

Quoddy Head

angled up about 30 degrees. It almost looks like frozen, seaweed-covered waves. It is one of the few places along the Bold Coast where the shoreline doesn't look like a random jumble of bedrock, cliff, and holes. And geologically it is something of a jumble, with many kinds of rock together and many more in the cobbles on the beaches.

Taking the time to explore the wild and irregular coast can be an all-day adventure. The return hike on the Thompson Trail goes much faster. Just 0.1 mile before the Thompson Trail dead-ends into the Inland Trail, a 0.3-mile round-trip side trail leads out to a boardwalk across a raised peat bog, also called a heath. It is a great place to find carnivorous pitcher plants and bog orchids. In the fall the laurel leaves curl up and hang limp from the branches; the next spring they will unfurl and turn green again. The bushes have small pink blooms in the summer. These Downeast bogs are unique and may have existed here and at other locations along the coast for as long as 9,000 years. They are found nowhere else in the United States and are closely related to bogs found much closer to the arctic.

Miles and Directions

0.0 Begin from the information sign on the coastal side of the parking lot. Follow the gravel path west along the shore.

0.2 The Coastal Trail follows along the rocky shore, with benches where you may stop and enjoy the view. You can see the lighthouse above the trees to the east. The trail comes to a cove with a small waterfall at its head.

0.3 The Coastal Trail junctions with the Inland Trail. Turn left and hike behind the cove with the waterfall. Around the cove the Inland Trail continues straight ahead and the Coastal Trail bears left and follows the coastline. Take the Coastal Trail toward Gulliver's Hole.

0.4 Reach Gulliver's Hole. From the trail you can see the deep narrow inlet and the sheer cliff on the far side. The trail continues up and around the inlet with obstructed views from the far side.

0.5 The trail reaches High Ledges, an open cliff top with fine views.

0.6 The trail appears to fork. Straight ahead is not a trail. Turn right and climb away from the shore.

0.8 There is a 300-foot-long, marked side trail out to Green Point that offers views and access the rocky shore.

1.8 Reach Carrying Place Cove. The trail turns north and follows along the shore of the cove.

1.9 Junction with the Thompson Trail. An unmarked trail continues straight ahead to the sandy beach at the head of Carrying Place Cove. To continue the hike, turn right onto Thompson Trail.

2.9 The Thompson Trail winds through the woods at the center of Quoddy Head, then comes to a junction with the Bog Trail. Turn left and take Bog Trail.

3.0 The Bog Trail becomes a boardwalk that loops through a bog surrounded by spruce forest.

3.2 Arrive back at the Thompson Trail. Turn left to continue the hike.

3.3 The Thompson Trail ends at the Inland Trail. Turn left to return to the parking area.

3.6 The Inland Trail junctions with the Coastal Trail twice; stay to the left each time to arrive back at the parking area in the shortest distance.

22 Bangor City Forest and Orono Bog Boardwalk

The loop hike around the outside of Bangor City Forest offers an easy hike with surprisingly good opportunities to see wildlife. The Orono Bog Boardwalk is unique in the state. It is nearly a mile long, looping out through a raised peat bog. The Orono Bog is part of the much larger Penjajawoc-Caribou Bog complex that extends from Bangor north beyond Pushaw Lake. The hike, using the Veazie Railroad Bed, links with other trail systems—particularly the Walden-Parke Preserve—in and around the wetland system.

Start: From the East trailhead at the north end of the parking area at the end of Tripp Drive
Distance: 5.2-mile loop and lollipop
Hiking time: 3 to 4 hours
Difficulty: Easy
Best seasons: City Forest Trails open year-round; Orono Bog Boardwalk open May to Oct
Trail surface: Graded path and boardwalk
Land status: Bangor City Forest and Orono Bog Preserve
Nearest town: Bangor
Other trail users: Bangor City Forest trails open to bikes and groomed for cross-country skiing in the winter; Orono Bog Boardwalk only open to foot traffic
Water availability: None
Canine compatibility: Dogs must be on a leash at all times; dogs not permitted on the Orono Bog Boardwalk
Fees and permits: No fees or permits required
Maps: DeLorme: The Maine Atlas and Gazetteer: map 23; USGS Veazie
Trail contacts: Bangor City Forest, (207) 992-4490; www.bangormaine.gov, http://cityforest .bangorinfo.com. Orono Bog Boardwalk, 581-1697; www.oronobogwalk.org.

Finding the trailhead: From I-95 exit 187, drive north for 0.6 mile on Hogan Road. Turn right onto Stillwater Avenue and drive 1.7 miles to Tripp Drive. There is a sign for the Bangor City Forest just before the intersection. Turn left onto Tripp Drive and drive to the parking area at the end of the road. The trailhead is at the north end of the parking area. There is a sign at the trailhead for the Orono Bog Boardwalk.
Trailhead GPS: N44 51.773' / W68 43.694'

The Hike

The Bangor City Forest and Orono Bog are part of the larger Penjajawoc-Caribou Bog complex. This extensive wetland extends from Essex Woods in Bangor north through the Penjajawoc wetlands, past the Bangor City Forest, north through Caribou Bog to the wetlands along Dead and Pushaw Streams northeast of Pushaw Lake. It is one of the largest and most important wetland systems in Maine; various government and private organizations are involved in its protection. There are a number of trail systems in areas that adjoin the wetlands. The East-West Trails loop is a good place to begin exploring this area. The Orono Bog Boardwalk is unique in the state for the size of the boardwalk and the untouched nature of the raised peat bog it passes through.

The author's daughter on the Orono Bog Boardwalk near where it reenters the woods.

Even though the hike is in the city of Bangor (most of the boardwalk is in Orono) and popular with hikers and bicyclists, the opportunities for wildlife viewing and seeing rare and unusual wildflowers are high. Of all the hikes in Maine, this may be the one where you are most likely to see a bear, for instance.

The Orono Bog Boardwalk has several interpretive signs that help you understand the nature of the raised peat bog and the plants and animals that live there. The best time to see the rose pogonia, grass pink, and white fringed orchids and carnivorous plants that grow in the bog is June and early July. All through the spring and summer there are wildflowers to see. The more time you spend on the boardwalk, carefully looking around you, the more you see. Many of the rarest plants, such as the carnivorous sundew and the bog cranberry, are very small and easy to miss.

As you hike farther into the Bangor City Forest beyond the Orono Bog Boardwalk, the fewer people you will see. Several smaller trails cut across the forest and are even less used. The forest is crisscrossed with narrow, winding trails. Only some of them are marked and named. Before the forest was developed for hiking, it was popular with mountain bikers, who made many of the City Forest's trails. Most of the trails that lead out, away from the forest, are mountain bike trails that intersect with the Veazie Railroad Bed. The East and West Trails meet at the back of the City Forest at Main Road just south of the Veazie Railroad Bed.

The Veazie Railroad, opened in 1836, was the second in the country. It was built to haul finished lumber from the mills in Old Town to downtown Bangor where it was loaded on ships to be sent around the world. For a time, in part because of the Veazie Railroad, Old Town was the lumber capital of the world and Bangor one of the richest cities in the country. Today you can still find hand-dug cuts through rock ledges and bridge supports sticking out of wetlands. Many of the trail systems in the Penjajawoc-Caribou Bog System intersect the railbed. You can use it as a means of getting, for example, from the Bangor City Forest to the Walden-Parke Preserve. Unfortunately, north of the City Forest, the railbed disappears beneath the waters of Caribou Bog for a distance, making the trails of the Orono Land Trust inaccessible from your hike.

Along the East-West Loop Trail.

On the return leg of the hike, along West Trail, you pass many of the same trails that you passed earlier. These trails can be used to create different loop hikes of varying distance and difficulty. Where the West Trail emerges from the woods at the edge of the arboretum, you pass the Old Dump Trail. The high grassy hill to the south is Bangor's old city dump. The trail crosses the dump and ends at Kittredge Road. Before the trail climbs the grassy hill, it passes a large beaver flowage that is a good place to find wading birds, ducks, and beaver.

Miles and Directions

0.0 Start from the East trailhead at the north end of the parking area at the end of Tripp Drive. There is a sign at the trailhead for the Orono Bog Boardwalk.

0.2 Pass a trail on the left that leads to Shannon Drive and a privy.

0.3 Junction with the Orono Bog Boardwalk. Turn right onto the boardwalk.

1.3 The Orono Bog Boardwalk is a lollipop that loops out into the open raised bog and back. After completing the circuit, turn right onto the East Trail.

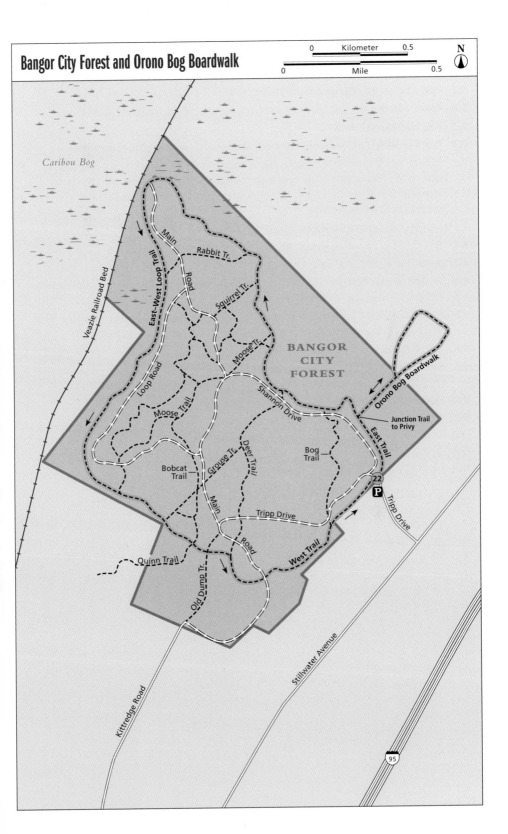

Bangor City Forest and Orono Bog Boardwalk

Caribou Bog

Veazie Railroad Bed

East-West Loop Trail

Main Road

Rabbit Tr.

Squirrel Tr.

Loop Road

Moose Tr.

Moose Trail

BANGOR CITY FOREST

Shannon Drive

Orono Bog Boardwalk

Junction Trail to Privy

East Trail

Bobcat Trail

Grouse Tr.

Deer Trail

Bog Trail

22

P

Tripp Drive

Main Road

Tripp Drive

Quinn Trail

Old Dump Tr.

West Trail

Kittredge Road

Stillwater Avenue

95

0   Kilometer   0.5

0   Mile   0.5

N

1.5 Pass the Bog Trail. This often wet and rough trail can be used to make a much shorter loop hike.

1.7 Pass the Deer Trail. This graded trail can be used to make a shorter loop hike.

1.9 Pass the Moose Trail. This fairly rough trail can be used to make a different loop hike.

2.1 Pass the Squirrel Trail.

2.2 Pass the Rabbit Trail. This fairly rough trail can be used to make a different loop hike.

2.7 Junction with Main Road to the right, which drops down to the Veazie Railroad Bed. The railroad bed gives access to the trails of the Bangor Land Trust's Walden-Parke and North Penjajawoc Preserves. The East Trail changes names here to the West Trail. Continue straight ahead on the West Trail.

3.1 Pass the other end of the Rabbit Trail.

4.1 Pass the other end of the Moose Trail.

4.3 Junction with the Grouse Trail.

4.4 Junction with the Quinn and Bobcat Trails. The Quinn Trail can be used to access the Veazie Railroad Bed and the North Penjajawoc Preserve.

4.5 Pass the Old Dump Trail. This trail drops down to a large beaver flowage before climbing the grassy dome of the old Bangor dump. Continue straight ahead on the West Trail.

4.6 Pass the other end of the Deer Trail.

4.7 Junction with Main Road. To the right is a parking area at the end of Kittredge Road. Continue straight ahead on the West Trail.

5.1 Pass the other end of the Bog Trail.

5.2 Arrive at the south end of the parking area at the end of Tripp Drive.

Honorable Mentions

D Bog Brook Cove Preserve

East of Cutler Public Reserved Land is Bog Brook Cove Preserve. This 1,500-acre wildland has three hiking trails. The 2.8-mile Norse Pond Trail goes past Norse Pond, winding among spines of bedrock to Bog Brook Cove and its pebble beach. The 2.3-mile Ridge Trail begins in an alder-choked bog and leads to a cobbled beach. The trail goes over a ridge of rough, tan rock with views of Moose Cove and the surrounding shore and country. The 0.5-mile Chimney Trail follows along the coast with views of Grand Manan Island. Along Moose River Road, which gives access to the Ridge and Chimney Trails, the preserve is managed as a commercial blueberry barren. The Norse Pond trailhead is on the south side of ME 191, 5.7 miles east of Cutler village. The other two trails are accessed from Moose River Road, 1.6 miles east of the Norse Pond trailhead. The two trailheads are at the end of Moose River Road, 1.3 miles from ME 191. For more information contact Maine Coast Heritage Trust, (207) 244-5100; www.mcht.org.

E Bald Bluff Mountain

Bald Bluff Mountain is in a group of low granite hills east of Bangor. The hike up Bald Bluff Mountain climbs gently over granite bedrock and through mossy spruce to an open summit of low spruce, blueberries, lichen, and wintergreen. The trail drops down across the summit to a cliff top overlook with views of the surrounding hills and the mountains of Mount Desert Island in the distance. It is an easy hike for such fine views. To get to the trailhead from the junction of ME 9 and ME 180 in Clifton, drive east for 9 miles on ME 9, passing Chick Hill and the first blue Amherst Public Reserved Land sign. Turn left onto Ducktail Pond Road at the second blue Amherst Public Reserved Land sign, just past the snowplow turnout. On Ducktail Pond Road drive past the Partridge Pond Trail parking area at 1.8 miles and the Ducktail Pond Trail parking area at 2.5 miles to an intersection at 3 miles. Turn left (the right-hand road is gated) and drive another 0.8 mile to an intersection. Turn left again and drive another 2.3 miles to the trailhead at the top of a rise. There is a brown state sign at the trailhead. For more information contact Amherst Public Reserved Land, (207) 941-4412, www.maine.gov/dacf/parks.

Mount Desert Island

Mount Desert Island is the largest of the Downeast islands; locals refer to it simply as "The Island" or "MDI." It is the second-largest island on the eastern seaboard—only New York's Long Island is larger. Most of the hikes are in Acadia National Park, which makes up about half the island. Acadia is the second most visited national park in the United States, getting more than 2.5 million visitors each year.

Valley Peak Trail on the cliffs on St. Sauveur Mountain's east face (hike 29).

MDI is a large granite pluton that was ground down by glaciers during the last ice age. On many of the mountains, you can find scratches that run northwest to southeast in the granite bedrock. These scratches were made by rocks embedded within the glaciers that were dragged across the bedrock by the moving ice. But the most notable effect of the glaciers on the island is the exposed granite mountaintops. The glaciers scraped off all the soil and loose rock, leaving bare granite domes. More than 10,000 years on, and there still has not been enough time to make and deposit soil on the mountains. It was these bare summits that lead Champlain to name the island "Ile des Monts Deserts" in 1604. The highest of the mountains, Cadillac, is the highest coastal mountain between Labrador and Brazil.

The island has been a popular vacation spot since the Civil War. At first the distance from population centers and its relative isolation made it popular with wealthy "rusticators," folks who wanted to get away from city life and experience nature or paint. MDI was popular with the painters of the Hudson School. In fact, it was their paintings that drew more and more people to the island. By the 1880s the richest and most famous Americans, including the Rockefellers, were summering on Mount Desert Island. They built huge mansions and called them "cottages." Luxurious hotels sprang up to serve the less wealthy.

As transportation improved—first trains and later automobiles—more and more middle class Americans began coming to MDI. In 1919 Sieur de Monts National Monument was expanded and upgraded to Lafayette National Park (the name was changed to Acadia in 1929). Much of the land for the park was donated by the Rockefellers, including 40 miles of carriage roads on the eastern half of the island.

World War II brought the golden age of Mount Desert Island to an end, and just when the tourists were starting to return in 1947 a large fire destroyed more than 17,000 acres of land, five of the grand hotels, and sixty-seven "cottages." The forest has regrown and Bar Harbor's "Millionaire's Row" has been rebuilt with shops and hotels. Today, MDI is as popular as ever. From many mountaintops you can see one or more cruise ships anchored off Bar Harbor among the Porcupine Islands, bringing thousands of visitors to the island. Fall foliage cruises are the most popular. Even with all this bustle, you can still find quiet and solitude in and around the mountains of Mount Desert Island.

23 Cadillac Mountain

Cadillac Mountain is the highest on Mount Desert Island. This hike climbs the South Ridge past several waterfalls. The summit of Cadillac Mountain can be reached by car, so expect crowds in the summer. This route avoids the crowded trails and takes in a lot of the mountain's highlights.

Start: From the Canon Brook trailhead across ME 3 from the parking lot
Distance: 6.2-mile lollipop
Hiking time: 4 to 5 hours
Difficulty: Strenuous
Best seasons: May to Oct; May and June for Canon Brook Falls
Trail surface: Woodland path and bare granite
Land status: Acadia National Park
Nearest town: Bar Harbor

Other trail users: None
Water availability: Canon Brook
Canine compatibility: Dogs must be on a leash at all times
Fees and permits: No fees or permits required
Maps: DeLorme: The Maine Atlas and Gazetteer: map 16; USGS Seal Harbor
Trail contact: Acadia National Park, (207) 288-3338; www.nps.gov/acad/index.htm

Finding the trailhead: From the town square park in Bar Harbor, take ME 3 south toward Seal Harbor. Drive 3.1 miles, passing the Jackson Laboratory, the Sieur de Monts entrance to the park, and The Tarn. As the road begins to climb away from the tarn, the trailhead parking is on the left. The trailhead is across the road from the parking lot.
Trailhead GPS: N44 20.887' / W68 12.140'

The Hike

Cadillac Mountain, at 1,530 feet, is the highest point in Acadia National Park and on Mount Desert Island. In fact, the mountain is the highest coastal mountain in the eastern United States. In the fall and winter, it is the first place in the United States that the rising sun touches each morning. (The rest of the year the sun touches either Mars Hill, Quoddy Head, or Katahdin first; it varies because the sun shifts where it rises through the year.) It has become popular to climb—or drive—up the mountain to watch the sunrise. Each New Year's Day, about sixty folks brave the bitter cold, snow, and wind to greet the first sunrise of the year.

People have always been interested in climbing Cadillac Mountain. The Penobscots had a trail to the summit that was turned into a carriage road after the Civil War. Later still, that road was paved and now cars can drive to the summit. From 1883 to 1890 there was a cog railroad—much like the one that still climbs Mount Washington—from Eagle Lake to the summit.

There are three hiking trails that reach the summit, but there are numerous ways to create a hike up Cadillac Mountain. This guide describes one that is far from the

Looking south to the Cranberry Islands from Cadillac Mountain's South Ridge.

easiest, but is the most scenic and passes several sights worth the work to see. This hike also minimizes the amount of backtracking you have to do.

The hike begins on ME 3 near The Tarn and the Sieur de Monts entrance to Acadia National Park. The hike follows the Canon Brook Trail around Dorr Mountain to a ledge falls. Beyond the falls the trail climbs steeply along Canon Brook up the South Ridge of Cadillac Mountain. The stream is mostly out of sight beneath rocks, but can be heard tumbling along. If you take the time to investigate, you'll discover that the stream follows several channels spread out across the rocky mountainside. The forest is very open with large birches and maples. It is a good place to take your time and enjoy the scenery and sounds of the woods.

As the trail climbs, the rocks get bigger and the trees more stunted. The trail switchbacks up an area of bare granite, then comes to the bottom of Canon Brook Falls. In the spring the whole mountainside of exposed rock flows with water, which is channeled off a drop and through a narrow cleft in the granite. By late summer the stream is often reduced to separate pools and trickles that barely connect to one another.

Above Canon Brook Falls the trail crosses the exposed granite and then enters the woods to climb the rest of the way up the ridge. Atop the ridge the Canon Brook Trail ends at the South Ridge Trail near the Featherbed, a small snowfed pond that usually turns to a soft, green meadow each summer.

GREEN MOUNTAIN RAILWAY

In 1881 Francis H. Clerque leased the summit of Cadillac Mountain—then called Green Mountain—from its owner with the intention of building a railway to the summit. There had been a carriage road to the summit for more than twenty years. Tourists could walk or ride to the summit for the day or stay at the small hotel there. Clerque was able to attract enough investors to build a cog railway from Eagle Lake to the summit in early 1883.

The railway was only the second cog railway in the United States—the first being the one to the summit of Mount Washington that still operates. It is called a cog railway because there is a third rail between the tracks that a cog wheel on the engine engages with. The cog wheel keeps the engine from slipping backward on the steep slope as the train inches forward.

Building the railway and getting the engines in place was quite an undertaking. A wide swath had to be cleared along the route and tracks laid. Wherever possible the rails were bolted right onto the bedrock. Cribwork was used to even out the undulations of the terrain. The result wasn't pretty, but it worked. The real challenge was getting the engines to the beginning of the tracks on the shore of Eagle Lake. The first engine was shipped to Bar Harbor on a schooner. Once in Bar Harbor the engine had to be dragged by horses and winched through the woods to the shore of Eagle Lake. It was then transported across the lake on the steamer *Wauwinnet*.

Once in place, tourists took a horse-drawn "barge" from Bar Harbor to Eagle Lake, crossed the lake on the *Wauwinnet*, and took the cog railway to the summit. It was a very popular excursion the first year it operated, but interest soon waned. The fact that it took so long to get from Bar Harbor to the summit probably worked against it. Also, the train ride itself was not particularly scenic. There was talk of connecting the cog railway to Bar Harbor by rail, but that never happened. In 1890 the Green Mountain Railway ceased running. Five years later the engines were sold to the company that operated the Mount Washington cog railway. The steamer that tourists took across Eagle Lake was scuttled; it still lies on the bottom of the lake.

The hike follows the South Ridge Trail over mostly bare granite to Cadillac Mountain's summit. Along this section, with its sweeping vistas and lack of trees, it's easy to feel like a real mountaineer on some high peak. The illusion is shattered when you reach the summit and can see down the path to the gift shop and parking lot, usually crowded with tourists who drove to the summit. The actual summit is not across the parking lot where the tourists congregate, but along the trail just before you drop down to the gift shop.

The hike picks up the Gorge Path across the parking lot. This trail descends down into the notch between Cadillac and Dorr Mountains. Down in the notch the trail goes between high cliffs and across rocky, uneven ground. As the trail begins to

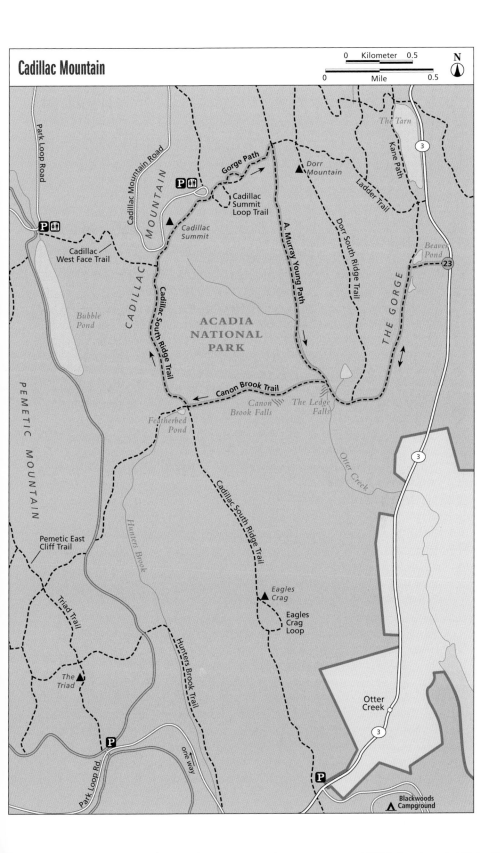

Cadillac Mountain

0 Kilometer 0.5
0 Mile 0.5

N

Park Loop Road

Cadillac Mountain Road

Gorge Path

CADILLAC MOUNTAIN

P

Cadillac Summit Loop Trail

Cadillac Summit

Cadillac West Face Trail

Dorr Mountain

Kane Path

The Tarn

3

Ladder Trail

A. Murray Young Path

Dorr South Ridge Trail

Beaver Pond

23

P

Bubble Pond

Cadillac South Ridge Trail

ACADIA NATIONAL PARK

THE GORGE

PEMETIC MOUNTAIN

Canon Brook Trail

Canon Brook Falls

The Ledge Falls

Featherbed Pond

Otter Creek

3

Cadillac South Ridge Trail

Pemetic East Cliff Trail

Hunters Brook

Triad Trail

Eagles Crag

Eagles Crag Loop

The Triad

Hunters Brook Trail

Otter Creek

3

P

one way

Park Loop Rd.

P

Blackwoods Campground

descend from the notch, you'll begin to hear water moving beneath the rocks you're walking on. Later in the summer the trickle begins farther down the mountainside, but even in August you can hear the stream long before it emerges from the rocks. The trail follows Otter Creek all the way back to the ledge falls you passed a mile into the hike.

Miles and Directions

0.0 Start at the Canon Brook trailhead, across the road from the parking lot. There is an information kiosk just down the trail. The trail drops gently down to and then winds around a beaver pond with a large lodge. The trail crosses the dam on bog boards.

0.3 Junction with the Tarn Trail. Turn left and stay on the Canon Brook Trail. The trail skirts around Dorr Mountain, following the boggy Otter Creek.

1.0 The trail turns away from the creek and climbs to a junction with the Dorr South Ridge Trail. Continue hiking straight on the Canon Brook Trail past a small waterfall.

1.2 The trail crosses a wet area then comes out onto a sheet of granite that Otter Creek flows across. The A. Murray Young Path comes in from the right, above the ledge falls. The Canon Brook Trail crosses Otter Creek and begins climbing the South Ridge of Cadillac Mountain, following Canon Brook. The brook falls through the open hardwoods in several braided channels that you more hear than see.

1.5 After a steep section the trail comes to the bottom of Canon Brook Falls, then climbs the rocks to the left of the falls. Above the falls the trail crosses the exposed granite to another falls. Above the second falls, it crosses the granite and enters the woods.

2.1 Canon Brook Trail ends at the Cadillac South Ridge Trail. Just beyond the intersection is a small pond called the Featherbed, which usually dries up during the summer and becomes a meadow. Turn right and follow the Cadillac South Ridge Trail up Cadillac Mountain, mostly over bare granite.

2.8 Junction with the Cadillac West Face Trail. The trail levels out from here as you continue straight ahead.

2.9 The trail skirts Cadillac Mountain Road, then turns right and enters the woods.

3.2 The trail reaches an unmarked open area that is the summit of Cadillac Mountain. The trail, more of a gravel road, drops down to the parking area.

3.3 The parking lot. Follow the sidewalk around the lot to the right. Take the second paved path up onto the developed summit area.

3.5 Turn left onto the Gorge Path at the sign. Gorge Path can be hard to follow initially. Follow the cairns and blazes down and to the north around a rock outcropping. The trail then turns to the south and begins dropping. The descent into the notch between Cadillac and Dorr Mountains is very steep in places.

3.9 The Gorge Path turns left (north) in the notch. Turn right (south) onto the A. Murray Young Path. After passing between cliffs on the sides of the two mountains, the trail begins dropping through boulders that have fallen from the cliffs. Otter Creek begins in these boulders. The descent lessens and the trail enters woods.

5.0 Arrive back at Canon Brook Trail. Go straight ahead to return to the trailhead.

6.2 Arrive back at the trailhead.

24 Dorr Mountain

Dorr Mountain is just to the east of Cadillac Mountain. The hike follows several historic trails up and across the mountain's east face. The Emery Path is a steep climb almost entirely on stone steps and granite bedrock with fine views to the east and north. The Schiff Path passes through a stunted oak-pine forest full of blueberries before turning west and climbing the mountain across a series of granite slabs. Across the summit the hike descends steeply into the notch between Dorr and Cadillac Mountains. In the notch you pick up the Gorge Path and descend down a mostly dry streambed past high cliffs and waterfalls. There are shorter ways to climb and descend Dorr Mountain, but this loop captures many of the mountain's most dramatic features and views.

Start: From the Emery Path trailhead behind the Nature Center

Distance: 4.0-mile loop

Hiking time: 3 to 4 hours

Difficulty: Moderate

Best seasons: May to Oct

Trail surface: Woodland path

Land status: Acadia National Park

Nearest town: Bar Harbor

Other trail users: None

Water availability: At the Nature Center

Canine compatibility: Dogs must be on a leash at all times

Fees and permits: No fees or permits required

Maps: DeLorme: The Maine Atlas and Gazetteer: map 16; USGS Seal Harbor

Trail contact: Acadia National Park, (207) 288-3338; www.nps.gov/acad/index.htm

Finding the trailhead: From the town square in Bar Harbor, take ME 3 south toward Seal Harbor. Drive 2.1 miles, passing Jackson Labs. Turn right at the Sieur de Monts entrance to Acadia National Park at the sign. Drive 0.1 mile and turn left into the Sieur de Monts area. The Nature Center is at the southwest end of the parking area. The Emery Path trailhead is behind the Nature Center, next to the spring.
Trailhead GPS: N44 21.704' / W68 12.483'

The Hike

Dorr Mountain is named for George Dorr, who is often called the father of Acadia. In 1901 he created a nonprofit to buy and preserve lands on Mount Desert Island. Dorr Mountain was at the heart of the original preserve that became Sieur de Monts National Monument in 1916. Many of the oldest and most interesting trails in the park are on Dorr Mountain's steep east face. Several of these trails were lost or abandoned at one time or another, including the Emery Path that this hike begins on. In 2009 the Park Service renamed several trails in the park, returning them to their original names. Friends of Acadia had previously begun reopening a number of abandoned trails. These changes most affected the east face of Dorr Mountain. In general, if a trail in Acadia National Park is called a "path," then it is one of the trails that has been regiven its original name.

The hike begins at the Sieur de Monts spring. The name is a misspelling of Champlain's navigator's name. The spring house next to the trailhead was originally built by George Dorr. In addition to the spring, the Sieur de Monts area also contains a nature center, the Abbe Museum, and the Wild Gardens of Acadia. Before the visitor center was built north of Bar Harbor near the Hull's Cove entrance, this area was the hub of visitor activities.

The Emery Path climbs steeply up Dorr Mountain's east face almost entirely on stone steps and ledges. The stonework was done by some of the same artisans who built bridges on the carriage roads. Similar stonework can be seen on Homans Path and Kurt Diederich's Climb—two other historic trails that climb Dorr Mountain's east face. The climb up the Emery Path offers fine views to the east across Indian Pass and north across Great Meadow. As you climb, the views open more to include Frenchman's Bay and the Gulf of Maine.

The Emery Path ends at the Schiff Path, which runs level to the south on Dorr Mountain's shoulder. The trail is shaded by twisted oaks and surrounded by abundant blueberry bushes. Beyond the Ladder Trail—another historic trail that no longer has any ladders on it, only seemingly endless stone steps and several iron rungs to help with climbs—the Schiff Path turns west and climbs across a series of granite slabs to the top of Dorr Mountain. To reach the actual summit, you have to hike 0.1 mile south on the Dorr Mountain North Ridge Trail.

The Schiff Path continues across Dorr Mountain and drops precipitously into the deep notch between Cadillac and Dorr Mountains. On most days you pretty much have Dorr Mountain to yourself; as you descend into the notch, you can see people swarming all over Cadillac Mountain's granite summit. In the notch the Schiff Path ends at the Gorge Path. This trail descends to the north down a steep gorge. Much of the trail makes use of a streambed that is mostly dry by summer. It is almost always possible to hike this trail without getting your feet wet. There are several waterfalls and high cliffs along the trail. As you descend, the gorge widens and the stream flows more strongly.

Stairs on a steep section of the Emery Path.

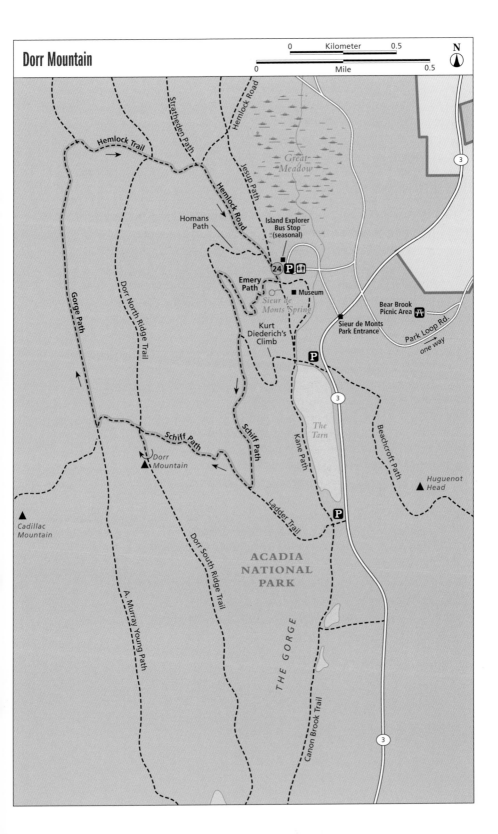

Dorr Mountain

0   Kilometer   0.5

0   Mile   0.5

N

3

Stratheden Path

Hemlock Road

Hemlock Trail

Jesup Path

Great Meadow

Homans Path

Hemlock Road

Island Explorer Bus Stop (seasonal)

24   P

Emery Path

Sieur de Monts Spring

Museum

Bear Brook Picnic Area

Sieur de Monts Park Entrance

Park Loop Rd.

one way

Kurt Diederich's Climb

Gorge Path

Dorr North Ridge Trail

P

3

The Tarn

Schiff Path

Schiff Path

Kane Path

Beachcroft Path

Huguenot Head

Dorr Mountain

Cadillac Mountain

Ladder Trail

P

ACADIA NATIONAL PARK

A. Murray Young Path

Dorr South Ridge Trail

THE GORGE

Canon Brook Trail

3

To complete the hike, you follow the Hemlock Trail to Hemlock Road—a gated woods road—to the Jesup Path, working your way east around Dorr Mountain's north ridge through towering hemlocks. Just before arriving back at the trailhead, you pass the back entrance of the Wild Gardens of Acadia. It's worth taking the time to explore this garden of the region's indigenous flora. The garden is organized by habitat type, and all the plants and trees are well labeled. The garden is popular with deer and rabbits, so you may see some wildlife as well.

Miles and Directions

0.0 Start from the Emery Path trailhead behind the Nature Center, next to the spring.

0.4 The Emery Path climbs steadily up stone steps to pass the Homans Path.

0.5 At a switchback there is an overlook with a granite bench.

0.7 The Emery Path climbs steadily on stone steps and between large boulders with views to the east and northeast. The trail ends at the Schiff Path. Go straight onto the Schiff Path.

1.3 The Schiff Path passes through an oak-pine forest of stunted trees with an understory of blueberries. The trail is relatively level to the junction with the Ladder Trail. Bear right, staying on the Schiff Path.

1.9 The Schiff Path climbs steadily, mostly on exposed granite slabs to the junction with the Dorr North Ridge Trail. Turn left onto that trail.

2.0 Reach the summit of Dorr Mountain with views in every direction. To continue the hike, return to the previous junction.

2.1 Arrive back at the junction of the Dorr North Ridge Trail and the Schiff Path. Turn left onto the Schiff Path, toward the Gorge Path. You can shorten the hike by 0.5 mile by descending the Dorr North Ridge Trail to the Hemlock Trail.

2.3 Descend steeply off Dorr Mountain into the notch between Dorr and Cadillac Mountains to the junction with the A. Murray Young Path and the Gorge Path. Turn right onto the Gorge Path.

3.2 The Gorge Path descends, steeply at times, through a narrow gorge with high cliffs. The trail is a streambed that usually is mostly dry in the summer. Once out of the gorge, the Gorge Path junctions with the Hemlock Trail. Turn right onto the Hemlock Trail.

3.4 Pass the Dorr North Ridge Trail.

3.6 The Hemlock Trail ends at Hemlock Road. Turn right onto Hemlock Road.

3.9 Turn right onto the Jesup Path.

4.0 The Jesup Path passes the Wild Gardens of Acadia before reaching the Nature Center.

25 Great Head

The Great Head Trail loops around the outside of Great Head with many fine views. The trail passes over the highest sea cliffs on the US Atlantic Coast. The hike also offers access to Sand Beach—one of the only sand beaches east of Penobscot Bay. This short, easy loop is one of the classic hikes in Acadia National Park.

Start: From the Great Head trailhead at the southwest corner of the parking area
Distance: 1.7-mile loop
Hiking time: 1 to 2 hours
Difficulty: Easy
Best seasons: May to June and Sept to Oct; accessible year-round
Trail surface: Woodland path
Land status: Acadia National Park
Nearest town: Bar Harbor

Other trail users: None
Water availability: None
Canine compatibility: Dogs must be on a leash at all times; dogs not allowed on Sand Beach, except during the winter
Fees and permits: No fees or permits required
Maps: *DeLorme: The Maine Atlas and Gazetteer:* map 16; USGS Seal Harbor
Trail contact: Acadia National Park, (207) 288-3338; www.nps.gov/acad/index.htm

Finding the trailhead: From the Hull's Cove entrance to Acadia National Park, drive south on Park Loop Road 3.1 miles to a T intersection. At the T turn left, toward Sand Beach, and drive 5.5 miles. Turn left toward Bar Harbor just before the park entrance gate and drive 0.1 mile to a Stop sign. Turn right onto Schooner Head Road; there are no street signs at the intersection. Drive 0.4 mile to the Great Head parking area on the left. The trailhead is at the southwest corner of the parking area.
Trailhead GPS: N44 20.028' / W68 10.718'

The Hike

There are very few sand beaches east of Penobscot Bay, so it's no surprise that Sand Beach in Acadia National Park is one of the most popular spots in the park. The west side of Great Head overlooks Newport Cove—with Sand Beach at its head. There is a short trail that connects the Great Head Trail with Sand Beach, so most people who hike Great Head do so from there. The advantage of starting from the Great Head trailhead is that you can avoid the traffic and congestion around Sand Beach and still enjoy the same scenery. Even when the Sand Beach parking lot is completely full, you can enjoy a quiet hike on Great Head.

The trail first passes close to the shore between the cliffs on Great Head and Oak Hill Cliffs to the north. There are two unmarked side trails that lead out to the rocky shore with fine views along the coast and across Frenchman's Bay. Out in the bay is Egg Rock Light; between the shore and the small island, lobster buoys bob in the water. Across the bay is Schoodic Peninsula—the tip of which is part of Acadia National Park.

The trail climbs gently through the woods to the high point on Great Head. The remains of an old foundation sit behind the elevation sign. At one time there was a lodge on this site. Now you can explore the high cliffs on the eastern tip of Great Head. Below you gulls wheel in the breeze as sea ducks bob on the swell. Lobster boats chug by, their diesel thrum penetrating even the thickest fogs that frequent Great Head. The cliffs here are the highest on the Atlantic coast in the United States. There are a number of rock climbing routes on the cliffs here, although the most difficult and well-known routes are farther south on Great Head at the sea cave. The climbs here are generally more difficult than those on Otter Cliffs, a popular climbing spot farther south along Park Loop Road.

The trail winds along the cliff tops at the edge of the woods. There are many opportunities to wander out to the edge of the cliffs. Just be sure to stay on bare rock when doing so; you wouldn't want to trample any of the fragile vegetation that clings to the rock. The irregular coastline offers varied views, including a good-size sea cave. Climbing down into the cave is dangerous. People have drowned in the cave with the incoming tide. It is best to enjoy the cave from a distance.

Sand Beach and The Beehive from the Great Head Trail.

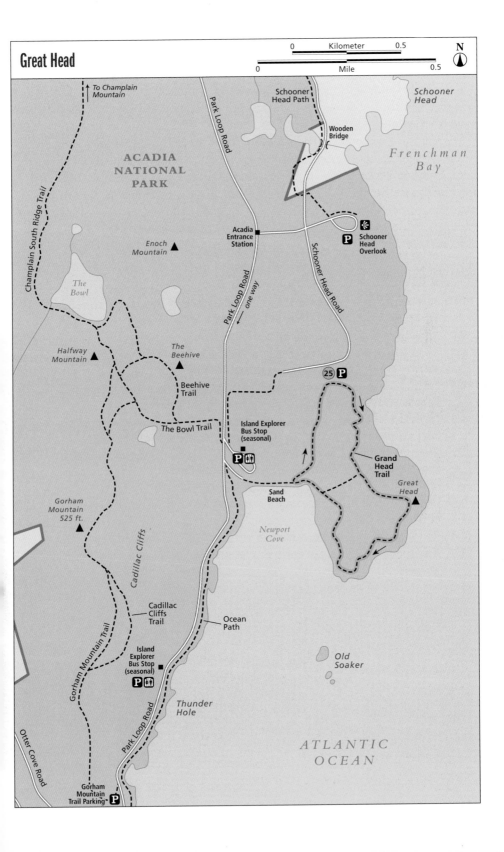

Great Head

0 Kilometer 0.5
0 Mile 0.5

N

To Champlain Mountain

Schooner Head Path

Schooner Head

Wooden Bridge

ACADIA NATIONAL PARK

Frenchman Bay

Park Loop Road

Champlain South Ridge Trail

Enoch Mountain

Acadia Entrance Station

The Bowl

Park Loop Road one way

Halfway Mountain

The Beehive

Beehive Trail

The Bowl Trail

Island Explorer Bus Stop (seasonal)

P

Schooner Head Overlook

Schooner Head Road

25 P

Grand Head Trail

Great Head

Sand Beach

Gorham Mountain 525 ft.

Cadillac Cliffs

Newport Cove

Cadillac Cliffs Trail

Ocean Path

Gorham Mountain Trail

Island Explorer Bus Stop (seasonal)

Old Soaker

Thunder Hole

Otter Cove Road

Park Loop Road

ATLANTIC OCEAN

Gorham Mountain Trail Parking

Beyond the cave area the cliffs are lower, with a number of places you can climb down to the shore at low tide. Again, stay safe by keeping well above where the waves are breaking at all times. Out beyond Great Head, you can see Old Soaker, a collection of rocks that rise above the high tide. The rocks are popular with seabirds and sometimes seals.

As you reach the southern end of Great Head, the cliffs get higher again and offer fine views west and north. Across Newport Cove and Sand Beach rise rocky mountains. From south to north you can see Gorham Mountain and its Cadillac Cliffs, The Beehive, Enoch Mountain, and Champlain Mountain with its line of cliffs. Behind the dunes on Sand Beach is a small freshwater lagoon. Some of the kids at the beach usually figure out that they can swim in the warm water of the lagoon just as easily as in the cold water of the ocean.

Miles and Directions

0.0 Start from the Great Head trailhead at the southwest corner of the parking area. In 200 feet turn left at the junction; the trail to the right is the return of the hike.

0.2 A short, unmarked side trail leads out to the rocky shore.

0.3 The trail climbs gently to a junction with the Great Head Cut-off Trail. Continue straight ahead on the Great Head Trail.

0.5 Emerge from the woods near the high point on Great Head. Beyond the high point are tall cliffs with views south and east.

1.0 The trail follows the cliffs on the south end of Great Head. The cliffs get lower as you hike— to a point where you can climb down to the water with views of Sand Beach.

1.2 The trail climbs through the woods past several side trails that go out to cliffs with views west to an intersection with the Great Head Cut-off Trail. Continue to the left on the Great Head Trail.

1.4 The trail descends down rock faces to a junction with a side trail that descends to Sand Beach.

1.5 The trail passes a trail on the left that goes out to the lagoon behind Sand Beach.

1.6 Arrive back at the junction that closes the loop of the hike. Go straight ahead to return to the trailhead.

1.7 Arrive back at the trailhead.

26 Pemetic Mountain–North Bubble Loop

This hike crosses three mountains—Pemetic Mountain, North Bubble, and Conners Nubble—all of which have open summits with fine views. The cliffs along North Bubble's summit ridge and Conners Nubble have sweeping views that few Acadia National Park visitors ever see. After climbing the three mountains, you have a hike along the shore of Eagle Lake with nice views and a good chance to see waterbirds. The hike starts at the Bubble Pond parking area because it is usually less crowded than the Bubble parking area.

Start: From the Pemetic North Ridge trailhead at the west end of the Bubble Pond parking area
Distance: 5.7-mile loop
Hiking time: 3 to 5 hours
Difficulty: Moderate
Best seasons: May to Oct
Trail surface: Woodland path and 0.4 mile on gravel carriage road
Land status: Acadia National Park
Nearest town: Bar Harbor

Other trail users: Bicycles allowed on the carriage roads
Water availability: Bubble Pond and Eagle Lake
Canine compatibility: Dogs must be on a leash at all times
Fees and permits: No fees or permits required
Maps: *DeLorme: The Maine Atlas and Gazetteer:* map 16; USGS Seal Harbor and Southwest Harbor
Trail contact: Acadia National Park, (207) 288-3338; www.nps.gov/acad/index.htm

Finding the trailhead: From the junction of ME 3 and ME 198 at the head of Mount Desert Island, bear left on ME 3 toward Bar Harbor. Drive 7.7 miles to the Hulls Cove entrance to Acadia National Park. Turn right into the park. Drive 0.1 mile to a Stop sign and turn left onto Park Loop Road. Drive 3 miles to a T intersection. Bear right at the T toward Cadillac Mountain and Jordan Pond. Drive 1.9 miles to the Bubble Pond parking area and turn left into the lot. The Pemetic Mountain North Ridge trailhead is at the west end of the parking area, across the carriage road toward Bubble Pond.
Trailhead GPS: N44 20.975' / W68 14.469'

The Hike

If you stand near the south shore of Jordan Pond, on the lawn behind Jordan Pond House, you'll get a fine view of the Bubbles at the north end of the pond. The two nearly perfectly round granite domes rise from the far shore of the pond, nestled in the steep-sided valley between Sargent and Pemetic Mountains. Standing, soaking in that classic view, you may get an overwhelming urge to climb the Bubbles. When you discover that there is a large erratic boulder perched on a cliff atop South Bubble, you'll head straight there. The only problem is that lots of other Acadia visitors have the same idea. The Bubbles parking area and the summit of South Bubble are often crowded.

Looking across Eagle Lake to Frenchman Bay from North Bubble.

The solution is to do a larger loop hike that goes across the Bubbles, but one for which you can park elsewhere, away from the crowds. This hike starts at the newly rebuilt Bubble Pond area. This pond has had several names over the years, and Bubble Pond may not be the most appropriate since it is across Pemetic Mountain from its namesake mountains.

The hike up Pemetic is steep, but the views along the way and from the summit are worth the effort. Pemetic sits between the two highest mountains in Acadia National Park—Cadillac and Sargent—and rises steeply on three sides. The trail off the summit to the Bubbles parking area is very steep. About halfway down, the trail splits at the top of a small canyon. You can either climb down a ladder and walk through the bottom of the narrow gorge or you can descend on steep bedrock next to the gorge with views into it and of the mountains to the west and north. There are several small gorges like this one in Acadia National Park, such as on Canon Brook and the Great Slide on the west side of Sargent Mountain. The one here is the easiest to hike through. Below the gorge is the steepest section of the entire hike.

Across the Bubbles parking area, you have a choice. You can first take a side trip up to the summit of South Bubble. The views are less obstructed than on North Bubble, and there is that erratic perched atop a cliff to try to climb. After sharing South Bubble with many other hikers, it's nice to enjoy North Bubble all alone. South Bubble partially blocks North Bubble's view of Jordan Pond, but there are plenty of other things to look at.

From the south both Bubbles look like round domes, but North Bubble is actually a long ridge with a rounded south end where it is highest. The Bubbles Trail heads north across this semi-open ridge, winding in and out of the woods. When out of the woods, the trail crosses high cliffs with sweeping views. It then gradually descends through birch to a carriage road. Across the carriage road you have a short, very steep climb to the summit of Conners Nubble. The unassuming little mountain has one of the best—and least known—views in the park. The nubble is nestled against the southwestern shore of Eagle Lake with views north across Frenchman's Bay, east to Cadillac Mountain, and south to the mountains around Jordan Pond.

After descending to the Eagle Lake Trail, you follow the shore of the lake south beneath the cliffs on Conners Nubble and around the south end of Eagle Lake, with views of the cliffs you crossed on North Bubble and Pemetic Mountain. The Eagle Lake Trail ends at the carriage road about half a mile from the trailhead.

Miles and Directions

0.0 Start from the Pemetic North Ridge trailhead at the west end of the Bubble Pond parking area. The trailhead is across the carriage road near the shore of the pond. In 500 feet turn right, staying on the Pemetic North Ridge Trail. The trail sign at this junction is incorrect. It says that the trail is the Pemetic NE Trail.

0.1 Cross the carriage road.

1.1 The trail climbs gradually at first, then steeply, through an evergreen forest with almost no understory. As the trail becomes rockier, the forest becomes stunted birch and evergreens with views to the east. The trail becomes more level and then you pass the Pemetic Northwest Trail.

1.2 Reach the summit of Pemetic Mountain with views in every direction. To continue the hike, retrace your steps back to the junction with the Pemetic Northwest Trail.

1.4 Arrive back at the Pemetic Northwest Trail. Turn left onto Pemetic Northwest Trail.

1.6 The trail descends to a fork. You can either descend a ladder and pass through a narrow gorge or hike above the gorge on steep granite bedrock. The two trails rejoin below the small gorge.

1.9 Below the gorge the trail becomes very steep, descending through the woods to Park Loop Road. Cross the road and the Bubbles parking area to the Bubbles Divide trailhead.

2.0 The Bubbles Divide Trail crosses the Jordan Pond Carry Trail.

2.2 Turn right onto the Bubbles Trail toward North Bubble. You can take a side trip 0.3 mile to the summit of South Bubble. South Bubble is famous for its view across Jordan Pond and the large erratic boulder perched atop a cliff near the summit.

2.4 The Bubbles Trail climbs steadily to the open summit of North Bubble. You have fine views in every direction but north.

2.6 The Bubbles Trail winds through the woods atop North Bubble to an open cliff top.

2.8 The trail winds in and out of the woods atop the cliffs and then begins descending toward Eagle Lake to the north.

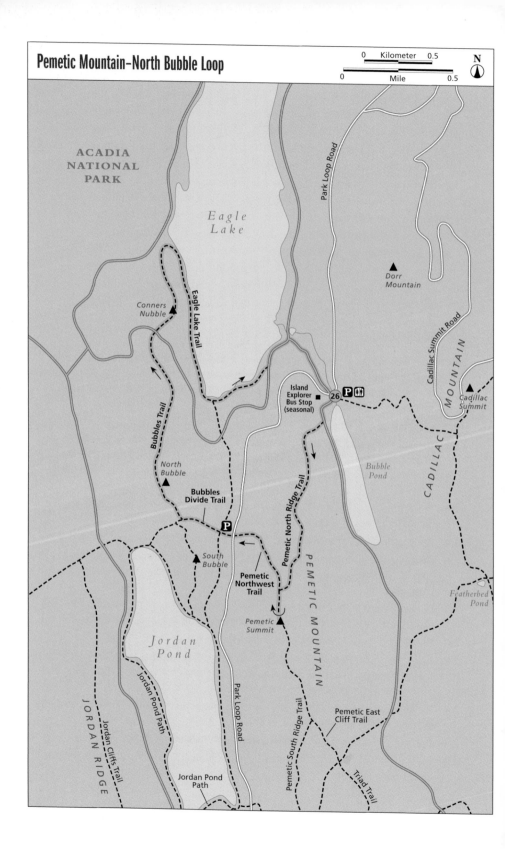

Pemetic Mountain–North Bubble Loop

0   Kilometer   0.5

0   Mile   0.5

N

ACADIA
NATIONAL
PARK

*Eagle
Lake*

Park Loop Road

▲ *Dorr
Mountain*

Conners
Nubble ▲

Eagle Lake Trail

Island
Explorer
Bus Stop
(seasonal)   ■   26   P 🚻

Cadillac Summit Road

CADILLAC MOUNTAIN

▲ *Cadillac
Summit*

Bubbles Trail

*North
Bubble* ▲

Bubbles
Divide Trail

Pemetic North Ridge Trail

*Bubble
Pond*

▲ *South
Bubble*   P

Pemetic
Northwest
Trail

PEMETIC MOUNTAIN

*Featherbed
Pond*

*Jordan
Pond*

*Pemetic
Summit* ▲

Park Loop Road

JORDAN RIDGE

Jordan Cliffs Trail

Jordan Pond Path

Jordan Pond
Path

Pemetic South Ridge Trail

Pemetic East
Cliff Trail

Triad Trail

3.3 Cross the carriage road.

3.4 Climb steeply to the open summit of Conners Nubble with views in every direction.

3.8 The Bubbles Trail continues north, descending to the Eagle Lake Trail. Turn right onto Eagle Lake Trail.

4.7 The Eagle Lake Trail follows the shore of the lake beneath the cliffs on Conners Nubble and then around a small bay at the south end of Eagle Lake. You then pass the Jordan Pond Carry Trail.

5.3 The trail follows along the south shore of Eagle Lake, then ends at the carriage road. Turn left onto the carriage road and walk 200 feet to Junction 7. Bear right at the intersection.

5.6 Cross Park Loop Road.

5.7 Arrive back at the trailhead.

The ladder at the head of the small canyon on the Pemetic Northwest Trail.

27 Norumbega Mountain

The hike up and over Norumbega is highly varied. The trail climbs steep granite bed-rock, winds through an open scrub pine forest along the summit ridge, and descends through a red pine forest. The hike then winds back to the trailhead along Lower Hadlock Pond, a beautiful section of Hadlock Brook, and through a mixed evergreen forest. There are fine views in every direction along the summit ridge, taking in a good portion of Mount Desert Island and the island-filled waters to the south.

Start: From the Norumbega Mountain trailhead at the north end of the parking area
Distance: 3.3-mile loop
Hiking time: 2 to 3 hours
Difficulty: Moderate
Best seasons: May to Oct
Trail surface: Woodland path and exposed granite
Land status: Acadia National Park
Nearest town: Northeast Harbor

Other trail users: None
Water availability: None
Canine compatibility: Dogs must be on a leash at all times
Fees and permits: No fees or permits required
Maps: *DeLorme: The Maine Atlas and Gazetteer:* map 16; USGS Southwest Harbor
Trail contact: Acadia National Park, (207) 288-3338; www.nps.gov/acad/index.htm

Finding the trailhead: From the junction of ME 3 and ME 198 at the head of Mount Desert Island, take the right fork toward Southwest Harbor, following ME 198 (the left-hand fork goes toward Bar Harbor). Drive 4.4 miles to a traffic light. Turn left, staying on ME 198, and drive 4.2 miles to the trailhead parking on the right. The trailhead is at the north end of the parking lot.
Trailhead GPS: N44 19.549' / W68 17.486'

The Hike

Norumbega Mountain is another feature that George Dorr renamed as Acadia National Park was being pieced together. The word *norumbega* is a Wabanaki word meaning "still water between falls"—evidently a reference to the Penobscot River above present-day Bangor. Early European settlers spent a lot of time and energy looking for a city of gold believed to be in Maine; much of their energy was spent searching along the Penobscot, and the mythical city became known as Norumbega.

There's no gold on Norumbega Mountain, but the hike climbs some nearly vertical granite, goes through a scrub pine forest, and descends through a large stand of mature red pine. The hike follows the Goat Trail to the summit. The trail ascends extremely steep granite almost the entire climb. The lower section was rebuilt, in 2013 with rock steps, wooden stairs, and pathways around some of the more dangerous sections. The trail is a lot less goat-y, but it's much safer now. It is one of the steepest trails in Acadia National Park that doesn't have any steel ladders or aids. From the top of the climb are fine views to the east; the summit is another 0.1 mile through scrub pine. There are only limited views from the actual summit.

Norumbega's summit is a long ridge that runs roughly north–south, covered with an open scrub pine forest. The trail winds over bare granite through the gnarled trees. The summit ridge tips gently to the south, making for a long, gradual descent. Hiking along, you get alternating views east across Upper Hadlock Pond to Sargent and Penobscot Mountains, and west across Somes Sound of Acadia and St. Sauveur Mountains. As the trail begins to descend in earnest, you get fine views south across Northeast Harbor to the Cranberry Islands.

Just as the panoramic views disappear, the trail enters the red pine forest. The tops of red pines look much like white pines with long, soft needles spread around a crown that towers above other trees. But

The Goat Trail crosses several open granite ledges.

the trunks look very different: White pines have fairly smooth bark, while red pines have orange bark that is cracked and broken into large flakes. The red pines extend all the way down to Lower Hadlock Pond.

At Lower Hadlock Pond, which is the town of Northeast Harbor's water supply, there are trails that lead into town. The hike follows north along the western shore of the pond to a small waterfall where Hadlock Brook drops into the pond. Take your time to explore the rocky watercourse as you hike along the stream. Not only is the stream beautiful, but it is also a good place to find wildflowers and birds.

SOMES SOUND

If you look at a map of Mount Desert Island, you'll notice that most of the ponds are long and narrow, oriented roughly north–south. That is how the glaciers shaped the valleys during the last ice age, scraping U-shaped valleys in the granite. Most of the mountains are long ridges with steep, rocky east and west flanks. The largest glacial valley on the island is Somes Sound. During the ice age, when it was formed, the sea level was much lower, and the valley was created like the others on the island. Later, after the ice melted, the sea level rose and flooded the valley, creating a fjord, the only fjord in the eastern United States. The nearly vertical slope of the valley continues well below sea level. If you watch the tide come in and go out along Somes Sound, you'll notice that the tide line moves up and down, not in and out.

The Goat Trail Connector parallels ME 198 through an open forest that varies between spruce and hemlock—some of which are quite big. The trail passes mossy cliffs that blend into the jumbled rocks on the forest floor.

Miles and Directions

0.0 Start from the Norumbega Mountain trailhead at the north end of the parking lot. Go straight on the Goat Trail. The Goat Trail Connector to the left is the return trail.

0.6 The steep climb on mostly bare granite ends before the summit with fine views to the east. The summit offers views in all directions, blocked somewhat by the scrub pines. The Goat Trail ends at the summit; the Norumbega Mountain Trail begins at the summit. Follow it south across the flat, rocky summit ridge.

1.8 The trail wanders across the summit ridge with alternating views east and west. As the trail begins to descend, you will have views south to the Cranberry Islands and the Gulf of Maine. The trail descends from the scrub pine forest on the summit through a mixed spruce forest into a rare forest dominated by red pines. The trail arrives at Lower Hadlock

Sargeant Mountain from the south ridge on Norumbega Mountain.

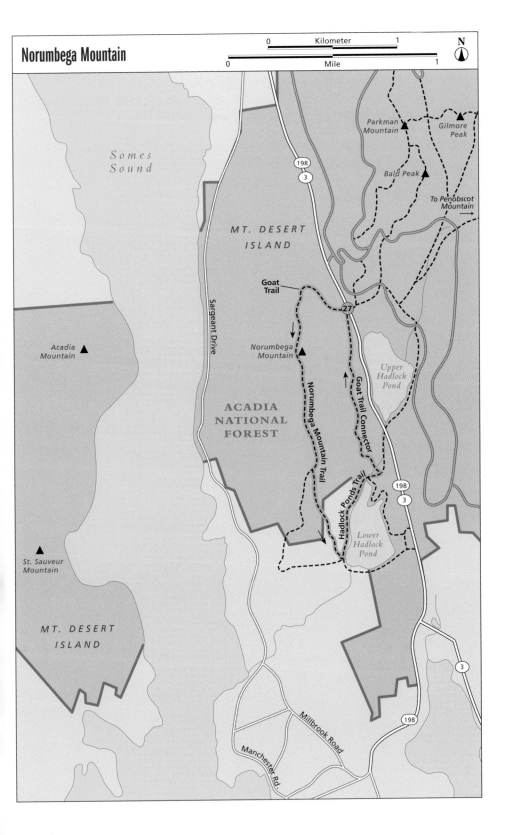

0   Kilometer   1

0   Mile   1

N

Somes Sound

Parkman Mountain

Gilmore Peak

198
3

Bald Peak

To Penobscot Mountain →

MT. DESERT ISLAND

Goat Trail

27

Acadia Mountain

Norumbega Mountain

Upper Hadlock Pond

Sargeant Drive

Goat Trail Connector

ACADIA NATIONAL FOREST

Norumbega Mountain Trail

198
3

St. Sauveur Mountain

Hadlock Ponds Trail

Lower Hadlock Pond

MT. DESERT ISLAND

3

Millbrook Road

198

Manchester Rd.

Pond. The Norumbega Mountain Trail ends here. Straight ahead is a short trail out onto the dam that raises the pond's water level. To continue the hike, turn left onto the Hadlock Ponds Trail and hike along the shore of Lower Hadlock Pond.

2.3 At the north end of Lower Hadlock Pond is a small waterfall where Hadlock Brook falls into the pond. Lower Hadlock Trail comes in from the east. To continue the hike, go straight, staying on the Hadlock Ponds Trail.

2.4 The trail follows the stream with a steep, high blank on the far side through a dense cedar woods to the junction with the Goat Trail Connector. Turn left onto this trail to hike back to the trailhead.

3.3 Arrive back at the trailhead.

28 Beech Mountain

The trails on and around Beech Mountain offer fine views for surprisingly little work. And once you hike away from Beech Cliff and the Beech Mountain summit, you are likely to have a surprising amount of solitude, even on a warm summer day. This loop hike crosses the summit of Beech Mountain and the cliffs on both its east and west flanks.

Start: From the Beech Mountain trailhead at the northwest corner of the parking area
Distance: 3.5-mile loop
Hiking time: 2 to 3 hours
Difficulty: Easy
Best seasons: May to Nov
Trail surface: Woodland path
Land status: Acadia National Park
Nearest town: Southwest Harbor

Other trail users: None
Water availability: None
Canine compatibility: Dogs must be on a leash at all times
Fees and permits: No fees or permits required
Maps: *DeLorme: The Maine Atlas and Gazetteer:* map 16; USGS Southwest Harbor
Trail contact: Acadia National Park, (207) 288-3338; www.nps.gov/acad/index.htm

Finding the trailhead: From the junction of ME 3 and ME 102/198 at the head of Mount Desert Island, bear right onto ME 102/198. Drive 4.4 miles to a traffic light; ME 198 turns left and ME 102 goes straight. Go straight, staying on ME 102. Drive 0.9 mile to Pretty Marsh Road and turn right. There is a sign at the intersection for Beech Mountain. Drive 0.2 mile on Pretty Marsh Road to Beech Hill Road. Again, there is a sign for Beech Mountain at the intersection. Turn right onto Beech Hill Road and drive 3.2 miles to the end of the road. The parking lot is on the right. The trailhead is at the northwest corner of the lot.
Trailhead GPS: N44 18.919' / W68 20.631'

The Hike

As you hike on and around Beech Mountain, the fine views from all along the hike may distract you from noticing that you see very few beech trees. At one time the lower slopes of the mountain were covered with beech trees, but no more. The beech may never have been a dominant feature of the mountain's appearance. Originally, locals named it Nipple Mountain because of its shape. It has also been known as Defile Mountain because of the steep cliffs on both its east and west flanks. As happened with the Bubbles, the name was changed to the more family-friendly Beech Mountain.

Because Beech Hill Road climbs most of the way up the mountain, the hike from the trailhead to the summit involves very little climbing. Instead, the trail skirts around the north and west sides of the mountain along cliffs high above Long Pond. Across the pond, Western Mountain rises almost as steeply as Beech Mountain. To the northwest you can see Blue Hill and even the Camden Hills on the horizon. To

Looking north from the cliffs above Long Pond on Beech Mountain's west face.

the south you can see across Southwest Harbor to the islands around Mount Desert Island.

The short climb to the summit, with its tower, offers views in every direction, but the best views aren't from the summit but from the cliffs around the summit that the hike crosses. The hike down the South Ridge Trail from the summit offers off and on views in every direction as you descend the rocky spine of the mountain. When you reach the end of the ridge, the trail drops steeply down through towering evergreens to the base of the cliffs that circle the mountain. The Valley Trail heads north, back toward the trailhead along the base of the cliffs on the mountain's south ridge. Huge boulders litter the forest, many capped with bright green moss and ferns. To your left the cliffs rise above the trees, and to your right the valley becomes narrower and steeper—almost a canyon.

At the head of the valley, the Valley Trail continues straight ahead to the parking area and the trailhead, but the hike turns right onto the Canada Cliffs Trail. The Canada Cliffs were so named because you could supposedly see all the way to Canada from them. The views are fine, and you can see well inland, but not nearly to Canada. Don't let that keep you from enjoying the hike up the ridge atop the cliffs.

At the top of the cliffs, the Canada Cliffs Trail turns right and descends on iron ladders toward Echo Lake. This section of trail was designed by Benjamin Breeze and built by the Civilian Conservation Corps in the 1930s. The hike does not go down this trail, but it's worth taking a few minutes to walk down to the top of the first ladder to see just how steep the trail is.

The hike continues, from Canada Cliffs, on the Beech Cliff Trail. You'll follow the trail out to the top of Beech Cliff, more than 700 feet almost straight above Echo Lake. The Beech Cliff Loop is sometimes closed because peregrine falcons nest on the cliffs below the trail. These skittish birds nest on a number of cliffs throughout the park, leading to trail closures to protect their nest sites. In the early years of the peregrines' return to Acadia, trails were not closed for the birds, and they would dive-bomb hikers and sometimes abandon their nests. The chance to see nestlings from a trail isn't worth the risk to the birds' well-being.

On this loop hike you get to climb Beech Mountain and stand atop three separate areas of cliffs, all with fine views. And even on days when the trails close to the trailhead are crowded, much of this hike can be walked in solitude. You can take time to eat blueberries on South Ridge, stop and gaze up at the cliffs along the Valley Trail, and count the mountains that you've climbed or want to climb from each of the overlooks. And maybe, if you look carefully, you'll even find a few beech trees.

Miles and Directions

0.0 Start from the Beech Mountain trailhead at the northwest corner of the parking lot. In 100 feet take the right fork.

0.4 The trail emerges from the woods onto high cliffs above Long Pond.

0.6 The trail reenters the woods and junctions with the West Ridge Trail. Bear left and stay on the Beech Mountain Trail.

0.7 Junction with the South Ridge Trail. Turn right and climb 125 feet to the tower on the summit of Beech Mountain. Continue past the tower south down the South Ridge Trail.

1.3 The South Ridge Trail descends gently over bedrock with some views. The trail then turns east and descends steeply.

1.5 The trail switchbacks down to end at the Valley Trail. Turn left and hike north on the Valley Trail.

1.7 The Valley Trail winds along the base of cliffs on Beech Mountain, passing the first of two boulder fields that include very large boulders.

2.1 The trail climbs up between the cliffs of Beech Mountain and an increasingly deep, steep-sided valley. Above the valley's head the trail junctions with the Canada Cliffs Trail. The Valley Trail continues straight ahead 0.2 mile to the parking area. Turn right onto the Canada Cliffs Trail.

2.3 The Canada Cliffs Trail forks. The right-hand fork descends along the base of Canada Cliffs to Echo Lake. The left-hand fork climbs gently to the top of Canada Cliffs. Take the left-hand fork.

2.8 The trail climbs to Canada Cliffs on exposed granite bedrock with increasing views.

2.9 Junction with the Beech Cliff Trail. The Canada Cliffs Trail descends on iron ladders to a steep trail down to Echo Lake. This is probably the steepest trail in Acadia National Park. This hike, though, goes straight onto the Beech Cliff Trail.

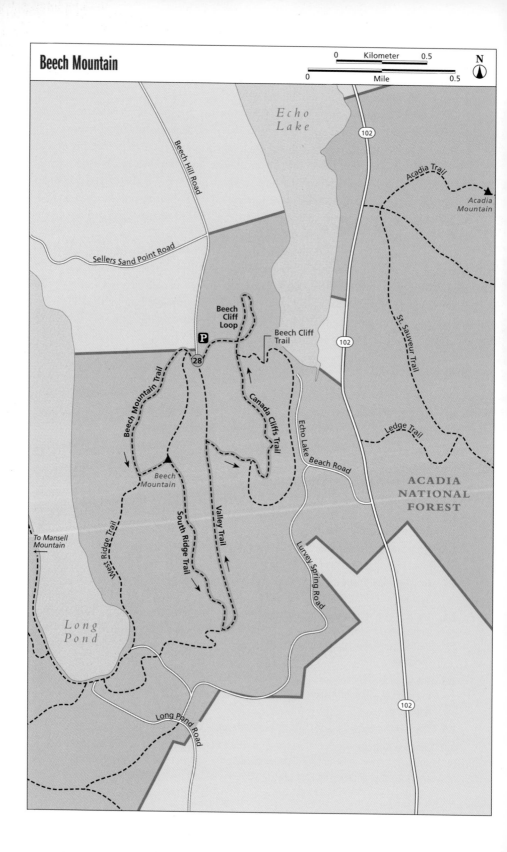

Beech Mountain from Canada Cliffs Trail.

3.0 Junction with the Beech Cliff Loop. If the trail is not closed because of nesting peregrine falcons, turn right onto the Beech Cliff Loop.

3.4 The Beech Cliff Loop goes out onto the top of Beech Cliff with views down to Echo Lake and east to the mountains between Echo Lake and Somes Sound. The trail loops back through the woods, ending at the Beech Cliff Trail. Turn right to head downhill to the trailhead.

3.5 Arrive at the Beech Cliff trailhead, across the road from the parking lot.

29 Acadia and St. Sauveur Mountains

This hike climbs Acadia and St. Sauveur Mountains on the western shore of Somes Sound. The views from the rocky summits, high above the sound, are among the best in the park. You can make use of other trails on and around the two mountains to either lengthen or shorten the hike. In the valley between the mountains flows Man O'War Brook, which falls down a rock face into Somes Sound. The brook was named because sailing ships could come close to shore at the brook's mouth and refill their water barrels. On the south side of St. Sauveur Mountain was a first, short-lived attempt by the French Jesuits to establish a mission in North America. The mission was burned by the English, but the mountain still bears the mission's name.

Start: From the Acadia Mountain trailhead across ME 102 from the parking area
Distance: 3.9-mile loop
Hiking time: 2 to 3 hours
Difficulty: Moderate
Best seasons: May to Nov
Trail surface: Woodland path
Land status: Acadia National Park
Nearest town: Southwest Harbor
Other trail users: None

Water availability: Man O'War Brook at mile 1.6
Canine compatibility: Dogs must be on a leash at all times
Fees and permits: No fees or permits required
Maps: *DeLorme: The Maine Atlas and Gazetteer:* map 16; USGS Southwest Harbor
Trail contact: Acadia National Park, (207) 288-3338; www.nps.gov/acad/index.htm

Finding the trailhead: From the junction of ME 3 and ME 102/198 at the head of Mount Desert Island, bear right onto ME 102/198. Drive 4.4 miles to a traffic light; ME 198 turns left and ME 102 goes straight. Go straight, staying on ME 102, and drive 3.5 miles to the trailhead parking on the right. The trailhead is across ME 102 from the parking area.
Trailhead GPS: N44 19.300' / W68 19.964'

The Hike

Acadia and St. Sauveur Mountains rise dramatically on the western shore of Somes Sound across from Norumbega Mountain. The two mountains are separated by a steep-sided valley that Man O'War Brook flows through. Most hikers climb Acadia Mountain and return to the trailhead up Man O'War Brook and never climb St. Sauveur. That's too bad. The cliffs on St. Sauveur are among the highest and most dramatic in Acadia National Park. Even on a sunny summer day, you can have them to yourself.

The trail crosses rocky woods to the base of Acadia Mountain where you begin your ascent with a rock scramble. The hike up Acadia Mountain is almost entirely on exposed granite bedrock. As you climb through the gnarled scrub pine and oak, you get occasional views across Echo Pond of Beech and Western Mountains. The climb is steady, steep in places, but never too difficult. Once at the top the view opens up in every direction. The smaller islands off Mount Desert Island are spread out below you across Flying Mountain and Somes Sound. Southwest Harbor lies behind the gentle curve of Valley Cove that St. Sauveur Mountain looms over.

The trail drops off the summit and crosses a shallow saddle to a lower summit that is directly above Somes Sound. The trail descends toward Man O' War Brook much more steeply than the climb up the west side of the mountain. There are many views before the trail descends from the gnarled trees fighting to grow on the bare rock into the forest. The trail is so steep that you almost appear to drop into the treetops.

Man O' War Brook runs from a boggy area at the west end of the valley to Somes Sound. The brook was named because sailing ships could come very close to the falls where the stream drops into the sound to refill their water barrels. In 1604 Samuel de Champlain, the French explorer, was the first to do so. He is the one who named

The summit of Acadia Mountain with Somes Sound and the Cranberry Islands in the background.

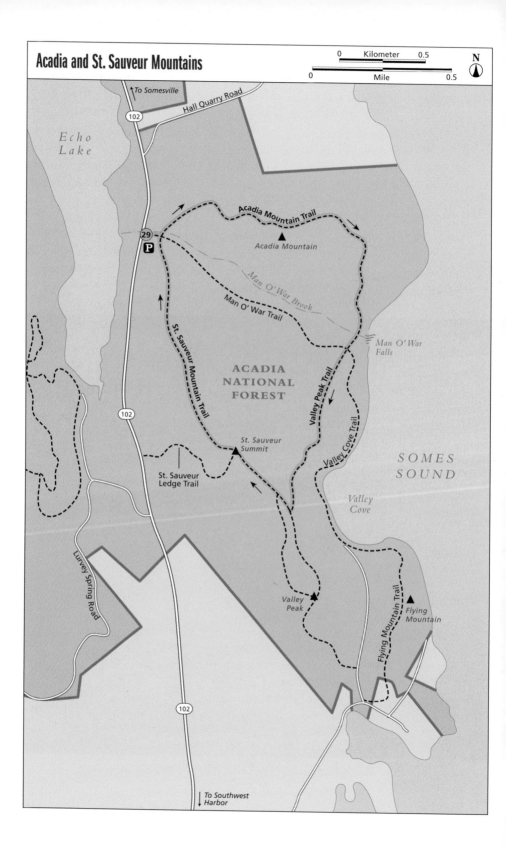

Mount Desert Island and was the first European to explore the waters around the island. Nine years later, several years before the Pilgrims landed at Plymouth, French Jesuits established their first mission in North America on Fernald Point on the south side of St. Sauveur Mountain. Two months later the English burned the settlement, but St. Sauveur Mountain still bears the name of the short-lived colony.

As you cross Man O'War Brook, dip your hands in the water. It is the same stream that your European forebears drank from 400 years ago. Just across the brook a side trail leads down to Somes Sound where Man O'War Brook tumbles down a rock face and into the sea. This is a good spot to see seals and other wildlife.

Beyond the stream the Acadia Mountain Trail ends at a four-way junction. The right fork leads directly back to the trailhead on Man O'War Trail. This is the hike most people take. It makes for a 3.1-mile loop. If you turn left, you can take the Valley Cove Trail along the base of the cliffs on St. Sauveur Mountain. You can then climb the mountain from the south side up the other end of the Valley Trail, making a 6.7-mile loop. The Valley Cove Trail is often closed in the summer to give the peregrines that nest on the cliffs the privacy they need. This hike continues straight on the Valley Peak Trail.

The Valley Peak Trail climbs steadily to the cliff tops overlooking Valley Cove on Somes Sound. You can stand on the cliffs and look almost straight down more that 600 feet to the water. These cliffs offer the best views on the hike. From the cliffs the trail ascends to the wooded summit of St. Sauveur Mountain and then gently descends to the trailhead through scrub pines with occasional views to the west.

Miles and Directions

0.0 Start from the Acadia Mountain trailhead across ME 102 from the parking area.

0.1 The trail climbs up onto and across a rocky ridge to a junction with the St. Sauveur Mountain Trail. You will come down this trail to complete the hike. Turn left and remain on the Acadia Mountain Trail.

0.3 Cross the Man O'War Trail.

0.8 Across the Man O'War Trail, the Acadia Mountain Trail begins climbing with increasing views as you get higher on Acadia Mountain. The summit offers fine 360-degree views.

1.2 The trail winds along the top of Acadia Mountain to a second, lower summit with fine views.

1.6 The trail descends off Acadia Mountain more steeply than it climbed. There are numerous steps and short climbs. The trail reaches the valley and crosses Man O'War Brook.

1.7 A side trail descends 0.1 mile to the shore of Somes Sound where Man O'War Brook cascades over a rock face and into the sea.

1.9 The Acadia Mountain Trail ends at a four-way intersection. To the left is the Valley Cove Trail that runs along the base of St. Sauveur Mountain. To the right is the Man O'War Trail that leads back to the trailhead in 1.2 miles; this trail can be used to shorten the hike. Straight ahead is the Valley Peak Trail that climbs St. Sauveur Mountain. Go straight on this trail.

2.3 The Valley Peak Trail climbs to the first overlook with views across Somes Sound 300 feet below you.

2.5 The trail emerges atop the cliffs with fine views. Somes Sound is nearly 600 feet almost straight below you.

2.6 The trail crosses the cliffs, then turns west and enters the woods. At a junction the Valley Peak Trail turns left and continues 0.3 mile to Valley Peak. Turn right onto the St. Sauveur Mountain Trail.

2.7 Come to another junction. Turn right again toward the summit of St. Sauveur Mountain.

2.8 The trail crosses the wooded summit of St. Sauveur Mountain.

2.9 Junction with the St. Sauveur Ledge Trail. Continue straight on the St. Sauveur Mountain Trail.

3.8 The trail descends gently to the junction with the Acadia Mountain Trail. Turn left to return to the trailhead.

3.9 Arrive back at the trailhead.

30 Western Mountain

Western Mountain is a group of mountains that includes Mansell and Bernard Mountains and Knight Nubble between them. The mountain is on the west side of Mount Desert Island—often called the "quiet side" by locals. The hike climbs all three peaks with fine views of the coastal islands and surrounding country. The hike can be lengthened or shortened, but however you do this hike it will involve steep climbing and descents and plenty of solitude.

Start: From the Long Pond trailhead on the west side of the pumphouse
Distance: 4.0-mile loop
Hiking time: 2.5 to 3.5 hours
Difficulty: Moderate
Best seasons: May to Oct
Trail surface: Woodland path, bare rock, and lots of granite steps
Land status: Acadia National Park
Nearest town: Southwest Harbor

Other trail users: None
Water availability: No reliable water
Canine compatibility: Dogs must be on a leash at all times
Fees and permits: No fees or permits required
Maps: *DeLorme: The Maine Atlas and Gazetteer:* map 16; USGS Southwest Harbor
Trail contact: Acadia National Park, (207) 288-3338; www.nps.gov/acad/index.htm

Finding the trailhead: Follow ME 3 onto Mount Desert Island. Once on the island go straight onto ME 102 when ME 3 bears left. Drive 10.3 miles into Southwest Harbor. Turn right onto Seal Cove Road and drive 0.5 mile. Turn right onto Long Pond Road and drive 1.3 miles to the end of the road. Park to the east of the water pumphouse; the trailhead is to the west of the pumphouse.
Trailhead GPS: N44 18.004'/W68 21.033'

The Hike

The group of mountains west of Long Pond, on the western side of Mount Desert Island, are collectively known as Western or Westward Mountain. There are four summits: Starting from the west they are West Peak, Bernard—one of seven mountains in Acadia National Park over 1,000 feet—Knight Nubble, and Mansell Mountain. Mansell Mountain was named by George Dorr, who renamed many of the island's mountains when he was helping to put the national park together. Sir Robert Mansell bought Mount Desert Island for 110 pounds in 1622. The French, who had previously claimed the island, had named it Mount Desert Island. Mansell renamed it Mount Mansell Island for himself. The name was used for about seventy years, then reverted back to the French name.

There are several trails up Western Mountain, offering several hikes of varying difficulty and length. This hike begins at the foot of Long Pond, behind the pumphouse. After a 0.2-mile stroll along the pond, the hike turns up Mansell Mountain on the Perpendicular Trail. This trail was constructed during the 1930s by the Civilian

An overlook along the Perpendicular Trail in a frozen fog.

Conservation Corps. The trail switchbacks through spruce woods up to a rock slide, then crosses the slide. The trail up the slide is mostly granite steps. Over the years the stonework has come to appear as almost a natural part of the mountainside. The open slide offers fine views across Long Pond of Beech Mountain and the coast to the south.

The trail skirts along a cliff face that often weeps water, keeping the trail damp and cool, then turns west and climbs along a seasonal stream. The Park Service, a few years ago, rerouted the trail away from the stream to an overlook atop a rock outcropping. Not only does the trail now offer better views, but it's also easier to follow. The side trail out to the viewpoint is short and relatively flat.

Beyond the overlook the Perpendicular Trail drops off the rock down into a swampy swale that is the source of the stream. Atop a short climb on the far side of the swale is the wooded summit of Mansell Mountain. The hike continues across the summit ridge to a junction. By continuing straight ahead, descending the Mansell Trail, you can make the hike a 2.4-mile loop. Continue the hike by turning right and descending into a deep notch between Mansell Mountain and the Razorback.

On the open top of the Razorback, you can turn left and descend the Razorback Trail to make the hike a 2.5-mile loop. This choice, while only 0.1 mile longer than the Mansell Trail loop, is much more strenuous, but offers views on the descent. To continue the hike, turn right (north) onto the Razorback Trail. The trail stays high on the exposed rock, then drops into Great Notch.

Once again you can shorten the hike by turning left (south) and descending the Great Notch Trail, making the hike a 3-mile loop. You can also turn right onto Great Notch Trail and circle around north of Mansell Mountain to Long Pond. This would be a 4.6-mile loop. To continue the hike, go straight (west) on the Bernard Mountain Trail, climbing Knight Nubble. A sign marks the wooded summit of Knight Nubble. The hike continues on, dropping down into Little Notch.

To climb Bernard Mountain, hike straight ahead up the steep mountainside. The summit offers limited views to the south. You can continue on to West Peak and down the west face of Bernard Mountain. Hiking that longest loop requires some road walking to get back to the trailhead. The upside is that the open western face of the mountain offers unique views across Blue Hill Bay. To continue the hike, from the summit of Bernard Mountain, retrace your steps back to Little Notch. Turn right (south) and descend the Sluiceway. This trail follows a stream down the mountain, getting steeper as you descend. Eventually the trail becomes a steep, granite staircase next to the stream that tumbles down the mountain in a series of cascades.

The trail crosses the stream twice on rocks, then junctions with the Gilley Trail. Take the Gilley Trail east, passing all the trails you passed hiking across the top of Western Mountain. In 0.3 mile past the Great Notch Trail, Gilley Trail intersects with a side trail that drops down to The Reservoir, a small dammed pond in a steep valley that was used to store water for fighting fires. The Gilley Trail ends at the Gilley Field parking area; the hike continues on the Cold Brook Trail across the parking lot. From Gilley Field it is a rather flat 0.4 mile back to the trailhead.

Miles and Directions

0.0 Start at the Great Pond trailhead on the west side of the pumphouse. The trail follows along the shore of Long Pond.

0.2 Turn left onto the Perpendicular Trail. The trail switchbacks up to a rock slide, then climbs across and up the slide, mostly on granite steps.

0.8 After turning west the trail begins climbing along a seasonal stream. The trail climbs away from the streambed to a junction with a side trail across the bare granite to an overlook.

0.9 From the end of the overlook trail, there are views to the east across Long Pond and to the south of Southwest Harbor and the islands beyond.

1.1 Mansell Mountain summit.

1.3 Turn right onto the trail to Great Notch. The trail drops steeply to a wooded notch, then climbs up the Razorback.

1.4 On the Razorback's open summit, turn right onto the Razorback Trail. Staying on exposed rock until it enters the woods, the trail drops down into the Great Notch.

1.6 Junction with the Great Notch Trail. Continue straight ahead, climbing Knight Nubble.

2.0 Reach the wooded summit of Knight Nubble.

Western Mountain

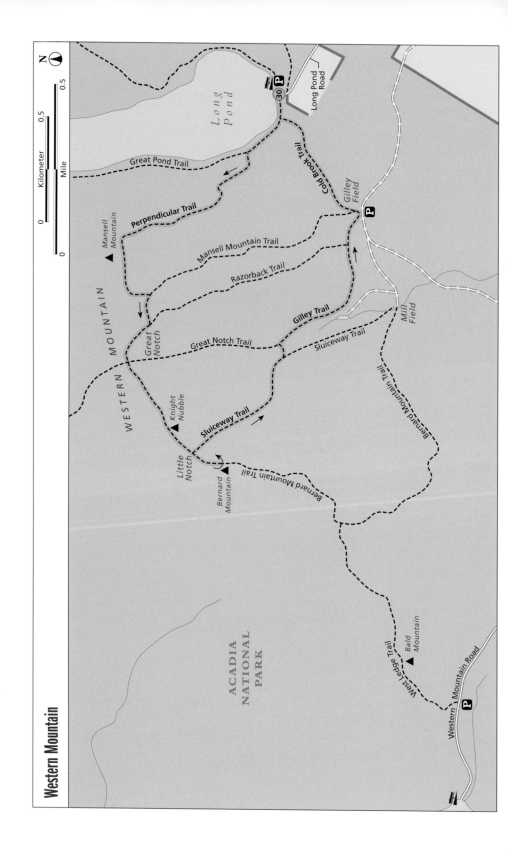

2.1 The trail drops off Knight Nubble into Little Notch. Continue straight ahead, climbing up Bernard Mountain.

2.25 Bernard Mountain summit. There are limited views to the south. Return to Little Notch.

2.4 In Little Notch turn right onto the Sluiceway. The trail drops gently at first, then more steeply along a seasonal stream.

2.9 Just before reaching the Gilley Trail, the Sluiceway drops down next to a series of waterfalls on steep granite steps. Turn left onto the Gilley Trail.

3.0 Junction with the Great Notch Trail. Turn right and stay on the Gilley Trail.

3.3 There is a short side trail that drops down to a parking lot with access to a small reservoir.

3.5 Junction with the Razorback Trail. Continue straight on the Gilley Trail.

3.6 Reach the Gilley Field parking area. Walk straight across the gravel lot and begin hiking the Cold Brook Trail.

3.95 Arrive back at the Great Pond Trail. Turn right to return to the trailhead.

4.0 Arrive back at the trailhead.

31 Ship Harbor Nature Trail

Ship Harbor is a small cove, connected to the ocean by a narrow, granite-lined channel. The cove is a roughly round, shallow pool surrounded by dense forest. The hike follows the shore of Ship Harbor to the rockbound coast. There is no beach at the shore, only a jumble of broken granite and low cliffs. Fingers of forest extend out into the jumble of rock. Visible in the distance are Great Gott Island, and farther east the Cranberry Islands. It is perhaps the most iconic landscape in Acadia National Park.

Start: From the Ship Harbor Nature Trail on the south side of the parking area
Distance: 1.5-mile lollipop
Hiking time: 1 to 2 hours
Difficulty: Easy
Best seasons: May to Oct; hike accessible year-round
Trail surface: Woodland path
Land status: Acadia National Park
Nearest town: Bass Harbor

Other trail users: None
Water availability: None
Canine compatibility: Dogs must be on a leash at all times
Fees and permits: No fees or permits required
Maps: *DeLorme: The Maine Atlas and Gazetteer:* map 16; USGS Bass Harbor
Trail contact: Acadia National Park, (207) 288-3338; www.nps.gov/acad/index.htm

Finding the trailhead: From the junction of ME 3 and ME 102 at the top of Mount Desert Island, take ME 102 toward Southwest Harbor. Drive 11.5 miles, passing through Southwest Harbor, to the junction with ME 102A. Turn left onto ME 102A, toward Seawall. Drive 4.5 miles—passing the natural seawall, Seawall Campground, and Wonderland Trail—to the parking for Ship Harbor on the left. The trailhead is on the south side of the parking area.
Trailhead GPS: N44 13.900' / W68 19.531'

The Hike

North of the parking area, across ME 102A from the trailhead, is a nearly impenetrable wall of alders and trees. It is the southern edge of the Big Heath, a large wetland that drains northwest into Bass Harbor. The land south of ME 102A that the Ship Harbor Nature Trail passes through is higher and drier. The trail first crosses a grassy meadow that slopes down to Ship Harbor.

According to historian Samuel Eliot Morisson, Ship Harbor got its name from an incident in the Revolutionary War. A local ship escaped and hid from an English man-of-war by slipping into the cove with the high tide. As the tide went out, the ship became grounded. Presumably the ship was refloated on the rising tide and sailed back out of Ship Harbor. The long, narrow inlet into Ship Harbor hardly seems wide enough to accommodate a ship; you can easily throw a rock across it. Many vessels plying the waters of Maine at the time would have been small fishing or trading ships

Looking out Ship Harbor at high tide.

that were smaller than we might imagine, and British warships were common on the coast of Maine during the Revolution. In fact, the first naval engagement of the war was at Machias on June 12, 1775. So the story is probably true.

The trail follows along the east side of Ship Harbor. The small cove is bounded by dense spruce right down to the high tide line. The intertidal zone is gravel, mud, and sea grass—good habitat for a number of wading birds. After turning east around a small inlet in the cove, the trail turns west and climbs a low, rocky ridge. There is a side trail that goes out to a gravel bar that tapers away from the granite wall of the channel to the ocean into Ship Harbor. Except at high tide it is a good place to get a view of the entire cove as well as the channel. The channel is bounded on both sides by low vertical walls of rose granite. Often sea ducks bob on the swell in the channel, diving regularly to feed.

The trail climbs to the top of the granite wall and follows it to the shore. The spruce forest opens to the rocky shore, the moss understory giving way to scattered beach plants such as sea roses and peas. At high tide the sea comes almost right up to the granite bedrock. As the tide ebbs, a jumble of granite boulders with pools between them emerges. There is no beach as such; it is a truly rockbound coast. Out across a wide channel is Great Gott Island.

As you scramble east along the shore, the Cranberry Islands become visible. Fingers of scattered spruce extend out the higher areas of bedrock. The dark green of the trees contrast with the blue of the sky and the orangish-pink of the granite. More than any other spot in Acadia National Park, this is the iconic Maine coast. This is the postcard view.

The trail leaves the coast and follows a low spine of weathered bedrock back toward the trailhead. The open rock is bounded by blueberries and other shrubs that turn scarlet in the fall. After returning to the trailhead, you may want to explore two nearby attractions. Farther west along the shore is Bass Harbor Head Light—a picturesque lighthouse atop a rugged cliff. A trail leads down to the edge of the water below the lighthouse. Another option, 0.4 mile east of the Ship Harbor trailhead, is the Wonderland Trail. This short, easy trail follows an old driveway out to the rocky coast. There are no cliffs on this hike, but an abundance of roses and granite blocks.

The granite coast east of Ship Harbor at high tide.

Ship Harbor Nature Trail

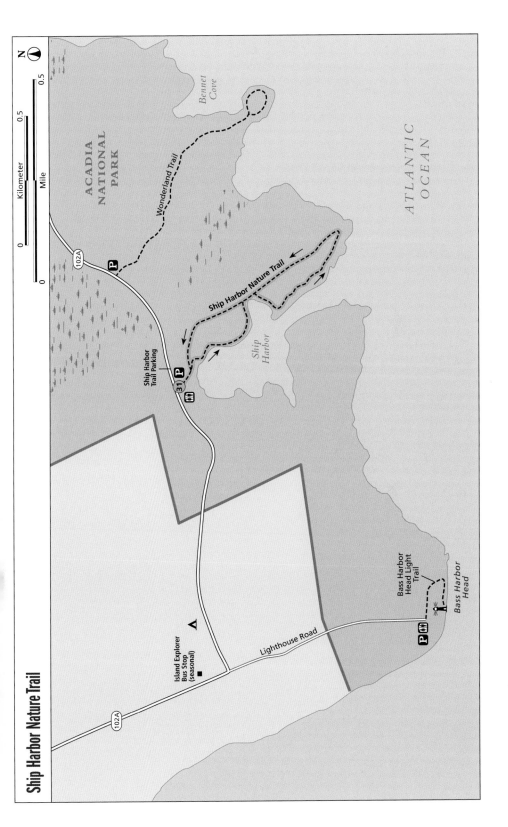

Miles and Directions

0.0   Start from the Ship Harbor Nature Trail on the south side of the parking area.

0.1   The trail passes through a meadow with Ship Harbor visible to the south, then enters the woods and comes to a fork. Take the right fork; you will return on the left fork.

0.2   The trail reaches the shore of Ship Harbor.

0.4   Follow the shore of Ship Harbor to an X intersection. Stay to the right along Ship Harbor.

0.5   The trail becomes more rocky, climbing up a rocky spine. A short side trail leads to a gravel bar where Ship Harbor enters the narrow channel that connects it to the ocean.

0.7   The trail follows along the granite shore of the channel to the open coast.

0.8   The trail follows among the jumbled granite blocks along the shore, then turns inland away from the coast. To complete the hike, follow the trail back to the trailhead, staying right at the two forks you come to.

1.5   Arrive back at the trailhead.

32 Hadlock Falls and Bald Peak

Hadlock Falls is the highest waterfall in Acadia National Park. It is on the shoulder of Cedar Swamp Mountain, just south of a group of low, bare peaks. The hike climbs all three peaks—Bald, Parkman, and Gilmore. The hike descends from the peaks along Maple Spring Brook through a narrow canyon. It then crosses two scenic bridges on a carriage road over Maple Spring and Hadlock Brooks before reaching the falls. Sargent and Penobscot Mountains are a constant backdrop for this hike.

Start: From the Hadlock Brook trailhead across the road from the parking area
Distance: 3.5-mile lollipop
Hiking time: 2 to 4 hours
Difficulty: Moderate to strenuous
Best seasons: May and June for the streams and waterfall
Trail surface: Woodland path and exposed granite
Land status: Acadia National Park
Nearest town: Northeast Harbor

Other trail users: None; bicycles and horses use the carriage roads
Water availability: Maple Spring and Hadlock Brook
Canine compatibility: Dogs must be on a leash at all times
Fees and permits: No fees or permits required
Maps: *DeLorme: The Maine Atlas and Gazetteer:* map 16; USGS Southwest Harbor
Trail contact: Acadia National Park, (207) 288-3338; www.nps.gov/acad/index.htm

Finding the trailhead: From the junction of ME 3 and ME 198 at the head of Mount Desert Island, take the right fork toward Southwest Harbor, following ME 198 (the left-hand fork goes toward Bar Harbor). Drive 4.4 miles to a traffic light. Turn left, staying on ME 198. Drive 4.2 miles to the trailhead parking on the right. The trailhead is across the road from the parking area.
Trailhead GPS: N44 19.551'/W68 17.481'

The Hike

Hadlock Falls is the highest in Acadia National Park. In spring the water pours down a high rock face onto a jumble of angular rocks. By midsummer the falls is but a trickle. The granite mountains of Acadia don't hold water well, so most brooks in the park nearly or completely dry up during the summer. Still, this hike takes in the highlights west of Sargent Mountain and east of ME 198. Even when Hadlock Falls is only a hint of itself, the hike still has a lot to offer.

There are a number of ways to shorten or lengthen this hike, depending on your abilities. You can hike directly to Hadlock Falls from the trailhead on the Hadlock Brook Trail and back the same way in 1.6 miles. By hiking up Bald Peak Trail, you get to climb three granite knobs with expansive views of the surrounding mountains and the islands off the coast. These open granite slopes are great blueberry habitat, so in late summer you can snack while you hike. Notice that there are two kinds of blueberries: Some are almost black in color; the rest look blue and are dusted with

Approaching the summit of Parkman Mountain.

fine white powder. These two varieties are in fact different species. The primary difference is the white powder that makes the one variety appear blue. They both taste great, though.

Your first chance to lengthen the hike comes atop Parkman Mountain. Instead of following the hike and taking the Grandgent Trail to the east, follow the Parkman Mountain Trail north. In 0.8 mile this trail dead-ends into the Giant Slide Trail, which you can follow south to the notch between Parkman Mountain and Gilmore Peak. The little gorge along the Giant Slide Trail between the Parkman Trail and the carriage road is the giant slide that the trail gets its name from.

If you stay with the hike, the Grandgent Trail off Parkman Mountain drops extremely steeply down into the notch and then climbs steeply up Gilmore Peak, the highest of the three mountains on this hike. You can shorten the hike by taking the Giant Slide Trail south from the notch and skip Gilmore Peak. This only saves 0.2 mile and misses the descent along Maple Spring Brook, one of the few in the park that runs all summer because it's spring fed.

▶ Because Mount Desert Island's granite mountains and thin soil don't retain water well, most of Acadia's streams and waterfalls disappear by late summer without regular rain.

You could climb Sargent Mountain by either Grandgent or Maple Spring Trails, or make a loop using them both. Sargent Mountain is the second highest in Acadia. Most people climb it from the east side, coming up from Jordan Pond. Even on a sunny summer day, you can find solitude on the west side of the mountain.

This hike follows Maple Spring Trail south along the stream as it tumbles over and around boulders, dropping toward Upper Hadlock Pond. At the junction with the southern end of the Giant Slide Trail, the stream enters a steep, narrow gorge that holds snow and ice into May. This little gorge is one of Acadia's hidden treasures. Below the gorge the valley opens to a view of the arch of a carriage road bridging high above the stream. This is the Hemlock Bridge. To get to Hadlock Falls, take the carriage road east 0.1 mile. As you walk along, look back the way you came. Bald

Hadlock Falls in May with a fairly high water flow.

Peak looms over the carriage road, a steep granite face that rises a couple of hundred feet almost straight up.

Hadlock Falls is best viewed from the Waterfall Bridge, another high bridge that is the twin to the Hemlock Bridge. The bridge has two rounded viewing platforms built into it. The hike follows the Hadlock Brook Trail past the falls and under the bridge. The rest of the hike is a stroll, gently descending across the Hadlock and Maple Spring Brooks valleys and back to the trailhead.

Miles and Directions

0.0 Start from the Hadlock Brook trailhead, across the road from the north end of the parking lot. In 100 feet pass the Parkman Mountain Trail. Continue straight ahead on the Hadlock Brook Trail.

0.2 Turn left onto the Bald Peak Trail. (**Option:** You can make the hike an easy 1.6 miles by going straight on the Hadlock Brook Trail all the way to Hadlock Falls. In doing so, however, you will miss all the mountaintops and their views.)

1.0 The Bald Peak Trail crosses two carriage road as it climbs Bald Peak. The open summit offers views in every direction.

1.2 Continue across the summit of Bald Peak and descend steeply into the notch between Bald Peak and Parkman Mountain. The trail levels out and ends at the Parkman Mountain Trail. Turn right and climb Parkman Mountain.

1.3 Parkman Mountain's open summit offers fine views in every direction. The Parkman Mountain Trail continues across the summit of Parkman Mountain. Our hike descends off Parkman Mountain on the Grandgent Trail, which descends the east side of the mountain.

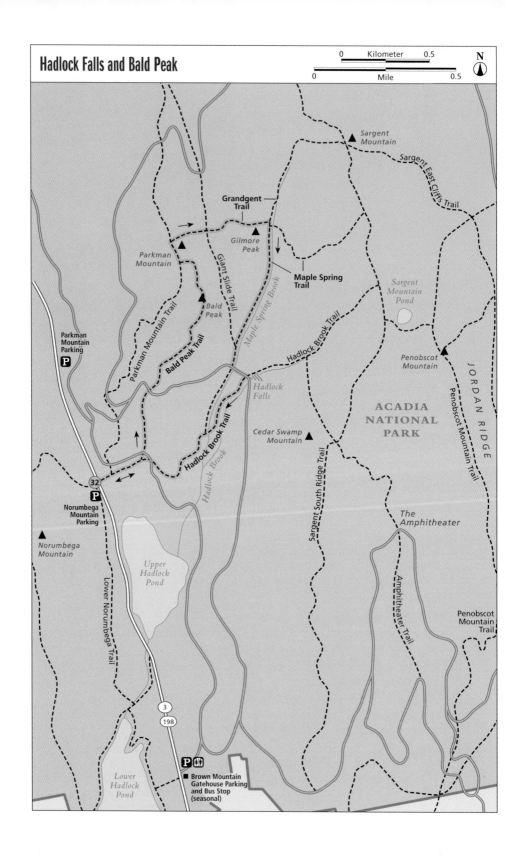

Hadlock Falls and Bald Peak

0   Kilometer   0.5

0   Mile   0.5

N

Sargent Mountain

Sargent East Cliffs Trail

Grandgent Trail

Gilmore Peak

Parkman Mountain

Maple Spring Trail

Giant Slide Trail

Maple Spring Brook

Parkman Mountain Trail

Bald Peak

Bald Peak Trail

Parkman Mountain Parking

Hadlock Brook Trail

Hadlock Falls

Sargent Mountain Pond

Penobscot Mountain

JORDAN RIDGE

ACADIA NATIONAL PARK

Penobscot Mountain Trail

Hadlock Brook Trail

Cedar Swamp Mountain

Hadlock Brook

Norumbega Mountain Parking

32

Norumbega Mountain

Sargent South Ridge Trail

The Amphitheater

Lower Norumbega Trail

Upper Hadlock Pond

Amphitheater Trail

Penobscot Mountain Trail

3
198

Lower Hadlock Pond

Brown Mountain Gatehouse Parking and Bus Stop (seasonal)

1.5 The Grandgent Trail drops gradually, then very steeply into the notch between Parkman Mountain and Gilmore Peak. Across the bottom of the notch the Grandgent Trail crosses the Giant Slide Trail. (**Option:** To make the hike 0.2 mile shorter and miss a 300-foot climb, turn right onto the Giant Slide Trail. This shortcut misses much of the hike along Maple Spring Brook.) To continue the hike, follow the Grandgent Trail up Gilmore Peak.

1.7 Gilmore Peak is the highest point on the hike at 1,030 feet.

1.9 Turn right onto Maple Spring Trail and descend along Maple Spring Brook.

2.4 Junction with the Giant Slide Trail. Continue straight ahead on the Maple Spring Trail, descending through a narrow gorge. This gorge is one of the hidden treasures of Acadia National Park.

2.6 Hike beneath the Hemlock carriage road bridge and take the side trail up to the carriage road. Turn right onto the carriage road and walk east. Behind you Bald Peak looms over the carriage road.

2.7 Arrive at Hadlock Falls. The carriage road goes past the falls across Waterfall Bridge. The Hadlock Brook Trail descends from the west end of the bridge to the base of the water-fall. This is the highest waterfall in Acadia National Park. Follow the Hadlock Brook Trail beneath Waterfall Bridge and across the Hadlock Brook.

3.1 The Hadlock Brook Trail follows the height of land between Hadlock and Maple Spring Brooks, then descends to and crosses Maple Spring Brook. Across the stream you pass Maple Spring Trail. Continue straight ahead to return to the trailhead.

3.5 In the last 0.2 mile you cross a carriage road, pass the Bald Peak Trail that you hiked up, and pass the Parkman Mountain Trail. Finally, arrive back at the trailhead.

Honorable Mentions

F The Beehive

The Beehive is one of the most popular hikes in Acadia National Park because of its proximity to Sand Beach and the views from the 1.4-mile lollipop hike. You get sweeping views of the shoreline from Bar Harbor south to Otter Cliffs and the mountains behind the shore as you make your way up the face of the mountain. Farther west you can see Dorr and Cadillac Mountains. The Beehive Trail crosses a secondary summit and then ends at The Bowl. The pond is a good place for a quick dip on a hot summer day. To return to the trailhead, take The Bowl Trail around the south side of The Beehive. To find the trailhead, drive south on Park Loop Road from the Hull's Cove entrance 3.1 miles to a T intersection. Turn left at the T, toward Sand Beach. Drive 3.6 miles to the fee gate. After paying the entrance fee, drive another 0.6 mile to the Sand Beach parking area on the left. The trailhead is on the right, just before the turn into the parking area. For more information contact Acadia National Park, (207) 288-3338; www.nps.gov/acad/index.htm.

G Champlain Mountain

The steepest trail in Acadia National Park is the Precipice Trail that climbs the cliffs on Champlain Mountain's east face. The trail is maintained as a nontechnical climbing route. Much of the steepest climbing on the trail is done on iron rungs, some with real exposure. The trail is not suitable for small children or people afraid of heights, and does not allow dogs. For everyone else it is an invigorating climb with spectacular views of the coast. It is not recommended that you hike down the Precipice Trail, so the hike should be done as a lollipop. You hike up the Precipice Trail to Champlain Mountain's open summit. From there you descend the Champlain North Ridge Trail, an open descent on bare rock with fine views. Down into the oak forest, you turn right onto the Orange and Black Trail, which slabs south along the cliffs of Champlain Mountain to the Precipice Trail. The hike is a very strenuous 2.4 miles. The Precipice Trail is closed during the summer to protect nesting peregrine falcons. The trail is unsuitable when wet or snowy; as a result the hike is only possible from August 15 until the first snow. To find the trailhead, drive south on Park Loop Road from the Hull's Cove entrance 3.1 miles to a T intersection. Turn left at the T, toward Sand Beach. Drive 4.6 miles on the one-way Park Loop Road to the Precipice parking area on the right. The trail begins up the stairs on the west side of the parking area. For more information contact Acadia National Park, (207) 288-3338; www.nps.gov/acad/index.htm.

Western Mountains

The Western Mountains are a region of high mountains and wide river valleys. Through the valleys flow some of Maine's largest rivers, carrying water from the mountains of New Hampshire and western Maine to the sea. There are fewer lakes here than in many parts of the state, although the Rangeley Lakes are among the most famous and storied in the state. North of the Rangeley Lakes, the country is remote and little visited. There is even a 3,855-foot mountain on the Quebec border without a name.

Along the Grafton Loop Trail on Puzzle Mountain (hike 36).

The highest mountains in Maine are mostly in an arc from Katahdin west across Moosehead Lake to the Canadian border, then south toward Evans Notch. Whitecap Mountain (hike J) is the only mountain over 3,000 feet that isn't along this arc. Of the mountains over 3,500 feet, most are at either end of the arc. In western Maine the highest mountains are either in the Mahoosuc Range or a loose group of mountains around Sugarloaf Mountain. The Appalachian Trail knits together the high peaks of western Maine along its winding route from New Hampshire northeast to the Kennebec River.

There are pockets of granite in western Maine, but the granite doesn't line up with the mountains. In fact, many of the region's highest mountains are not granite. The Bigelows (hike 35), for example, are made of schists and gneisses. These are mineral-bearing bedrocks that formed at contact zones between granite and other rock types. In western Maine many of the mountains are composed of hard, weather-resistant rocks associated with contact zones. This makes for a more varied geology. On many of the hikes in western Maine, you can find quartz boulders, mica, and a variety of minerals. In many places these minerals have been commercially mined. Even today, prospectors comb the mountains and streams of western Maine for tourmaline and gold.

Many of Maine's highest and most spectacular waterfalls are in western Maine. Because of the complex and varied bedrock, each waterfall is unique. Even falls only a few miles apart, such as Dunn Falls (hike I), Screw Auger Falls, and Step Falls are very different.

New Hampshire's White Mountain National Forest spills over into western Maine between Fryeburg and Gilead—in the Evans Notch region. It was here that LL Bean learned to hunt and fish at his family's camp. On one such trip he came up with the idea for his now-famous boot. It was also here that a devastating forest fire in 1903 forced the country to come to terms with its lack of forest stewardship, leading eventually to the national forest system.

33 Mount Blue

The cone-shaped Mount Blue offers fine 360-degree views from the tower on its summit. The hike climbs steadily on the old fire warden's trail, passing the remains of the cabin. The last section of the climb is over exposed bedrock through increasingly stunted spruce trees. There are several short side trails emanating from the summit that were the only way to get views before the tower with its viewing platform was built.

Start: From the Mount Blue trailhead at the north end of the parking area
Distance: 3.1 miles out and back
Hiking time: 2 to 4 hours
Difficulty: Moderate
Best seasons: May to Oct
Trail surface: Woodland path
Land status: Mount Blue State Park
Nearest town: Weld
Other trail users: Hunting allowed in Mount Blue State Park

Water availability: Spring behind old fire warden's cabin at mile 0.5
Canine compatibility: Dogs must be under control at all times
Fees and permits: No fees or permits required
Maps: *DeLorme: The Maine Atlas and Gazetteer:* map 19; USGS Mount Blue
Trail contact: Mount Blue State Park, (207) 585-2347 (summer), (207) 585-2261 (winter); www.maine.gov/dacf/parks

Finding the trailhead: From the junction of US 2 and ME 156 in Wilton, drive north on ME 156 for 4.5 miles to Weld. In Weld, at the junction of ME 156 and ME 142, turn right onto Center Hill Road. There is a sign for Mount Blue at the intersection. Drive 3.5 miles, passing the Center Hill area of Mount Blue State Park. Turn right onto Mount Blue Road; there is a sign for Mount Blue at the intersection. Drive 3.5 miles to the end of the road. The trailhead is at the north end of the parking area. There is a privy and picnic area south of the parking area.
Trailhead GPS: N44 43.385' / W70 21.709'

The Hike

Mount Blue is a tree-covered pyramid that rises from the hills east of Webb Lake. The mountain dominates the landscape for a large area, even more so than Jackson and Tumbledown Mountains, its taller neighbors to the west. East of Mount Blue is the Temple Stream valley, made famous by poet Theodore Enslin. He was followed up Temple Stream to the flanks of Mount Blue by Robert Kimber and Bill Roorbach. Each wrote about Mount Blue in his own poetic way. Naturalist Bernd Heinrich also contributed to the literature of Mount Blue. His cabin made famous in his book *A Year in the Maine Woods* is on the southern flanks of Mount Blue. Heinrich wandered and jogged around the region training for ultramarathons and observing nature. His cabin became the center of years of study of Maine's wildlife.

The climb up Mount Blue, though, is from the west side, following the old fire warden's trail. The trail climbs steadily through hardwoods dominated by maples to

Mount Blue across Webb Lake.

the remains of the fire warden's cabin. Houghton Brook burbles down the hillside, unseen in the woods to the north. Behind the cabin is the spring that keeps the stream flowing all summer. There, from a cool pool the fire warden got his water, and so can you. Above the cabin the trail climbs onto a more open ridge. The widely spaced hardwoods let in enough light for wildflowers and ferns to carpet the forest floor. The air takes on a yellowish hue from the pale leaves overhead and ferns all around. There are only hints of views to the north.

The trail climbs more steeply into spruce, the loose gravel of the trailbed replaced by bedrock. Where the trail levels off near the summit, a short side trail leads south to an overlook facing west. You can see across Webb Lake to the mountains around Grafton Notch and beyond. To the north are the Jackson Mountains and Tumbledown.

▶ **Beginning in 1905 fire towers were constructed on hills and mountains in Maine. Fire wardens spent their days atop the towers scanning the surrounding country for fires. In all, 143 sites had towers constructed on them. By the 1960s the use of staffed towers to watch for fires had been replaced by airplanes. Today, fifty-eight towers are still standing; most are either unused or have been converted to communications towers or retrofitted with observation decks for hikers to use. Many of the trails the fire wardens used to get from their cabin to their tower are still used by hikers.**

Mount Blue

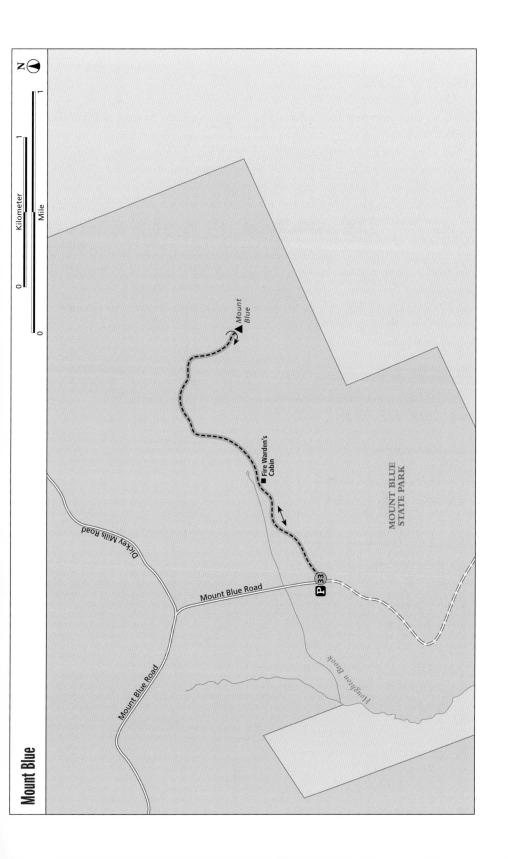

They angle away to the northwest, becoming lower and steeper until Tumbledown seems to end abruptly.

There are several side trails leading away from the summit to overlooks in each direction. Until recently they offered the only views from Mount Blue's wooded summit. Now there is a communications tower with an observation deck above the spruce. The tower is cleverly disguised as a fire tower, complete with a cabin at the top. If you look closely, you'll see that the cabin is a skin around the antennas. In this way the view of Mount Blue from Farmington and the other towns around the mountain are more like they were one hundred years ago when fire wardens manned the tower on Mount Blue.

From the observation deck you can see the long line of mountains to the north that the Appalachian Trail crosses, including Saddleback. To the south and west, row after row of mountains in western Maine fade into New Hampshire's White Mountains. On clear days early in the season, Mount Washington, still snow-covered, shines like a beacon on the horizon. To the east, isolated hills and mountains are separated by wide valleys with towns and farms along streams and rivers flowing toward the Kennebec River.

Miles and Directions

0.0 Start from the Mount Blue trailhead at the north end of the parking area.

0.5 The trail climbs steadily to the old fire warden's cabin. A short side trail leads north around the cabin to a spring.

0.9 The trail passes through a more open forest and begins to climb more steeply on a rockier trail.

1.4 Just before the summit there is an overlook to the south.

1.5 Reach the summit. There is a communications tower disguised as a fire tower on the summit with a viewing platform. Several short side trails lead away from the summit to overlooks—the only way to get views before the tower was built in 2012. To complete the hike, return the way you came.

3.1 Arrive back at the trailhead.

34 Tumbledown Mountain

Tumbledown Mountain is not the highest in the line of mountains that stretches from Mount Blue east to Tumbledown, but it is the most spectacular. The climb up the Loop Trail is one of the most challenging in Maine, but the views from the top of the trail and then at Tumbledown's summit are worth the work. The hike along Tumbledown's summit ridge to Tumbledown Pond offers fine views and interesting bedrock beneath your feet. The pond sits in a rounded bowl between Tumbledown and Little Jackson Mountains. It is a popular place to rest and soak in the mountain scenery.

Start: Start from the Loop trailhead on the north side of Byron Notch Road

Distance: 6.1-mile loop

Hiking time: 4 to 6 hours

Difficulty: Strenuous, with some exposure near the top of the Loop Trail

Best seasons: June to Oct

Trail surface: Woodland path and exposed bedrock

Land status: Tumbledown-Mount Blue Public Reserved Land

Nearest town: Weld

Other trail users: Hunting allowed on Maine Public Reserved Lands

Water availability: Tumbledown Pond and Tumbledown Brook

Canine compatibility: Sections of the Loop Trail not suitable for dogs

Fees and permits: No fees or permits required

Maps: *DeLorme: The Maine Atlas and Gazetteer:* map 19; USGS Roxbury and Jackson Mountain

Trail contact: Mount Blue State Park, (207) 585-2347 (summer), (207) 585-2261 (winter); www.maine.gov/dacf/parks

Finding the trailhead: From the junction of US 2 and ME 156 in Wilton, drive north on ME 156 for 4.5 miles to Weld. At the junction of ME 156 and ME 142, go straight (north) onto ME 142. Drive 2.4 miles to Webb Corner and turn right onto Byron Road. Drive 0.5 mile and turn right onto the gravel Byron Notch Road. There is a sign at the intersection for Tumbledown. Drive 4 miles to the Brook trailhead. You will come down this trail on the hike and road walk the rest of the drive to complete the loop hike. Drive 1.4 miles to the Loop trailhead. The trail is on the right opposite a small parking area. There is more parking on the right beyond the trailhead.
Trailhead GPS: N44 43.896' / W70 33.481'

The Hike

The Loop Trail begins innocently enough, winding through the woods and climbing gently along West Brook. The trail alternates between high, rocky areas where pines dominate and low, wet areas with hardwoods. The trail crosses more than one glade where you can find bog plants and mosses. Then the trail comes to a boulder the size of a suburban home, skirting around the boulder and climbing a rock slide. The trail is very steep with loose rock. Just when the climbing seems too much, the trail levels out and crosses Great Ledge. From the open ledge you have views of the 600-foot cliffs on

The view from the top of the Loop Trail.

the south face of Tumbledown Mountain. Darker areas on the face are where sections of rock have broken off more recently. The two summits of Tumbledown are clearly visible with a notch between them. The Loop Trail goes up a steep gully into the notch.

The trail drops off Great Ledge to a small stream, then begins climbing. The climb up to Great Ledge was just a warm-up for the climb into the notch. The trail becomes increasingly steep and rocky. In spring and after rains, the trail becomes a stream pouring down from a bog in the saddle between Tumbledown's two summits. In places this section feels more like rock climbing than hiking. The gully becomes increasingly narrow as you climb. When you turn out away from the mountain, you have a fine view across a wide valley of hardwoods. In fall the view is a patchwork of reds and yellows.

The trail appears to end above a waterfall where several large boulders have fallen into the notch and gotten stuck, blocking the way. This is what is known as Fat Man's Misery. The gully here is only about 30 feet wide. Blazes show the way to climb up through the boulders with the aid of iron rungs. This section is not safe for small children or dogs. There is some exposure and the rock is often wet and slippery. There is nothing else quite like the Loop Trail in Maine.

Above Fat Man's Misery it is a short walk to the end of the Loop Trail. There are fine views out over the gully along the cliffs of Tumbledown and out to Webb

Lake. The hike turns left onto the Tumbledown Trail and climbs on exposed bed-rock up to the west summit. This small dome of rock offers 360-degree views. To the north a long line of mountains runs from horizon to horizon; the Appalachian Trail winds along these mountains. To the south the open, rocky ridges of Tumble-down and Little Jackson Mountain hold Tumbledown Pond in a deep bowl out of sight.

The Tumbledown Trail runs from the west summit across the east summit and down to the pond. As you hike over the exposed rock, notice the variability of its color—from gray to pink to green. In places it looks like frozen waves arcing across the mountain, or even swirls and eddies frozen in place. This bedrock is composed of sediments that were hardened and deformed by contact with magma. These hard rocks better withstood the millennia of weathering than the surrounding rock; thus Tumbledown and the surrounding mountains are higher than the country they rise from. You may also notice that the bedrock on the summits is different from much of the exposed rock you scrambled up on the Loop Trail.

Tumbledown Pond nestled against Little Jackson Mountain.

Tumbledown Mountain

Little Jackson Mountain ▲

Tumbledown Pond

Tumbledown Mountain ▲

Tumbledown Trail

Fat Man's Misery

GREAT LEDGE

Loop Trail

Tumbledown Brook

Brook Trail

Pond Link Trail

Little Jackson Mountain Trail

To Jackson Mountain

Parker Ridge Trail

Byron Notch Road

Little Jackson Connector

34

To (142)

From Tumbledown Pond the hike descends on Brook Trail alongside Tumbledown Brook, which falls dramatically for the first half mile or so. The trail crosses the stream below a 30-foot waterfall, then crosses and recrosses it again. As the descent becomes more gentle, the trail keeps the stream out of sight to the north, but you can still hear it. The Brook Trail ends at Byron Notch Road. The road walk back to the Loop trailhead is a stroll through a hardwood forest. Just before the trailhead, on the south side of the road, there is a large beaver flowage that is a good place to see wildlife.

Miles and Directions

0.0   Start from the Loop trailhead on the north side of Byron Notch Road.

0.8   The trail winds through the woods, crossing and recrossing a stream but not climbing very much. The trail goes around a house-size boulder and then begins climbing steeply up a rock slide.

1.0   Reach an open flat area known as Great Ledge, with views of the 600-foot vertical face of Tumbledown Mountain.

1.6   The trail drops off Great Ledge to cross a small stream, then climbs very steeply up a gully. In the spring and after rains, the gully runs with water, making the climb slippery. The gully appears to end where several large boulders have fallen from above and blocked the way up. This is known as Fat Man's Misery. The trail, using iron rungs, climbs up through the boulders.

1.7   The Loop Trail ends at the Tumbledown Trail. Turn left to climb to Tumbledown's west summit.

1.9   The trail ends atop the small open summit with 360-degree views. To continue the hike, return to the junction with the Loop Trail.

2.1   Arrive back at the Loop Trail. Continue straight ahead on the Tumbledown Trail.

2.2   The trail climbs to the east summit of Tumbledown Mountain on exposed bedrock.

2.7   The trail crosses the open east summit and then descends on exposed bedrock to Tumbledown Pond.

2.8   Just after crossing Tumbledown Brook where it leaves the pond, you come to an intersection where the Little Jackson, Tumbledown, and Brook Trails all end. There is no sign here. Turn right onto the Brook Trail and begin descending.

4.7   The Brook Trail descends steeply next to Tumbledown Brook, past several waterfalls. As you descend, the trail becomes less steep and crosses the stream less frequently. The Brook Trail ends at Byron Notch Road. Turn right and walk up the road to the trailhead.

6.1   Arrive back at the Loop trailhead.

Option

Leave a second vehicle at the Brook trailhead at Byron Notch Road to make a 4.7-mile one-way shuttle hike.

35 The Bigelows

The Bigelows contain four peaks above 3,500 feet, two of them above 4,000 feet. This hike goes to 4,088-foot Avery Peak, but the hike can be modified to include all four summits, or you can add just West Peak, the highest in the range. Each peak has a large, rocky area above treeline that offers fine views in every direction. The hike up the Fire Warden's Trail is very steep, climbing more than 3,100 feet, but the views and the open summit are worth the effort.

Start: From the Fire Warden's trailhead at the end of Stratton Brook Pond Road
Distance: 9.4 miles out and back
Hiking time: 6 to 8 hours
Difficulty: Strenuous
Best seasons: June to Oct
Trail surface: Woodland path
Land status: Bigelow Preserve Public Reserved Land
Nearest town: Stratton
Other trail users: Hunting allowed on Maine Public Reserved Lands; mountain bikes allowed on the first 0.8 mile of the hike

Water availability: Stratton Brook at mile 0.4, Moose Falls at mile 3.3, and springs at miles 4.1 and 4.3.
Canine compatibility: Dogs must be under control at all times
Fees and permits: No fees or permits required
Maps: *DeLorme: The Maine Atlas and Gazetteer:* map 29; USGS The Horns
Trail contact: Bigelow Preserve Public Reserved Land, (207) 778-8231; www.maine.gov/dacf/parks

Finding the trailhead: From the junction of ME 16 and ME 27 in Kingfield, drive north on ME 16/27. At 15.2 miles you will pass the entrance to Sugarloaf Ski Resort; at 17.9 miles you will pass where the Appalachian Trail crosses the highway. At 0.6 mile past the AT, turn right onto Stratton Brook Pond Road; just before the turn is a black Bigelow Preserve Public Reserved Land sign. Drive 1.6 miles on Stratton Brook Pond Road to the parking area at the end of the road. The trail begins on the woods road on the north side of the parking area.
Trailhead GPS: N45 06.595' / W70 20.228'

The Hike

Millions of years ago, the collision of two tectonic plates created an area of geologic violence in what is now Maine. Soft sedimentary rock was pushed several miles beneath the surface. At that depth and under great pressure, the rock was chemically transformed. Many of western Maine's mountains, including the Bigelows, are made of these metamorphic rock types. Notice, high on the mountain, that the rock is fractured into relatively square block of all sizes. The very fine-grained rock resists weathering, but water that seeped into cracks pried the rock apart when it froze. The result is a mountain that is a jumbled pile of irregularly shaped rock. The

The Appalachian Trail across Avery Peak with West Peak in the background.

chemical changes that created these hard rock types also created new substances; many of western Maine's mountains contain mine-able quantities of metals, garnets, and tourmaline.

More than one hundred years ago, in 1905, the first fire tower was built on Avery Peak. A fire warden's trail was cut from the valley to the col between West and Avery Peaks. Like most fire warden trails in Maine, it is relentlessly steep, with no effort to make the climb easier by making it somewhat longer. The hike follows this trail from the Fire Warden's Trailhead to the summit, where only the foundation of the fire tower remains.

The Bigelows are named for Major Timothy Bigelow, who was a commander under Benedict Arnold on his ill-fated attempt to surprise attack the British in Canada during the Revolutionary War. The expedition went up the Dead River—now dammed as Flagstaff Lake—in October 1775. Major Bigelow climbed the mountain now named for him to observe the surrounding country the soldiers were passing through. It must have been quite a climb from the Dead River to the summit without a trail. It really makes you appreciate the steep fire warden's trail.

The trail is relatively flat for the first 0.8 mile to and then along Stratton Brook Pond—which looks more like a wide, winding stream than a pond. The pond winds through a wide meadow that is a good place to see moose and other wildlife. Then the trail turns toward the mountain and begins climbing, gently at first. Beyond Horns Pond Trail, the trail climbs more steeply to the Moose Falls campsite. Above Moose Falls the trail becomes very steep; in fact, for nearly a mile it is a giant rock staircase. As you climb the stairs, take time to stop and enjoy the ever-opening views.

Near the col are two unusual springs. Before the Appalachian Trail there is a marked side trail to a spring that comes out of a rock face; this is the water source for the campsites in the col. On the AT, above the col, there is a spring right in the trail. This second spring has a wooden box built over it, but it still often runs dirty.

From the open summit you have fine views in every direction. Across the Carrabassett Valley is Sugarloaf Ski Resort on Maine's second-highest mountain. Plans to develop a similar ski area on the Bigelows led to a statewide referendum in 1976 that created the Bigelow Preserve. To the west the slightly higher West Peak blocks the view of The Horns, but you can see the receding line of the Bigelows all the way to Stratton. To the east, at a slight angle, is the long ridge of Little Bigelow. Nestled against the north slope of the entire range is Flagstaff Lake, created by damming the Dead River. Across the lake are ever-more-hazy mountains all the way north to Canada and beyond and east to Katahdin—which is visible on the clearest days.

Miles and Directions

0.0   Start from the Fire Warden's trailhead next to the kiosk on the north side of the parking area.

0.4   The woods road ends where Stratton Brook flows out of Stratton Brook Pond. The trail crosses the stream on rocks that will be under water during high water.

0.8   The trail follows the shore of Stratton Brook Pond to a campsite. The mountain bike trail goes straight, and the Fire Warden's Trail goes left. There is a sign at this junction.

2.0   Junction with the Horns Pond Trail. (**Option:** You can make the hike a 14-mile lollipop that crosses all three major peaks of the Bigelows by taking the Horns Pond Trail to the Appalachian Trail and following the AT north to Avery Peak. Not only is this route 3.6 miles longer, but it adds two climbs.) Continue straight on the Fire Warden's Trail. In the next 2.1 miles the trail climbs more than 2,600 feet.

3.3   At the Moose Falls campsite, there is a 250-foot side trail to Moose Falls.

3.5   The trail becomes a giant staircase that is the steepest 0.5 mile of the hike. You begin to get views to the west.

4.1   A short side trail leads to a spring that flows out of a rock face.

4.2   Turn right onto the Appalachian Trail. (**Option:** You can add 0.6 mile to the hike by taking a side trip up West Peak, the highest of the Bigelow peaks, before climbing Avery Peak.) Turn left onto the southbound AT to climb Avery Peak.

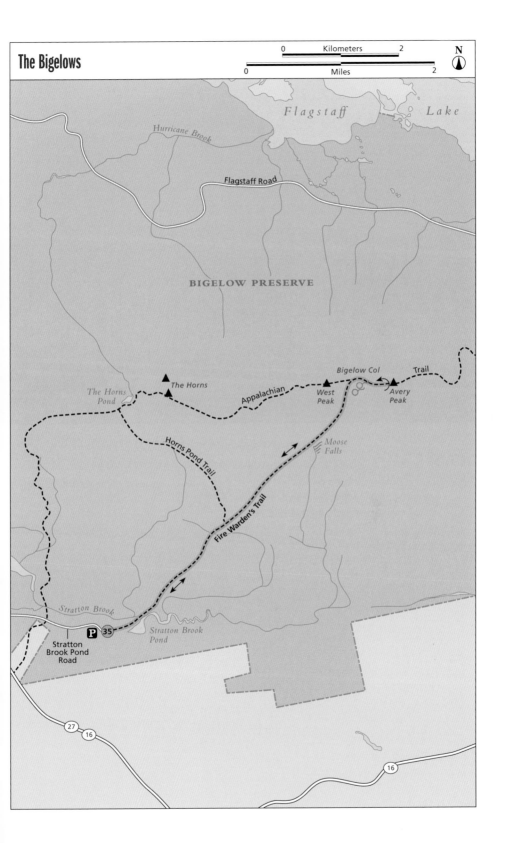

The Bigelows

0 Kilometers 2
0 Miles 2

N

Flagstaff Lake

Hurricane Brook

Flagstaff Road

BIGELOW PRESERVE

The Horns

The Horns Pond

Appalachian

Bigelow Col

Trail

West Peak

Avery Peak

Horns Pond Trail

Moose Falls

Fire Warden's Trail

Stratton Brook

P 35

Stratton Brook Pond Road

Stratton Brook Pond

27 16

16

West Peak from above Bigelow Col.

4.3 On the lower section of the rocky climb to Avery Peak, there is a spring in the trail.

4.7 The trail crosses the open summit and reaches Avery Peak. All that is left of the summit building is its foundation. There are fine views in every direction. To complete your hike, retrace your steps back to the trailhead.

9.4 Arrive back at the trailhead.

36 Puzzle Mountain

The hike up Puzzle Mountain follows the Grafton Loop Trail. The hike zigzags up through hardwoods, crossing and recrossing small streams before climbing in earnest to open ledges. From the ledges you have fine views of Grafton Notch, the Mahoosucs, and the Presidential Range. The trail continues climbing over granite that glitters in the sun because of mica flakes embedded in the rock. The summit and ledges below the summit have 360-degree views.

Start: From the Grafton Loop trailhead at the north end of the parking area
Distance: 6.1 miles out and back
Hiking time: 4 to 5 hours
Difficulty: Moderate
Best seasons: May to Oct
Trail surface: Woodland path
Land status: The first 1.9 miles of the hike are on private land and the rest is a Mahoosuc Land Trust preserve, all managed as part of the Grafton Loop.
Nearest towns: Bethel and Hanover
Other trail users: None

Water availability: Several small streams in the first 1.8 miles
Canine compatibility: Dogs must be under control at all times
Fees and permits: No fees or permits required
Maps: *DeLorme: The Maine Atlas and Gazetteer:* map 18; USGS Puzzle Mountain
Trail contacts: Maine Appalachian Trail Club; www.matc.org. Mahoosuc Public Reserved Land, (207) 778-8231; www.maine.gov/dacf/parks. Appalachian Mountain Club; www.outdoors.org.

Finding the trailhead: From the junction of US 2 and ME 26 North in Newry, drive north on ME 26 toward Grafton Notch State Park. Drive 4.7 miles to the trailhead parking for the Grafton Loop. The parking area is on the right just after a sign. The trailhead is at the north end of the parking area.
Trailhead GPS: N44 32.366' / W70 49.777'

The Hike

In 1859 a graphite mine was opened on Plumbago Mountain—just southeast of Puzzle Mountain. Plumbago is another, older name for graphite. The quality and purity of the graphite was favorably compared to the best veins in the world. During the 1860s there was a large boardinghouse for miners and all the attendant buildings that went along with a money-making mining operation. About that time, a man from Newry was hunting on a nearby mountain when he became lost. In climbing down a rock ledge, he dropped his axe and it became stuck in the rock. The hunter realized that he had found a new graphite vein. With dreams of getting rich, he found his way home. Unfortunately, he could never refind the graphite vein, so the mountain where he had been lost was renamed Puzzle Mountain. The hunter has faded into obscurity, but his dreams of riches are memorialized in the mountain's name.

Looking through Grafton Notch from the ledges on the shoulder of Puzzle Mountain.

The trail up Puzzle Mountain was built as part of the Grafton Loop. Robert Stewart built a trail through his land to ledges on the mountain with views of Grafton Notch and the White Mountains. Wanting to share the views with others, Stewart contacted the Appalachian Mountain Club and the Maine Appalachian Trail Club with the idea of creating a trail from ME 26 to the Appalachian Trail on East Baldpate Mountain. The result was the Grafton Loop. Much of the trail that this hike uses passes through private property or Stewart's land—which is now a Mahoosuc Land Trust preserve.

The lands around Grafton Notch are dominated by granite, but unlike the granite on Mount Desert Island or around Katahdin, the granite here is varied and infused with other minerals. Near the trailhead a large, white quartz boulder sticks out of the trail to remind us. There are boulders like these on nearby Old Speck Mountain as well. No matter how hot or dry the weather, the quartz always looks cool and damp—more like ice than rock.

The trail zigzags up the mountain, crossing and recrossing several small streams. The hardwood forest is cool and dark during the summer; earlier in the year, wild-flowers carpet the forest floor in a mad rush to mature and bloom before the trees leaf out. The trail begins to climb in earnest above the last stream crossing. The trail passes from private land into the Stewart Preserve just as the trail levels out and the forest fully transitions from hardwoods to evergreens.

TEABERRY

As you hike around Maine, you may notice a groundcover with waxy green leaves and small red berries—commonly called teaberry or wintergreen—growing in acidic soil; in Maine that often means you'll find it in spruce and pine forests, especially on granite bedrock. The plant favors sunny areas, so look for it along the trail, edging areas of open granite, and where the forest canopy is broken.

Native Americans and European settlers steeped the leaves to make tea, thus "teaberry." If you pick a leaf and break it or chew on it, you can smell and taste the wintergreen flavor. The name wintergreen derives from the fact that the leaves stay green all winter. The leaves are eaten by many animals, from squirrels and chipmunks to deer and grouse. The berries are edible too, having a minty taste.

At the first ledges you get fine views north into Grafton Notch and across Sunday River Whitecap of Sunday River Ski Resort and the Presidential Range beyond that. As you climb above the ledges, notice that the bedrock sparkles in the sun. There are bits of mica embedded in the granite. In several places you can see blocks of the thin reflective rock sticking out of the trail. If you stop to look at the small rocks that litter the trail and mountainside, you can find all kinds of interesting combinations of granite, mica, quartz, and other minerals.

As you climb, the semi-open ledges offer partial views, including one of Puzzle Mountain's rounded summit above you. A short, marked side trail leads to where several large slabs of rock have slid down and slumped against the mountainside, creating narrow caves. The trail passes directly above the caves—you'd never know it if it weren't for the sign directing you to the "boulders and caves." After another short climb the trail reaches a large, flat rock that hangs out over the mountainside, offering

The Grafton Loop Trail winding through a boulder field.

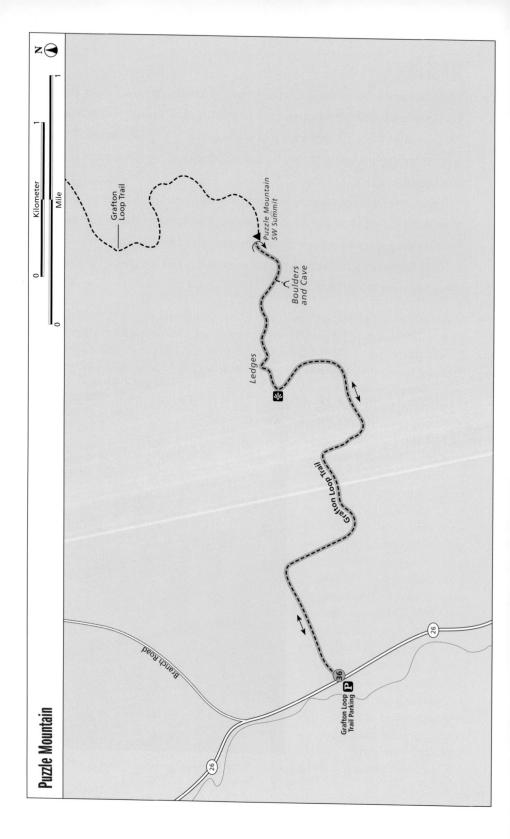

views in every direction. A short hike across the semi-wooded summit leads to the high point, where you can stand on a boulder and turn around and see unobstructed in every direction.

Miles and Directions

0.0 Start from the Grafton Loop trailhead at the north end of the parking area.

0.2 The trail crosses a private lane.

1.8 The trail climbs gently, crossing and recrossing several streams. After climbing alongside a stream, the trail climbs away from this last stream.

2.0 After leveling out, the trail enters the Stewart Family Preserve and comes to the first overlook with views west.

2.2 The trail crosses an open ledge with views north through Grafton Notch and west of Sunday River Whitecap and the mountains beyond, including the Presidential Range.

2.4 Junction with the Woodsum Spur Trail. This trail loops around Puzzle Mountain's southwest summit to the south and rejoins the Grafton Loop between the southwest and main summits of Puzzle Mountain.

2.6 A marked side trail leads 150 feet to where several large boulders have slumped against the mountainside, creating several small caves.

2.9 The trail passes a large, flat rock overlook.

3.1 The hike ends atop the unmarked southwest summit of Puzzle Mountain. The open summit offers 360-degree views. To complete the hike, retrace your steps back to the trailhead.

6.1 Arrive back at the trailhead.

37 East Royce Mountain

East Royce Mountain forms the western wall of Evans Notch. The East Royce Trail doesn't climb the mountain within sight of the vertical wall of the notch, but the emptiness beyond the woods that the trail climbs through is evident. The hike is relentlessly steep, but mercifully short. The views from the open summit are expansive. You can see from the Presidentials in the west, across the Carter and Mahoosuc Ranges, around to Caribou and Speckled Mountains to the east. Beyond them, and to the south beyond Baldface Mountain, is the low, rolling country of southwestern Maine.

Start: From the East Royce trailhead at the west end of the parking area
Distance: 3.0 miles out and back
Hiking time: 2 to 3 hours
Difficulty: Strenuous; hike is short, but very steep
Best seasons: May to Oct
Trail surface: Woodland path
Land status: White Mountain National Forest
Nearest town: Bethel
Other trail users: None

Water availability: Small stream between miles 0.1 and 0.5
Canine compatibility: Dogs must be under control at all times
Fees and permits: No fees or permits required
Maps: *DeLorme: The Maine Atlas and Gazetteer:* map 10; USGS Wild River
Trail contact: White Mountain National Forest, (603) 536-6100; www.fs.usda.gov/whitemountain

Finding the trailhead: From the junction of US 2 and ME 113 in Gilead, take ME 113 south. Drive 7.9 miles to the East Royce trailhead parking on the right at the small brown hiker sign. The trailhead is at the west end of the parking area.
Trailhead GPS: N44 18.314' / W70 59.408'

The Hike

The White Mountains are famous for their deep, vertical-walled notches. Evans Notch—the only one in Maine—is no exception. The west side of the notch is a nearly vertical wall of exposed bedrock that extends south from East Royce Mountain, towering over the Cold River valley. The east side of the notch is rolling hills, climbing toward Caribou and Speckled Mountains. The geography of the notch is a reminder that this section of the White Mountains is its edge, a transition from the high granite peaks to the low lake country of southwestern Maine.

The East Royce Trail climbs the mountain from the west, north of the notch, following the small stream that is one of the headwaters of the Cold River. The stream tumbles down the steep mountainside over boulders and slabs of bedrock. As you climb, you will notice that you can see blue sky through the trees to the south of the trail. It's an odd feeling to be climbing steeply through the woods along a small stream and be able to see vultures and ravens soaring below you through the trees. Above the stream the trail climbs away from the escarpment. The climb is relentlessly steep, but mercifully short.

At a small flat the Royce Connector Trail comes in from the west. This trail leads into New Hampshire with access to trails in the Cold River valley, the Wild River valley, and on West Royce Mountain. The East Royce Trail climbs away from the junction, mostly on granite bedrock. You quickly climb out of the mixed forest and into evergreens as the soil thins near the mountain's summit. The summit is an open granite dome with fine views. To the south you can see the arc of mountains around Evens Notch, ending with South Baldface. Across West Royce Mountain is the Presidential Range, often cloaked in either snow or clouds. More to the north, across the Wild River valley, is the Carter Range—a line of jagged peaks. North, a bit farther away, is the Mahoosuc Range. To the east are Caribou and Speckled Mountains.

The Carter-Moriah Range across the Wild River valley from East Royce Mountain's summit.

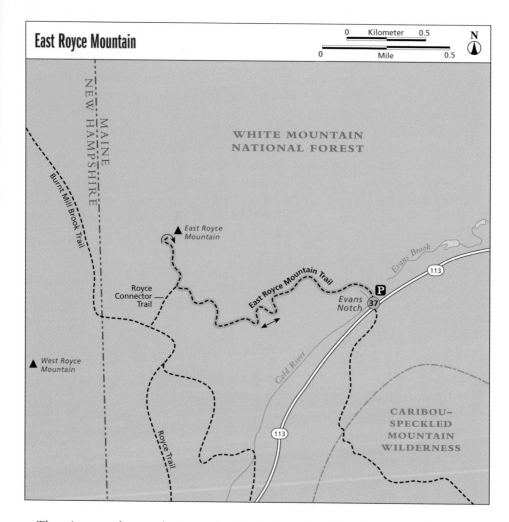

The view to the north is mostly blocked by East Royce's summit ridge. An unmarked, but easy to follow, trail leads from the summit out the ridge to ledges with fine views north and west. The north end of the ridge drops into the Wild River valley. The valley was once owned by LL Bean's family. It was at a small camp below where you stand that LL learned to hunt and fish, and where he got the idea for his famous boots. This river valley has gone from wild forest to working forest—with rail lines to haul logs out to Hastings—to burned-over wasteland and back again. In 2007 most of the valley was officially designated a wilderness.

Miles and Directions

0.0 Start from the East Royce trailhead at the west end of the parking area.

0.1 The East Royce Trail climbs to cross a small stream above a good-size waterfall.

West Royce Mountain foregrounds a view of the Presidential Range.

0.5 The trail climbs near the stream, crossing two small tributaries before climbing away from the stream.

0.9 The trail levels out just before the junction with the Royce Connector Trail. Turn right and continue to climb on the East Royce Trail.

1.2 The trail climbs, mostly on bedrock slabs, to the open summit.

1.5 Just beyond the summit cairn is a white sign at the top of a small rock face. (***Option:*** An unofficial trail continues at the bottom of the rock face, crossing the summit ridge to a north overlook. The trail beyond the summit is unblazed, but easy to follow.) To complete the hike, return the way you came.

3.0 Arrive back at the trailhead.

38 Caribou Mountain

Caribou Mountain is in the heart of one of Maine's only federally designated wildernesses. The hike up the mountain along Morrison Brook passes numerous waterfalls, including 30-foot Kees Falls. The falls drops from an exposed, flat ledge into a deep pool. The open summit of Caribou Mountain offers fine views in every direction. To the west, across the mountains around Evans Notch and the Carter Range, you can see the Presidential Range. At your feet the exposed bedrock is ringed by abundant blueberries. In the low areas you can find mountain cranberries. The descent off the mountain is steeper than the climb. Once down off the higher slopes, the trail follows Mud Brook.

Start: From the Caribou trailhead at the north end of the parking area
Distance: 6.7-mile loop
Hiking time: 4 to 5 hours
Difficulty: Moderate
Best seasons: May to Oct
Trail surface: Woodland path
Land status: White Mountain National Forest
Nearest town: Bethel
Other trail users: Hunting allowed in White Mountain National Forest

Water availability: Morrison Brook at miles 0.3 and 1.9; Mud Brook between miles 4.9 and 6.5
Canine compatibility: Dogs must be under control at all times
Fees and permits: No fees or permits required
Maps: *DeLorme: The Maine Atlas and Gazetteer:* map 10; USGS Speckled Mountain
Trail contact: White Mountain National Forest, (603) 536-6100; www.fs.usda.gov/whitemountain

Finding the trailhead: From the junction of US 2 and ME 113 in Gilead, take ME 113 south and drive 4.9 miles. Turn left onto the short road to the parking area at the brown sign for the trailhead. The trailhead is at the north end of the parking area.
Trailhead GPS: N44 20.159' / W70 58.516'

The Hike

Caribou Mountain is in the heart of the Caribou-Speckled Mountain Wilderness, one of only three federally designated wilderness areas in Maine (the other two are both in the Moosehorn National Wildlife Refuge in Washington County). The two mountains that the wilderness is named for are crossed by several trails. The region is mostly rolling hills and low mountains cut through by several deep notches. The region was heavily logged until the 1960s; the forest that has returned is mostly mixed hardwoods with white pine. The higher elevations, with their exposed bedrock and thin soils, are forested with spruce and stunted birch. Caribou Mountain was named in honor of the last woodland caribou in the region, which was shot by hunters on the mountain in 1854.

The hike follows the Caribou Trail along Morrison Brook from ME 113 to the notch between Gammon and Caribou Mountains. The trail climbs gently through

Looking north to the Mahoosuc Range from Caribou Mountain's summit.

the hardwood forest. Before the trees fully leaf out, this is a good area for wildflowers. There are several small waterfalls, culminating in the 30-foot Kees Falls. The trail passes across the top of the falls, where you can look down into the deep pool the water drops into. Above Kees Falls, Morrison Brook falls through a series of small drops and pools. The trail is often out of sight of the stream because of the dense underbrush along this section of the stream.

The trail continues to climb eastward beyond the upper reach of Morrison Brook through a wide vale. The widely spaced hardwoods give the forest an open feel, and the light seems especially yellow. The notch between Gammon and Caribou Mountains is a wide bowl with a flat floor. When you turn onto the Mud Brook Trail, you begin to climb immediately. Quickly the trail climbs out of the hardwood forest into evergreens.

Caribou Mountain's summit is a long, semi-open ridge that runs roughly northeast to southwest. Much of it is exposed granite rimmed by thick-growing spruce. The spruce and rock are bordered by abundant blueberries. In the low areas look for mountain cranberries too. The actual summit offers fine views in every direction. To the west, beyond the mountains along Evans Notch, rises the Presidential Range. It is easy to pick out Mount Washington with its tower on the summit—when it's not capped by a cloud. The Presidentials are especially striking early in the summer

Caribou Mountain

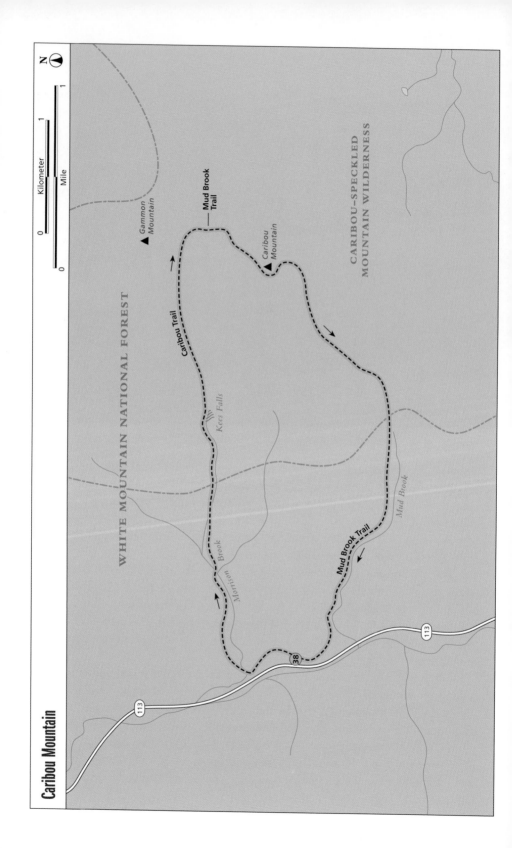

when they still hold snow. To the south, beyond Speckled Mountain, is the irregularly shaped Kezar Lake at the edge of what appears to be an infinite green plain.

The drop off the summit on Mud Brook Trail is much steeper than the ascent. The trail crosses open ledges and then turns into the woods for good. Mud Brook seems no muddier than Morrison Brook, but it flows in gentle curves through a low valley. Its banks are sunny, a good place to look for summer wildflowers and butterflies.

Miles and Directions

0.0 Start from the Caribou trailhead at the north end of the parking area.

0.3 The trail descends gently to cross Morrison Brook.

1.5 The trail climbs gently along Morrison Brook to the Caribou-Speckled Mountain Wilderness boundary.

1.9 The trail crosses Morrison Brook just above Kees Falls. Above the falls the brook drops through a series of small falls and pools.

3.0 The trail climbs above Morrison Brook to the notch between Caribou and Gammon Mountains. On the flat floor of the notch, the Caribou Trail junctions with the Mud Brook Trail. Turn right onto the Mud Brook Trail.

3.5 The trail climbs steadily out of the hardwood forest and into spruce before reaching the open summit.

4.0 The trail drops off the summit dome to the south and turns west to cross the mostly open summit ridge. The trail is poorly marked; stay high and to the left across the summit ridge; there are occasional faded yellow blazes on the rock and small cairns. The trail reaches the end of the summit ridge and descends steeply into the woods. The last open area is the top of a cliff that the trail crosses.

4.9 The trail crosses Mud Brook for the first time.

5.2 The trail leaves the wilderness area.

6.5 The trail turns north away from Mud Brook.

6.7 The Mud Brook Trail ends at the south end of the parking area.

39 Bald Mountain (Oquossoc)

Bald Mountain rises on a narrow neck between Mooselookmeguntic and Rangeley Lakes. From the observation tower on the summit, you can see mountains and lakes in every direction. It is a fairly easy hike to get one of the best views in the state.

Start: From the Bald Mountain trailhead at the east end of the parking area
Distance: 2.4 miles out and back
Hiking time: 1 to 2 hours
Difficulty: Moderate
Best seasons: May to Oct
Trail surface: Woodland path
Land status: Bald Mountain Public Reserved Land
Nearest town: Oquossoc

Other trail users: Hunting allowed on Maine Public Reserved Lands
Water availability: None
Canine compatibility: Dogs must be under control at all times
Fees and permits: No fees or permits required
Maps: *DeLorme: The Maine Atlas and Gazetteer:* map 28; USGS Oquossoc
Trail contact: Bald Mountain Public Reserved Land, (207) 778-8231; www.maine.gov/dacf/parks

Finding the trailhead: From Rangeley drive north on ME 4. Drive past the junction with ME 16 North after 6.9 miles and ME 17 South after 7.2 miles. Continue driving on ME 4 through Oquossoc until it ends, 8.4 miles from Rangeley. Turn right onto Bald Mountain Road and drive 0.9 mile. The trailhead parking is on the left at the blue Bald Mountain Public Reserved Land sign. The trailhead is at the east end of the parking area.
Trailhead GPS: N44 57.109' / W70 47.484'

The Hike

Bald Mountain rises from the narrow neck that separates Rangeley and Mooselookmeguntic Lakes. The mountain is only 2,443 feet high, but because it is nearly surrounded by water, the views from the summit are among the best in the state. You can see well into New Hampshire, including the Presidential Range to the southwest and the Connecticut Lakes country to the west. To the northwest are the Meguntic Mountains in Quebec. And everywhere around you are the mountains of western Maine.

The lakes around Bald Mountain almost looked very different. In 1907 the region became embroiled in a national conservation debate that pitted the tourist industry against the downstream mill owners. The mill owners wanted to change the level of the Rangeley Lakes with a dam to ensure year-round water power for their textile and paper mills on the Adroscoggin River. The tourist industry, led by Edward Ricker, owner of Poland Springs, claimed that the industrial development would ruin the aesthetic quality of the Rangeley Lakes, drive down local property values, and keep the tourists and their dollars away. Mainers have always had a love-hate relationship

Mooselookmeguntic Lake and the mountains to the southwest from Bald Mountain's summit.

with out-of-state tourists and their activities. They needed their money, but didn't like their tendency to look down on Maine's rural people and their culture. While Mainers tended to fish the Rangeley Lakes for food, the tourists fished for sport and criticized the locals' methods. There was even attempts to ban the use of lures on the lakes in order to limit the amount of fish locals could catch. Typically, local folks sided with industry against out-of-state tourists. But in 1907 anti-corporate feelings were running high in the United States. It was the beginning of the Progressive Era, which was marked by a push back against monopolistic capital. In the end the state legislature failed to pass the legislation to okay the dam. The Rangeley Lakes were saved. Ironically, the mill owners got their dam in the end; they built one farther upstream on the Magalloway River—in a true wilderness that lacked guides and folks from elsewhere to protect it.

What the battle for the Rangeley Lakes did was show that the economic and political power of the tourist industry could rival that of Maine's traditional extractive and manufacturing industries. This affected the outcomes of other proposals that were brewing at the time for Chesuncook, Brassau, and Sebago Lakes. These tensions between Mainers and tourists and summer folks from elsewhere, and between industry uses of the land and tourism continue. Today the battles are more likely to be over wind farms on remote mountaintops, motorized access to wildlands, or whether or

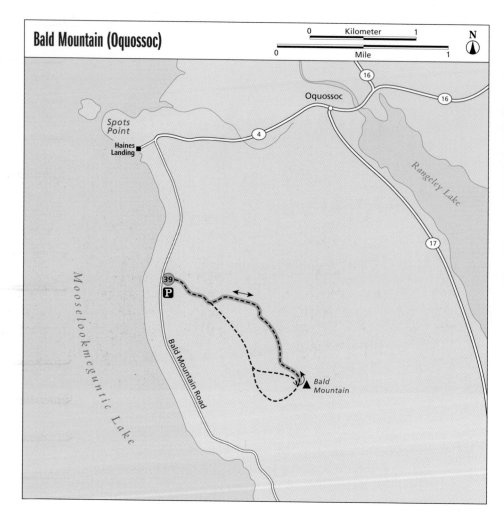

not to create a national park in the North Woods. In these fights the rural Mainers usually side with industry. Occasionally, though, the local people's interests line up with those of the conservationists—as with the proposal to build an east–west highway across northern Maine. In many ways the Maine Public Reserved Land system is an attempt to answer the needs of both the local communities and the recreationalists.

The trail up Bald Mountain in the Bald Mountain Public Reserved Land climbs gently through an open forest—a good place to find wildflowers and mushrooms in season in the cool, moist shade beneath the high canopy. About halfway to the summit, the trail bends to the south and begins climbing more steeply. The trail becomes rockier, often crossing slabs of bedrock, and the forest is dominated more by spruce. You begin to get occasional, partial views of Mooselookmeguntic Lake.

The summit is spruce covered, but with enough open rock so that there are views in every direction. There are a number of picnic tables on the summit, put there by the Rangeley Lakes Heritage Trust. The trust also built an observation tower on the summit. You can climb the steel stairs above the spruce forest and turn and see the lakes and mountains in every direction.

Miles and Directions

0.0 Start from the Bald Mountain trailhead at the east end of the parking area.

0.2 A side trail leads out to a trailhead on ME 4 (which is a much longer hike than this one).

1.2 The trail climbs steadily, then more steeply to reach the summit. There are several picnic tables on the summit, and a tower that rises above the spruce forest for 360-degree views. To complete the hike, return the way you came.

2.4 Arrive back at the trailhead.

Honorable Mentions

H The Grafton Loop

The Grafton Loop is a 40-mile loop hike through a patchwork of public and private lands. The trail climbs all the major mountains around Grafton Notch including Puzzle, East and West Baldpate, Old Speck Mountains and Sunday River Whitecap. It is a challenging hike with several very large climbs. There are backcountry campsites spaced regularly to accommodate either a three- or four-day trip. The loop includes 8 miles of the Appalachian Trail between the summits of East Baldpate and Old Speck Mountains. These two mountains can be day hiked separately on the AT from Grafton Notch. This popular section includes expansive views and geologically interesting climbs. But the real jewel of the Grafton Loop is Sunday River Whitecap with its views through Grafton Notch and of the surrounding mountains, including the Presidentials to the southwest. To find the trailhead, drive north for 4.7 miles on ME 26 from the junction with US 2 in Newry. The trailhead parking is on the right. There is a sign at the parking area. For more information contact Maine Appalachian Trail Club, www.matc.org, or Appalachian Mountain Club, (800) 372-1758; www.outdoors.org.

I Dunn Falls

Dunn Falls is one of the most spectacular in Maine. Just below Dunn Notch the West Branch Ellis River crosses the Appalachian Trail then drops 30 feet into a pool trapped between vertical rock walls. At the east end of the pool, the stream seems to disappear between the walls. From this vantage you can hear Dunn Falls, but not see it. The stream drops more than 80 feet straight down between vertical walls more than 100 feet high. The 1.9-mile loop hike to the falls begins on the southbound Appalachian Trail where it crosses East B Hill Road. You drop down to a small stream and turn left onto the Cascade Trail. This trail follows the stream down past numerous small and medium-size waterfalls. The trail then cuts through the woods to the West Branch Ellis River and follows it upstream. After crossing the stream you come to a fork. The trail to the right leads to the base of Dunn Falls where you can see the main drop. You then backtrack to the fork and take the trail up to the AT. To complete the hike, turn right on the AT and follow it back to East B Hill Road. To get to the trailhead, drive north on ME 5 for 10.6 miles from the junction with US 2 near the Rumford/Hanover town line. Where ME 5 ends in Andover, turn left onto Newton Street—which becomes East B Hill Road when you leave town. Drive 5.4 miles to where you pass the marked Cataract Trail; this is not the trail you want. Continue driving on East B Hill Road another 2.9 miles to a gravel parking area on the right just past the AT crossing. For more information contact Maine Appalachian Trail Club, www.matc.org.

Central Highlands

The Central Highlands encompass the area south of Baxter State Park between the Kennebec and Penobscot Rivers. South and east of the Piscataquis River it is a region of low, rolling country with small towns, second-growth forest, and lakes. North of the Piscataquis River is some of the wildest and remote areas in Maine. Several of the trailheads in this region are more than 25 miles from a paved road. Many of the lakes and ponds have few camps

This small waterfall on Little Wilson Stream is typical of the falls in the Central Highlands (hike 43).

and no good road access. Of the eight Debsconeag lakes and ponds (hikes 46 and 48), only Fourth Debsconeag Lake has road access or a camp on it, for example.

The section of the Appalachian Trail from Monson to Abol Bridge on the Golden Road across the Penobscot River is known as the "100 Mile Wilderness." Not that the region is a true wilderness; much of it is working forest. The name was given because it is the longest section on the entire AT without a paved road crossing or resupply opportunity. Several hundred thousand acres of land here have been preserved by various governmental and private organizations in a coordinated effort to preserve this region's wildness. Nahmakanta Public Reserved Land is one of the state's largest single holdings; it abuts both The Nature Conservancy's Debsconeag Lakes Wilderness and the Appalachian Mountain Club's 60,000-acre preserve.

Thru hikers have left most folks with the impression that the wilderness is flat, but as the hikes in this guide attest, there are plenty of mountains. The mountains may not be as high or rugged as those in Baxter State Park or western Maine—there's only one mountain in the region over 3,000 feet, Whitecap Mountain (hike J)—but there is plenty of good hiking on scenic mountains.

The Central Highlands are unique in that there is very little granite bedrock; most of the region is underlain by slate. The black slate is most in evidence at the region's many waterfalls (hikes 40, 43, and 44). Much of the slate bedding is dramatically upended. The hard, black slate is still mined commercially in the region. As you drive through Monson on ME 15, you will see pallets of slate stacked and ready to ship. There is some granite: Moxie Bald (hike 41) is mostly granite, and the granite of Katahdin extends down to the area around Nahmakanta Lake (hikes 45, 46, and 47).

40 Moxie Falls

Moxie Falls is one of the largest waterfalls in New England. None so powerful is as high in Maine. The easy walk to the viewing platforms around the falls passes through a hardwood forest that abounds in spring wildflowers. The black slate cliffs around Moxie Falls and its 80-foot main drop make it the most dramatic in Maine.

Start: From the Moxie Falls trailhead on the north side of the parking area
Distance: 1.8 miles out and back
Hiking time: About 1 hour
Difficulty: Easy
Best seasons: May and June for maximum water flow and wildflowers; July to Oct for average water flow
Trail surface: Graded woodland path and boardwalk
Land status: Private timberland and state preserve

Nearest town: The Forks
Other trail users: Hunting allowed in the surrounding woods
Water availability: None
Canine compatibility: Dogs must be under control at all times
Fees and permits: No fees or permits required
Maps: *DeLorme: The Maine Atlas and Gazetteer:* map 40; USGS The Forks
Trail contact: None

Finding the trailhead: From US 201 in The Forks, take Lake Moxie Road east and drive 1.8 miles. The trailhead parking is on the left at a brown state sign for Moxie Falls. The trailhead is on the north side of the parking area.
Trailhead GPS: N45 21.242' / W69 56.426'

The Hike

The Forks is in the heart of Maine's whitewater country. The Kennebec River rages through its gorge between Indian Pond and the town. In summer, rafts and kayaks crowd the river on their wet, wild rides. The Dead River, which empties into the Kennebec River at The Forks, is just as popular. It drops from Flagstaff Lake through miles of churning whitewater to the Kennebec. Just outside of town, on Moxie Stream, is one of New England's largest waterfalls.

The hike to Moxie Falls passes through a hardwood forest that abounds with spring wildflowers. Don't rush to the waterfall; take your time to enjoy the woods along the way. The best time to enjoy both the woods and the waterfall is late May, when Moxie Stream is still high and the trees haven't fully leafed out yet. This season has the added advantage that you are likely to have the trail to yourself. Because Moxie Stream flows out of Moxie Pond, supplying it with a steady water flow, the falls remains strong all through the summer. You can hear its roar as soon as you get out of your car at the trailhead.

▶ In Maine there is a Moxie Mountain, Moxie Bald, Moxie Stream, and Moxie Pond. The name is Abanaki for "deep water," so all the names came from that of the pond. Though never proven, it is believed that the tonic—and later, soda—called Moxie was named for the lake. Dr. Augustin Thompson, the drink's inventor, was originally from Union, Maine, in Waldo County. The word "moxie" was derived from the drink.

The trail first comes to the upper falls, a stair step cascade that drops 30 feet across a series of ledges spanning the stream. The maples hang densely out over the water; the stream is a narrow, churning corridor through the woods. Around a bend of calm water is the main falls. There is a railed deck right at the top of the falls. The stream leaps out and drops to a deep pool surrounded by black cliffs. The bedrock here is slate that has been upended, creating towering cliffs with smooth faces. Below the pool is another, smaller waterfall, easy to miss in the mist that hangs in the air.

From above the falls to the Kennebec River, Moxie Stream drops 300 feet in less than a mile. The main drop, right in the middle of this descent, is 80 feet. Not the highest waterfall in Maine, but none are as high with the water flow that Moxie Stream maintains. The falls are all the more dramatic because of the way the black slate bedrock frames the falls. The slate bedding is stood on end, making sheer walls below the falls on both banks. The mist from the falls keeps the rock wet and inky black. The lush vegetation atop the cliffs leans out over the void soaking up the sun and spray.

The trail continues around to two viewing platforms atop the cliffs with views across the pool of Moxie Falls. Many people try to make their way down to the stream from here, but there is no trail and no safe way down to Moxie Stream. The hillside is too steep and covered with loose rocks. The trail continues on, along the nearly vertical hillside as far as the confluence of Moxie Stream with the Kennebec River. Far below, Moxie Stream churns over jumbled rocks. Not part of this hike, the trail beyond the falls is worth exploring for at least a short distance.

Moxie Falls from one of the viewing platforms at the end of the hike.

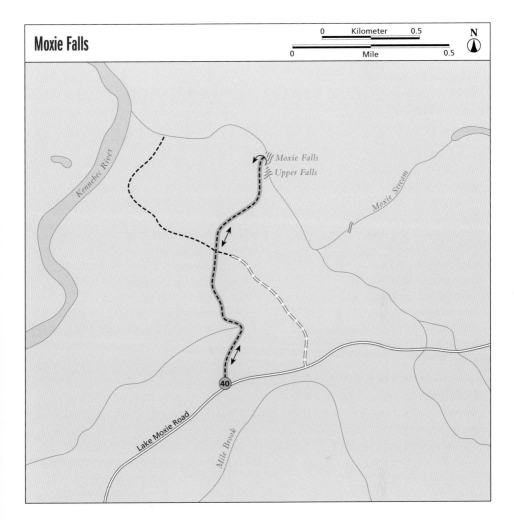

Miles and Directions

0.0 Begin from the Moxie Falls trailhead on the north side of the parking area.

0.5 The trail crosses an ATV trail; on the other side of the trail is a state sign for Moxie Falls.

0.8 The trail reaches a wooden deck with views upstream on Moxie Stream of the upper falls.

0.9 The trail reaches a deck at the top of Moxie Falls with views of the falls and the slate gorge downstream.

0.95 The official trail ends at two decks atop cliffs with views of Moxie Falls. A rough trail continues along the nearly vertical hillside all the way to the confluence of Moxie Stream and the Kennebec River. There is no safe way to reach the stream below the falls. To complete the hike, return the way you came.

1.8 Arrive back at the trailhead.

41 Moxie Bald

This granite peak offers fine views in every direction from its open summit. The trail climbs through a beech forest, then spruce over bare rock. The trail passes the rock formation known as the Devil's Doorstep. You can extend the hike by visiting the north summit and a waterfall south of the trailhead along the Appalachian Trail.

Start: From the Northbound Appalachian Trail where it crosses Moxie Bald Road
Distance: 4.1-mile lollipop
Hiking time: 2 to 4 hours
Difficulty: Moderate
Best seasons: Late May to Oct
Trail surface: Woodland path
Land status: Appalachian Trail
Nearest town: Bingham
Other trail users: Hunters use the woods around the AT corridor; logging along the roads to the trailhead

Water availability: Bald Mountain Brook at trailhead parking and a spring on the mountain at mile 2.3
Canine compatibility: Dogs must be under control at all times
Fees and permits: No fees or permits required
Maps: *DeLorme: The Maine Atlas and Gazetteer:* map 30; USGS Moxie Pond
Trail contact: Maine Appalachian Trail Club (MATC), PO Box 283, Augusta, ME 04332; www .matc.org

Finding the trailhead: From the junction of ME 15 and ME 16 in Abbot, take ME 16 west toward Bingham. Drive 19.4 miles. Just past a Recreational Trail Crossing sign and the Moscow town line, turn right onto Town Line Road. Drive 2.6 miles to the end of Town Line Road and turn right onto Deadwater Road. Drive 4.2 miles to a fork in the road. Take the left fork onto Trestle Road, staying along the power lines, and drive 2.9 miles. Turn right onto the unmarked Little Austin Pond Road just past Baker Dimmock Road on the left, which has a bridge over Moxie Stream. Drive uphill on Little Austin Pond Road 0.8 mile to a fork in the road. Take the left fork onto the unmarked Moxie Bald Road. Drive 3 miles to a small bridge over Bald Mountain Brook. Park on the right just across the bridge. *Do not* drive the additional 0.1 mile to the Appalachian Trail. The road quickly deteriorates, and there is no good place to turn around. The trailhead is the northbound AT 0.1 mile farther down the road from the bridge over Bald Mountain Brook.
Trailhead GPS: N45 15.542' / W69 47.903'

The Hike

The Appalachian Trail crosses Moxie Bald between Moxie Pond and Bald Mountain Pond. The official name of the mountain is Bald Mountain, but Maine has several so everyone calls this one Moxie Bald. To add to the confusion, there is a Moxie Mountain southwest of Moxie Bald. The ponds on either side of the mountain reflect the mountain's two names. The mountain is a granite island among the more common slate of the Central Highlands. To the northwest, Moxie Falls (hike 40) drops into a

Moxie Bald's open summit on a sunny November day.

slate gorge. Pleasant Mountain to the south on the AT is mainly slate. To the east the AT follows the West Branch Piscataquis River's slate gorge.

The standard way to climb Moxie Bald is to follow the AT north from the road crossing at Joe's Hole on Moxie Pond. The problem is that the trail crosses Moxie Stream, which the pond backs up into. Much of the year a hundred yards of trail are flooded with no easy way to cross. Beyond the stream the trail winds through hardwood forest, crossing two beaver flowages. By starting 2 miles farther north on the AT where Moxie Mountain Road crosses the trail, you avoid all these water hazards and shorten the hike by 4 miles. The only downside is that Moxie Mountain Road is rough in places, but always passable.

The hike begins climbing immediately, through a hardwood forest dominated by beech. In late spring the new leaves give the air a yellow cast; wildflowers bloom along the trail. Look for painted trillium, blue bead lilies, and wild lily-of-the-valley. Soon the trail climbs into a spruce forest. The trail has worn down through the moss and thin soil to the bedrock—a ribbon of granite climbing through the mossy forest.

▶ **Beech trunks: Almost all the large beech trees in Maine have rough bark with large cankers, caused by a fungus that infects almost all the beech trees in New England. Notice that most small beech trees don't show signs of infection yet.**

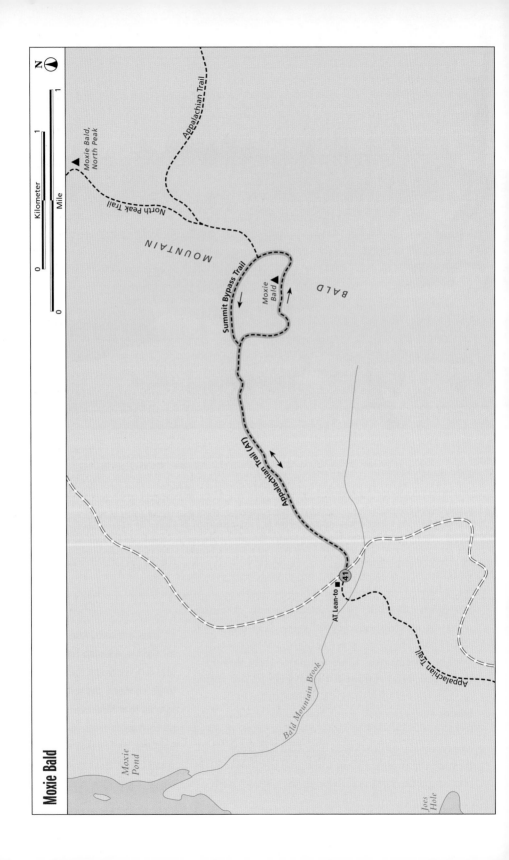

Moxie Bald

N

Kilometer

Mile

Moxie Bald,
North Peak

North Peak Trail

Appalachian Trail

MOUNTAIN

Summit Bypass Trail

Moxie
Bald

BALD

Appalachian Trail (AT)

AT Lean-to

41

Bald Mountain Brook

Moxie
Pond

Appalachian Trail

Joes
Hole

Above the Summit Bypass Trail, the AT passes beneath rounded cliffs, at one point passing under overhanging rocks. As you approach them, cool air engulfs you. The rocks must hide pockets of ice that remain into summer and cool the surrounding air. The trail then climbs the cliffs and breaks out of the woods onto bare granite, following a spine of rock up the mountain to the summit. From the summit you have fine views in every direction. Beneath your feet the granite appears like frozen waves passing across the mountaintop. In the wave troughs are boggy areas of sphagnum and stunted spruce.

The trail descends off the east side of the summit along a long, slender spine of rock known as the Devil's Doorstep. At the junction with the Summit Bypass Trail, a short side trail leads to a spring set against the flank of the mountain. To the right the northbound AT passes over an area of open rock and sphagnum moss. At 0.7 mile to the north, just after the AT drops back down into the woods, a side trail leads 0.7 mile to the north summit of Moxie Bald. The north summit is a larger, open granite expanse with more pronounced waves. The views are about the same as from the higher main summit, except that you can see the main summit's rounded dome to the south.

As you make your way back to the trailhead along the Summit Bypass Trail, the rocky north face of Moxie Bald is visible through and above the trees. Then you descend into the spruce forest and enter that quiet mossy world, and the landscape shrinks to the woods around you.

Miles and Directions

0.0 Begin on the northbound Appalachian Trail 100 yards down the road from the parking area.

1.3 Reach a junction of the AT and the Summit Bypass Trail. Turn right and climb on the AT.

1.5 The trail climbs the slabs around cliffs with limited views to the west to the Devil's Doorstep, a rock feature the trail goes through and under.

1.9 The trail climbs through rocky woods, then breaks out onto bare granite among stunted spruce. The trail follows a rock spine to the summit, which is 100 feet to the northeast of the trail.

2.3 Continue northbound on the AT, descending off the summit along a granite ledge to the north end of the Summit Bypass Trail. To the left a short side trail leads to a spring. To the right the AT continues north. (**Option:** To reach the north summit of Moxie Bald, hike 0.7 mile north on the AT across alternating bog and granite. Just after the trail drops back down into the woods, take a marked side trail north 0.7 mile to the north summit. This side trip adds 2.8 miles to the hike.) To complete the hike without the side trip, turn left onto the Summit Bypass Trail.

2.8 Junction with the AT. Go straight on the southbound AT to return to the trailhead.

4.1 Arrive back at the trailhead. (**Option:** If you continue southbound on the AT 0.1 mile beyond the trailhead, you will come to an AT lean-to. On Bald Mountain Brook, in front of the lean-to, is a waterfall worth taking a side trip to see.)

42 Borestone Mountain

Borestone Mountain's bare double summit is visible from as far south as Charleston even though the mountain is less than 2,000 feet high. The summit offers stunning views in every direction of the surrounding mountains and lake country. The hike climbs steadily through spruce to Sunrise Pond where there is a visitor center and museum. Once around the pond and past the Fox Pen Loop Trail, the hike climbs again. This second climb is steeper and rockier, ending in a section that involves some exposure.

Start: From the Borestone Mountain access road, across Mountain Road from the trailhead parking
Distance: 4.1-mile lollipop
Hiking time: 2 to 3 hours
Difficulty: Moderate
Best seasons: May to Oct
Trail surface: Woodland path and rock
Land status: Audubon Borestone Sanctuary
Nearest town: Monson

Other trail users: None
Water availability: None
Canine compatibility: Dogs not allowed in the sanctuary
Fees and permits: Fee collected at visitor center Memorial Day through Columbus Day
Maps: *DeLorme: The Maine Atlas and Gazetteer:* map 41; USGS Barren Mountain West
Trail contact: Maine Audubon, (207) 781-2330; maineaudubon.org

Finding the trailhead: From the center of Monson on ME 15, drive 0.6 mile north. Turn right onto Elliotsville Road; there is a sign for Borestone Mountain just before the turn. Drive 7.6 miles to the bridge over Big Wilson Stream. Across the bridge turn left onto Mountain Road; there is a gray sign pointing to Borestone Mountain. Drive 0.7 mile up the hill and across the railroad tracks. The parking area is on the left, across the road from the trailhead and Borestone Sanctuary sign.
Trailhead GPS: N45 22.672' / W69 25.808'

The Hike

Borestone Mountain's name was originally spelled "Boarstone." It seems that from the north the mountain's rounded, rocky flank rising above Onowa Lake looked like a certain part of a boar's anatomy to the loggers who named the mountain. Some time early in the twentieth century, the name was changed to the more family—and tourist—friendly "Borestone." The tourists never came, but the new spelling stuck. The valley remains largely undeveloped, and the town at the east end of the lake has been abandoned; nothing is left but a few collapsing buildings.

The three ponds on the mountain's flank—Sunrise, Midday, and Sunset—were named by the Moore family, who managed a fox farm on the mountain. The Fox Pen Loop Trail you pass on the Summit Trail as you hike around Sunrise Pond winds through the woods among the remains of the pens used to raise the foxes. The fox pelts were shipped to New York from the nearby Canadian Pacific rail line—you

Looking north from the West Peak across an autumn forest.

crossed the railroad on Mountain Road as you approached the sanctuary. If you look carefully, you can see the high trestle over the southeast corner of Onawa Lake where the railroad passes through the village. The fox pelts raised on Borestone Mountain had a reputation for their high quality. They must have drawn consistently high prices, because the Moores hired a well-known architect to design the Adirondack-style lodge on Sunset Pond. It was the Moore family that donated the land to Maine Audubon for the sanctuary. The mile-long Fox Pen Loop Trail is worth checking out on your way down off the mountain.

After hiking up the Base Trail and walking out the access road to Sunrise Pond, you need to stop at the visitor center to pay the entrance fee. There is a museum of local flora and fauna that is kid-friendly. The visitor center also sells guidebooks, shirts, and water.

Once around Sunrise Pond the Summit Trail is fairly steep; the last section before West Peak does have some exposure, but with care is doable even by small children. The views from the two peaks are well worth the work. The higher East Peak has two signs on the summit with maps of the mountains that you see all around you. You can see as far west as Sugarloaf Mountain and the Bigelow Range; to the east are the flat Penobscot and Piscataquis river valleys with the hills southeast of Bangor on the horizon. Katahdin would be visible but for the Barren-Chairback Range and

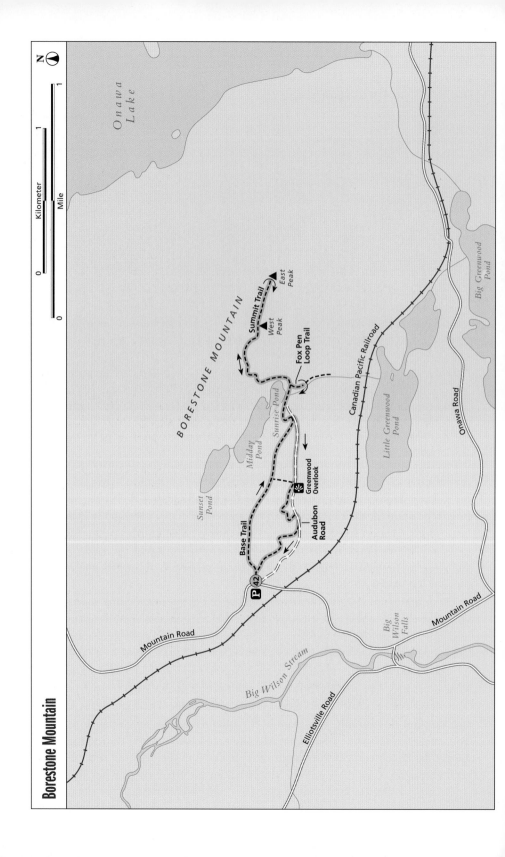

Whitecap Mountain behind it—Maine's famous 100 Mile Wilderness. In the spring hikers often mistake Whitecap's snow-covered summit for Katahdin. To the north are the mountains around Moosehead Lake.

On your return hike it is easier to take the access road instead of the Base Trail. The hike is a little shorter, and you pass by the Greenwood Overlook. On the hike up the mountain, you passed through forest dominated by evergreens. Along the more gentle south flank of the mountain, the access road passes through beech and especially maple. The maples are tapped each spring; the trail passes the sugar shack just before reaching the trailhead. One weekend each spring the sugar shack is open so visitors can watch the maple syrup being made.

Miles and Directions

0.0 Start by walking through the gate on the access road across Mountain Road from the parking lot. In about 350 feet the Base Trail begins on the left at an information sign. Begin climbing away from the access road.

0.5 After climbing through spruce and over slate and small seasonal streams, the trail junctions with the Greenwood Overlook Trail. Continue straight ahead; this overlook is part of the return hike.

0.8 The trail descends off the ridge the Base Trail climbed and meets the access road. Turn left onto the road and hike past the privy toward the visitor center and Sunrise Pond.

1.0 The access road ends at the visitor center on the shore of Sunrise Pond. If the visitor center is open, you need to go in to pay the fee. There is also a small gift shop and museum. The hike continues on the Summit Trail, which begins along the pond beyond the visitor center.

1.1 Junction with the Fox Pen Loop Trail. This side trail goes south down a slope, across a boggy area, then makes a loop through the area where foxes were once commercially raised. To continue climbing Borestone Mountain, follow the Summit Trail the rest of the way around Sunrise Pond.

1.5 The Summit Trail reaches the foot of a climb up to West Peak. This is the steepest section of the hike, and does entail some exposure.

1.6 Reach the open West Peak. Continue following the green blazes across the summit to get to the higher East Peak.

1.9 Reach the open East Peak. There are two metal signs on the summit that show you what mountains you are seeing around you. To complete your hike, return to the junction with the Base Trail the way you came.

3.1 Arrive back at the Base Trail. You can return on that trail or hike down on the access road. The road walk is 0.1 mile shorter, is easier, and passes the Greenwood Overlook.

3.4 Reach the Greenwood Overlook Trail. Turn left and hike 200 feet out to the overlook with views of Little and Big Greenwood Ponds and the flat country beyond. To hike back to the trailhead, return to the access road and turn left.

4.1 Arrive back at the trailhead.

43 Little Wilson Falls

Little Wilson Falls, at 75 feet, is one of the highest in Maine. Little Wilson Stream drops from a calm pool into a narrow, black slate gorge overhung with dark cedars. Below the falls the stream cascades over a series of smaller waterfalls before flowing into Big Wilson Stream. The hike passes several of these falls and offers access to the rest.

Start: From the northwest corner of the parking area at the end of Little Wilson Falls Road
Distance: 2.6 miles out and back
Hiking time: About 2 hours
Difficulty: Easy
Best seasons: May to Nov; during May and early June, the falls have more water
Trail surface: Woodland path with lots of roots and rocks
Land status: Elliotsville Plantation and Appalachian Trail

Nearest town: Monson
Other trail users: None
Water availability: Little Wilson Stream
Canine compatibility: Dogs must be under control at all times
Fees and permits: No fees or permits required
Maps: DeLorme: The Maine Atlas and Gazetteer: map 41; USGS Barren Mountain West
Trail contact: Elliotsville Plantation, (207) 581-9462; www.keepmebeautiful.org

Finding the trailhead: From the center of Monson on ME 15, drive 0.6 mile north. Turn right onto Elliotsville Road; there is a sign for Borestone Mountain just before the turn. Drive 7.6 miles on Elliotsville Road. Just before the bridge over Big Wilson Stream, there is an unmarked gravel road on the left. Turn down Little Wilson Falls Road and drive 0.5 mile to a fork in the road. At the fork go straight and drive another 0.3 mile to the end of the road. The trail leaves the northwest corner of the parking area along the stream. At first the trail looks more like a small, gravelly streambed than a trail.
Trailhead GPS: N45 22.511' / W69 26.937'

The Hike

Monson is the center of Maine's slate industry. The black slabs of rock are harvested from several quarries around the town; in town you can see slate stacked, ready to be sold. Many of the streams in this part of Maine cut through slate gorges, drop over slate ledges, or have piles of broken slate along their banks. Nearby Big Wilson Falls—across Elliotsville Road from the dirt road back to the trailhead—is a good example. To the west in Blanchard, the Piscataquis River cuts through a shallow slate gorge below Abbott Road; at the head of the gorge is Barrow's Falls. Northeast of Little Wilson Falls is the most famous slate gorge, Gulf Hagas.

In most of these cases, the sheets of slate are stood on end. Across Little Wilson Falls from the trail, the cliffs show this vertical bedding. You can see the same thing when you hike Gulf Hagas. Along the trail to Little Wilson Falls are several places where fins of slate stick out of the hillside. Near the falls, the top of the gorge has several large fins of slate that jut out into space. The blackness of the slate, the vertical bedding, and the forest closing over the gorge and falls all make Little Wilson Falls the most dramatic in Maine.

The trail begins at a no-longer-used state campsite. Originally the trail was a shortcut used by locals to get to the falls. In the summer of 2013, the Appalachian Mountain Club improved and blazed the trail for Elliotsville Plantation, the land's owner. The trail begins along the stream at the large pool below a waterfall and follows the stream up past another good-size falls. Notice that the huge boulder sitting on the slate ledge across the stream is not the same kind of rock—it is an erratic dropped here by the retreating glaciers. Beyond the sec-

The top half of the falls from the slate ledges beside Little Wilson Falls.

ond falls the trail begins to gently climb the hillside, staying withing earshot and often view of Little Wilson Stream. The trail turns away from the stream after it flattens out atop a ridge and just before junctioning with the Appalachian Trail.

To hike to Little Wilson Falls, turn left and hike southbound on the AT up a rocky and rooty climb alongside the slate gorge. When you reach the sign-in box just before the falls, there is a place to climb out onto the rocks to see the falls from partway down. Remember, while climbing around on the rock, that slate is slippery when wet. After exploring the falls, you may want to explore the slate gorge and the stream below the gorge. To do so, pass the Little Wilson Falls Trail and continue northbound on the AT as it drops down to Little Wilson Stream just below the gorge. To get the best view back up the gorge, you need to ford the stream or cross on the log that spans it. To explore a horseshoe bend and falls downstream, follow the rough trail on the west bank of Little Wilson Stream for 0.1 mile. When the water is low in late summer, you can cross and recross the stream on the slate at the falls. In the spring the water rushes over and around the rocks.

Miles and Directions

0.0 Start at the northwest corner of the parking area. The unmarked trail looks like a small, rocky streambed that stays close to Little Wilson Stream.

1.1 The trail follows along the stream, passing several waterfalls, then begins to climb. The trail ends at the white-blazed Appalachian Trail. Turn left to hike toward Little Wilson Falls.

Little Wilson Falls

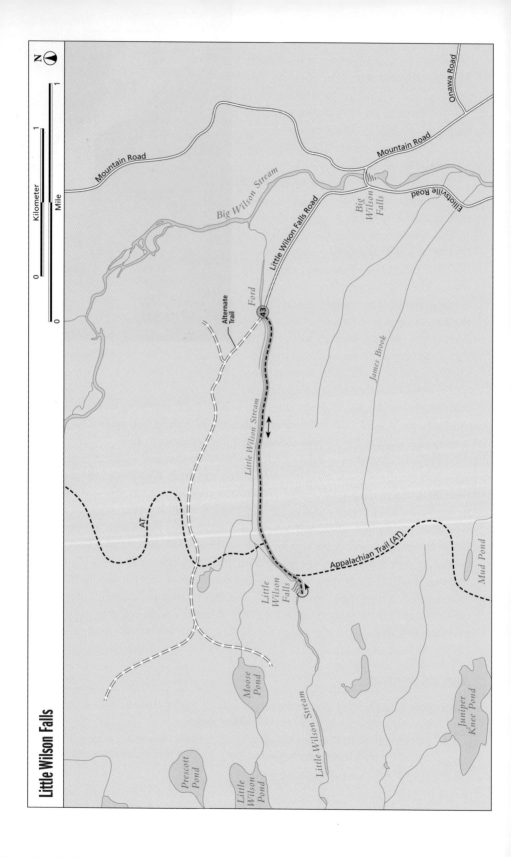

N

Kilometer
0   1

Mile
0   1

Mountain Road

Mountain Road

Big Wilson Stream

Little Wilson Falls Road

Elliotsville Road

Big Wilson Falls

Onawa Road

Ford

43

Alternate Trail

Little Wilson Stream

James Brook

AT

Appalachian Trail (AT)

Mud Pond

Little Wilson Falls

Little Wilson Stream

Moose Pond

Prescott Pond

Little Wilson Pond

Juniper Knee Pond

1.3 After hiking along the end of the gorge below the falls, you arrive at the top of the falls. When climbing around on the rocks, remember that slate is slippery when it's wet. To return to the trailhead, retrace your steps.

1.5 Arrive back at the Little Wilson Falls Trail. Turn right to return to the trailhead. (***Option:*** Hike straight ahead on the AT, descending to where the trail crosses the stream. This gives you a good view back up the dark gorge and, by bushwhacking downstream 100 yards, access to a horseshoe bend on Little Wilson Stream that is a great place for lunch or just to explore. If you take this option, you'll need to retrace your steps back up to the Little Wilson Falls Trail to get back to the trailhead.)

2.6 Arrive back at the trailhead.

44 Gulf Hagas

Gulf Hagas is one of Maine's deepest canyons. The hike follows the West Branch Pleasant River as it drops 400 feet in 4 miles through the Gulf. There are numerous waterfalls and rapids. The walls of the Gulf rise vertical at times as much as 140 feet. Below Gulf Hagas the hike follows Gulf Hagas Brook up past numerous waterfalls, including Screw Auger Falls—the highest on the hike.

Start: From the Head of the Gulf trailhead across the road from the parking area
Distance: 10.2-mile lollipop
Hiking time: 5 to 8 hours
Difficulty: Moderate
Best seasons: Mid-May to Oct, especially after heavy rains
Trail surface: Woodland path
Land status: Appalachian Mountain Club's North Woods Recreation and Conservation Area and Appalachian Trail Corridor
Nearest towns: Brownville and Greenville
Other trail users: None

Water availability: West Branch Pleasant River at miles 0.5 and 2.0; Gulf Hagas Brook at miles 5.8 and 6.1
Canine compatibility: Dogs must be under control at all times
Fees and permits: Fee paid at Katahdin Iron Works or Hedgehog gate
Maps: *DeLorme: The Maine Atlas and Gazetteer:* maps 41 and 42; USGS Barren Mountain East
Trail contacts: Appalachian Mountain Club, Greenville office, (207) 695-3085; www.outdoors.org. Maine Appalachian Trail Club; www.matc.org. KI-Jo Mary Multi-Use Forest, (207) 435-6213; www.northmainewoods.org

Finding the trailhead: From Brownville: Drive north on ME 11 for 4.8 miles from the bridge over the Pleasant River. Turn left onto K-I Road at the sign for Katahdin Iron Works and Gulf Hagas. Drive 6.5 miles to the gate where you pay your fee. Cross the Pleasant River and turn right; drive 3.5 miles to a fork in the road. Take the left fork, following the signs to Gulf Hagas. Pass the Gulf Hagas parking 2.9 miles beyond the fork, and the Appalachian Trail 3.5 miles beyond the fork. Turn right onto Little Lyford Ponds Road 7.3 miles past the fork (10.8 miles from the K-I gate). Drive 0.9 mile to the Head of the Gulf parking area on the left just past the trailhead.

From Greenville: From the blinking light in Greenville, drive north on Lily Bay Road. Almost immediately turn right onto Pleasant Street. As you leave Greenville the road becomes East Road. At the airport the pavement ends. At Lower Wilson Pond the road becomes K-I Road. There are numerous side roads—that change from year to year with the needs of the logging companies. The AMC has put up signs directing you to their lodges at most side roads. Follow the signs to the AMC lodges, staying on K-I Road. At 12.1 miles from the blinking light in Greenville, you get to the Hedgehog checkpoint where you pay the fee. Past the checkpoint drive 2.9 miles, then turn left onto Little Lyford Ponds Road. Drive 0.9 mile to the Head of the Gulf parking area on the left just past the trailhead.
Trailhead GPS: N45 29.908'/W69 21.418'

The Hike

No one is sure of the origin of the name Gulf Hagas. It has been suggested that it is a corruption of an Abanaki word or phrase, but the Penobscot name for Gulf Hagas is *Mahkonlahgok,* which doesn't lend itself to being corrupted to Gulf Hagas by the nineteenth-century loggers who named it. In the White Mountains are several "gulfs"—a word associated with oceans that is used in the names of cirques to describe the large empty space created by glaciers. Gulf Hagas is Maine's best known and deepest canyon, so "gulf" makes a certain amount of sense. But "hagas," because it is a homophone with *haggis,* sounds Gaelic. *Haggis* does mean "chopped," so maybe there is a connection there. It seems as reasonable an explanation as falling back on the reliable corruption of an Abanaki term. Whatever the origin of its name, Gulf Hagas is one of Maine's natural wonders.

The West Branch Pleasant River flows through the 4-mile-long canyon, dropping almost 400 feet. The walls of the Gulf are slate that at times rise vertically from the river for more than 100 feet. In places the canyon is less than 20 feet across. At The Jaws it was less than 8 feet wide until loggers blasted away rock, making it more than 20 feet wide. Loggers did it so the logs they floated down the river in the spring freshet to Katahdin Iron Works wouldn't get jammed up at The Jaws. This was a dangerous stretch of river for loggers; at least one river driver is known to have been killed in Gulf Hagas.

The hike begins at the west end of the Gulf along the West Branch Pleasant River, which runs deep and silent above the Head of the Gulf. The advantage of beginning the hike here rather than at the Gulf Hagas trailhead you passed on your drive in is that you avoid two river fords. Coming in from the east requires fording the West Branch Pleasant River below the Gulf. The crossing is more than 100 feet across, and the river bottom is slippery, round rocks. The water is usually cold enough to numb your calves and feet. Only in the driest times can the ford be done by hopping from rock to rock. And when the river is that low, the falls in the Gulf are much less dramatic. You also have to ford Gulf Hagas Brook above Screw Auger Falls. This crossing is only 30 feet across, but is deeper. The west end of the

Looking upstream from Billings Falls near the head of Gulf Hagas.

Gulf is generally less crowded, too. Many folks that hike in from the east don't make it much past Screw Auger Falls.

At the Head of the Gulf, the West Branch Pleasant River and Bear Brook come together and separately drop into a large pool, then the river drops twice in quick succession as it makes a sharp bend to the east. This is Stair Falls. There are several side trails off the Rim Trail that allow you to climb around on the rock along the river. Below Stair Falls the Gulf begins to get deeper and deeper. The steep, at times sheer, sides of the canyon are overhung with spruce and cedar trees. The river churns over rocks on its way to Billings Falls.

There is a short side trail out to the top of Billings Falls. You can stand on the uneven rock and look straight down on the river as it plunges into a large pool. Farther along the Rim Trail is an overlook of Billings Falls from across that pool. After following along the Gulf for another mile—the canyon varying from 50 to 140 feet deep and the river running rapid after rapid—you come to Buttermilk Falls. As at Billings Falls there is an overlook above the falls and another looking back at it.

Below Buttermilk Falls the walls of the Gulf narrow and are more vertical. Along this section are the two narrow pinches known as The Jaws. Past The Jaws a side trail leads down to the river at Cole's Corner where you can look back upstream through the narrowest part of the canyon. There is an area of quiet water here that is often used as a swimming hole in summer. During the spring the water is too high and moves too fast.

After Cole's Corner the Rim Trail climbs up and away from the Gulf. The forest changes from evergreens to hardwoods. The canyon is at its deepest here, but the sides are somewhat less vertical. A side trail leads to an overlook above Hammond Street Pitch, named for the street in Bangor. Most of the loggers spent the winter in the woods cutting and hauling wood. After the logs were floated down the river, the loggers made their way to Bangor to spend their wages. Bangor was, at that time, a wild frontier town of great wealth. It was considered unsafe for women, with all the taverns and entertainments for the loggers. A logger remembering stumbling down Hammond Street, as it dropped toward downtown, must have been inspired to name Hammond Street Pitch.

The Rim Trail leaves the Pleasant River and follows Gulf Hagas Brook up past several waterfalls. There are side trails to the lower falls and to Screw Auger Falls. In the 0.3 mile that the trail follows Gulf Hagas Brook, the stream drops 150 feet. Above Screw Auger Falls the Rim Trail ends. To the right, across the stream, is the Appalachian Trail that leads to the Gulf Hagas trailhead. To the left, 4 miles west on the Pleasant River Road Trail, is the Head of the Gulf trailhead where you started.

Miles and Directions

0.0   Begin at the Head of the Gulf trailhead across the road from the parking area.

0.5   Follow the Head of the Gulf Trail to a gravel road. Turn right and cross the West Branch Pleasant River.

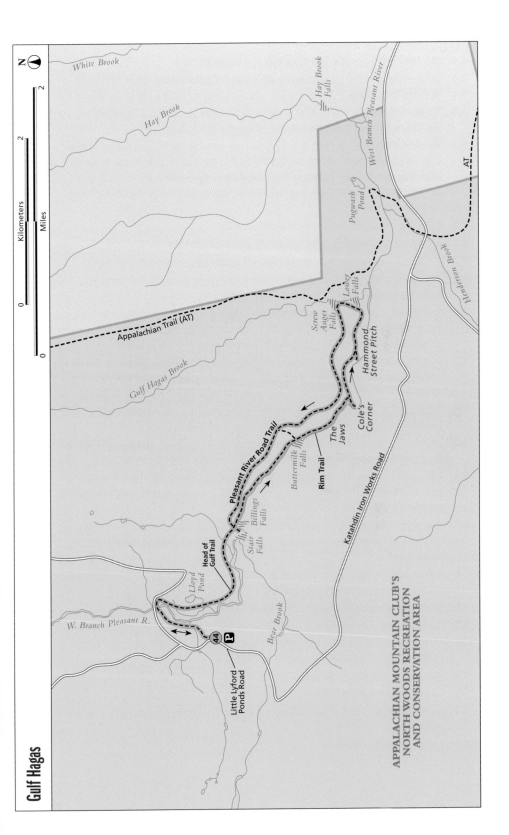

Gulf Hagas

White Brook

Hay Brook

Hay Brook Falls

West Branch Pleasant River

Pugwash Pond

AT

Lower Falls

Screw Auger Falls

Hammond Street Pitch

Gulf Hagas Brook

Appalachian Trail (AT)

Cole's Corner

The Jaws

Henderson Brook

Pleasant River Road Trail

Buttermilk Falls

Rim Trail

Stair Falls

Billings Falls

Katahdin Iron Works Road

Head of Gulf Trail

Lloyd Pond

W. Branch Pleasant R.

Bear Brook

44

P

Little Lyford Ponds Road

N

Kilometers

Miles

APPALACHIAN MOUNTAIN CLUB'S
NORTH WOODS RECREATION
AND CONSERVATION AREA

0.6 At a cairn and a sign, the trail turns right and leaves the road.

1.0 The trail skirts around the west and south shore of Lloyd Pond; there is a 100-foot-long side trail to the pond.

1.9 The Head of the Gulf Trail ends at the junction with the Pleasant River Road Trail and the Gulf Hagas Rim Trail. Turn right onto the Gulf Hagas Rim Trail.

2.0 Reach Head of the Gulf. There is a short side trail out onto the rocks at the top of Stair Falls. All signs for side trails on the Gulf Hagas Rim Trail face away from you as you hike. Most side trails have an upstream and downstream connection to the Rim Trail, with the sign near the downstream side trail. On this hike you will mostly use the upstream, upmarked side trails.

2.1 A side trail leads out onto the rocks below Stair Falls.

2.2 A short side trail leads to a cliff top directly above Billings Falls.

2.3 A 150-foot side trail leads to an overlook with a view upstream to Billings Falls.

3.3 After Billings Falls numerous unmarked side trails lead to overlooks and cliff tops, all worth exploring. Arrive at a cliff top overlook of Buttermilk Falls.

3.4 Junction with a cut-off trail that leads in 0.6 mile to the Pleasant River Road Trail. (**Option:** You can shorten the hike to 6.7 miles by taking this cut-off and then turning left onto the Pleasant River Road Trail.) To continue the hike, go straight on the Rim Trail.

3.7 After the cut-off trail the Rim Trail passes several short side trails to overlooks. This section of the Gulf is particularly deep and narrow. The last of these is just upstream from The Jaws.

4.0 A 0.1-mile side trail leads down to the river where there is a view upstream of The Jaws. At The Jaws the opposite walls of the canyon are only 20 feet apart.

4.8 Junction with a second cutoff trail to the Pleasant River Road Trail. (**Option:** You can take the cut-off and make the hike 8.4 miles.) To continue the hike, stay on the Rim Trail.

5.0 A 0.1-mile side trail leads to an overlook of Hammond Street Pitch. This is the deepest section of the Gulf. The trail appears to continue up and away from the cliff, but it peters out above a rocky area.

5.7 Past Hammond Street Pitch the Rim Trail turns away from the rim of the Gulf and passes through a hardwood forest to a side trail that leads 0.1 mile to the lower falls on Gulf Hagas Brook.

5.9 A short side trail leads to an overlook of Screw Auger Falls. You can climb down from the overlook to the pool between the two falls.

6.0 The trail passes along the rocks at the top of Screw Auger Falls.

6.1 The Gulf Hagas Rim Trail ends at the junction of the Pleasant River Road Trail and the trail across Gulf Hagas Brook that leads to the Appalachian Trail and the main Gulf Hagas trailhead. Turn left onto the Pleasant River Road Trail.

6.7 Pass the second cut-off trail.

7.5 Cross the first cut-off trail.

8.3 Arrive back at the Head of the Gulf Trail. Go straight and retrace your steps back to the trailhead.

10.2 Arrive back at the trailhead.

45 Nesuntabunt Mountain

Nesuntabunt Mountain rises in a wilderness of irregular hills and ponds. The short hike leads through an old-growth forest of white pine and red spruce to a spectacular view of Katahdin. The trailhead may be 25 miles from the nearest paved road, but it's worth the trip.

Start: From the Appalachian Trail crossing on the east side of Wadleigh Pond Road, across from the parking area

Distance: 2.4 miles out and back

Hiking time: 1 to 2 hours

Difficulty: Moderate

Best seasons: May to Oct

Trail surface: Woodland path

Land status: Appalachian Trail within Nahmakanta Public Reserved Land

Nearest town: Brownville

Other trail users: Hunting allowed on Maine Public Reserved Lands

Water availability: None

Canine compatibility: Dogs must be under control at all times

Fees and permits: Fee paid at the Jo Mary gatehouse to drive to trailhead

Maps: *DeLorme: The Maine Atlas and Gazetteer:* maps 50 and 42; USGS Wadleigh Mountain

Trail contacts: Nahmakanta Public Reserved Land, (207) 941-4412; www.maine.gov/dacf/parks. KI-Jo Mary Multi-Use Forest, (207) 435-6213; www.northmainewoods.org.

Finding the trailhead: From the bridge over the Pleasant River in Brownville, drive north on ME 11 for 15.7 miles. Turn left onto Jo Mary Road at the Jo Mary Campground sign. The gate where you pay the fee is 0.1 mile from ME 11. From the gate drive 5.9 miles to a fork in the road. Bear right onto Wadleigh Pond Road. At 11.4 miles from the gate, you cross a stream and the Appalachian Trail. At 14.1 miles from the gate you pass another gate that is remotely controlled from the gate where you paid your fee. At 15.8 miles from the first gate, you pass the Turtle Ridge Trail. At 19.7 miles from the first gate, you come to a T intersection. Turn right, staying on Wadleigh Pond Road. At 20.6 miles from the first gate, the road bends left and a smaller road goes straight; bear left, staying on Wadleigh Pond Road. At 20.6 miles from the first gate, you pass a road on the right that leads to the south end of Nahmakanta Lake and beyond into the Debsconeag Wilderness. At 24.9 miles from the first gate is a small, unmarked parking area on the left. Turn in here and park. The Appalachian Trail is 50 feet farther down the road. The hike follows the southbound AT on the east side of the road, across from the parking area.

Trailhead GPS: N45 45.809' / W69 10.540'

The Hike

Nesuntabunt Mountain is a small, rocky summit among rolling hills and scattered ponds. Its eastern face, much of it exposed cliffs, drops to Nahmakanta Lake. The mountain is 25 miles from the nearest paved road in the heart of the Nahmakanta Public Reserved Land, which is surrounded by protected lands owned by The Nature

Conservancy, the Appalachian Mountain Club, and others. The Appalachian Trail passes over the summit of the mountain on its way to Katahdin, 21 trail miles to the north.

The hike follows the southbound AT from Wadleigh Pond Road through a mixed forest dominated by maple and beech. Be on the lookout for spring wildflowers, especially blood trilium and trout lilies, blooming before the hardwoods leaf out and cast the forest floor into shade for the summer. As the trail gently climbs, the hillside becomes rockier and the forest is more spruce and fir. Across a seasonal stream that cuts a wide swath through the woods, the trail comes to a ledge of granite overlooking Nahmakanta Lake. Across the lake, some 13 miles away, Katahdin looms. In some years, even as late as July, its crown remains snow-covered. Through the summer the bare granite mountain creates its own weather and is often capped by a cloud even on bright sunny days. As you contemplate the view, look for the white specks of common terns flying low over Nahmakanta Lake. These gull-like birds nest on rocks sticking out of the lakes and ponds in the area. They congregate into loud colonies, adults flying in and out while their nestlings squawk for more food.

A snow-covered Katahdin is visible from Nesuntabunt Mountain.

Nesuntabunt Mountain

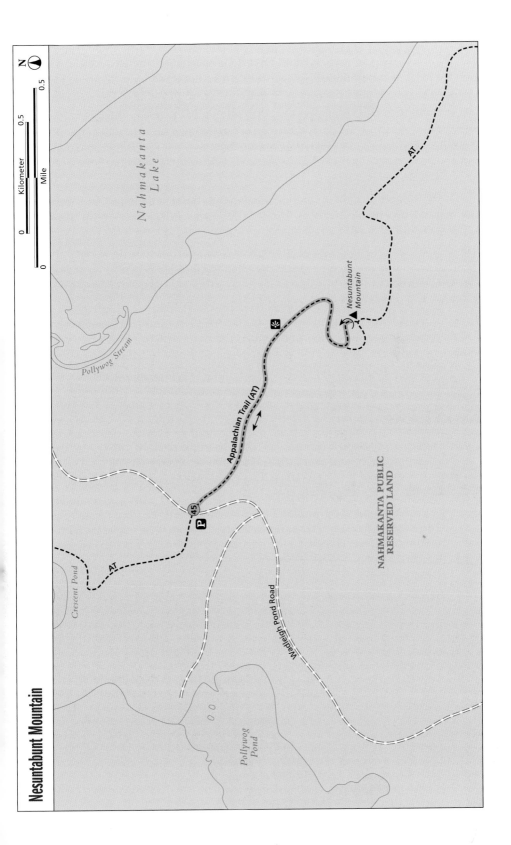

The AT leaves the overlook, turning toward Nesuntabunt's summit across a wide, wooded ledge between the cliffs down to the lake and those up to the mountain's summit. The granite cliffs are giant stairs from the lake to the summit. The trail climbs one step and then slabs around to the north side of the mountain through an open forest of old-growth white pine and red spruce. Because of the thin soil on this steep slope, the trees don't look large enough to be hundreds of years old. They stand tall and straight, marching up the increasingly steep slope and around the west side of the mountain with little growing beneath them.

The trail climbs straight up through the forest to the summit. The AT turns west and descends the mountain to the shore of Nahmakanta Lake, where on a sandy beach spring water bubbles to the surface. The hike leaves the AT at the summit and follows a side trail 0.1 mile out to an overlook. The view is similar to the one from the ledges earlier in the hike, but more open and expansive.

At the north end of Nahmakanta Lake, whose Penobscot name suggests the lake is full of togue (lake trout), is a commercial camp on the site of Joe Francis's fishing camp, a famous Penobscot guide. Today the lake has only a carry-in boat launch, so you may see a canoe slowly moving through the water, but you will never hear a motorboat. From the lake you can see that Nesuntabunt Mountain has three summits—the hike only crosses the highest one—along the shore of the lake. Its name means "three humps."

Miles and Directions

0.0 Start at the southbound Appalachian Trail 50 feet up the road from the parking area. There is a rough sign at the road and an official AT sign 100 feet down the trail.

0.6 The AT climbs gently to a cliff top with fine views across Nahmakanta Lake to Katahdin.

1.1 The AT crosses a wide, wooded ledge between the cliffs down to the lake and those up to the summit of Nesuntabunt Mountain. The trail climbs, then skirts around to the north side of the mountain. There the AT climbs steeply through the woods to the summit. The southbound AT continues to the right; the hike turns left onto a side trail to a cliff top overlook.

1.2 From the overlook you have an expansive view across Nahmakanta Lake of Katahdin and beyond. To complete the hike, return the way you came.

2.4 Arrive back at the trailhead.

46 Debsconeag Backcountry

This hike through remote woodlands is difficult only because of its length. The hike visits four of the Debsconeag lakes and ponds. Each is very different, but all offer execellent wildlife viewing opportunities. The surrounding woods, much of it towering mature trees, also offers good chances to see wildlife, especially moose. From the ledges above Seventh Debsconeag Pond, you get fine views to the west, north, and south. The trail is lightly maintained, but fairly easy to follow because of good blazing.

Start: From the parking area on the north side of Nahmakanta Stream Road, 1 mile from the bridge over Nahmakanta Stream
Distance: 9.6-mile lollipop
Hiking time: 5 to 7 hours
Difficulty: Moderate
Best seasons: June to Oct
Trail surface: Woodland path
Land status: Nahmakanta Public Reserved Land
Nearest town: Brownville
Other trail users: Hunting allowed on Maine Public Reserved Lands; anglers use the trails for access to the ponds

Water availability: 3 streams and 5 ponds along the hike
Canine compatibility: Dogs must be under control at all times
Fees and permits: Fee paid at the Jo Mary gatehouse to drive to trailhead
Maps: *DeLorme: The Maine Atlas and Gazetteer:* map 50; USGS Nahmakanta Stream and Rainbow Lake East
Trail contact: Nahmakanta Public Reserved Land, (207) 827-1818; www.maine.gov/dacf/parks

Finding the trailhead: From the bridge over the Pleasant River in Brownville, drive north on ME 11 for 15.6 miles. Turn left onto Jo Mary Road; there is a large sign for Jo Mary Campground at the intersection. Drive 0.1 mile to the gate; stop and pay the fee. Drive 6 miles to a fork in the road; turn right, staying on Jo Mary Road. Drive 8.2 miles to the Hedgehog gate. This gate is no longer staffed; it will be opened remotely by the person at the Jo Mary gate. Drive 1.7 miles to the trailhead parking for Turtle Ridge and Tumbledown Dick Falls. Continue driving 4 miles to an intersection. Turn right, staying on Jo Mary Road and drive 0.9 mile to Nahmakanta Stream Road. Turn right and drive 1 mile. The road bears right at a fork. Drive another 2 miles, passing the side road to the boat launch at the foot of Nahmakanta Lake. At 0.1 mile beyond the side road, Nahmakanta Stream Road crosses the Appalachian Trail and then Nahmakanta Stream. Across the stream the road is much rougher, but still passable by most cars. From the bridge, drive 1 mile to the parking lot on the left. The road continues down to the Fourth Debsconeag Lake; do not drive down the hill to the lake. The hike starts down the hill on the road.
Trailhead GPS: N45 44.723' / W69 05.478'

The Hike

The lower Debsconeag Lakes are within The Nature Conservancy's Debsconeag Lakes Wilderness; the upper ponds, which this hike visits, are within the Nahmakanta Public

Looking northwest from the ridge above Seventh Debsconeag Pond toward Nesuntabunt Mountain with Katahdin on the horizon.

Reserved Land. Together these units are a huge tract of remote woodlands with limited road access. This means fewer users and an abundance of wildlife. The trailhead is up the hill, west of Fourth Debsconeag Lake. The first 0.7 mile is along the woods road that leads to Debsconeag Lake Wilderness Camps on the north shore of the lake. Their cabins are the only structures on any of the eight Debsconeag lakes and ponds.

The Debsconeag Backcountry Trail leaves the woods road and follows the stream that flows from Fifth to Fourth Debsconeag Lake, passing through a mature hemlock forest. Along the way, you pass a waterfall where the stream flows down a chute along a cliff green with moss. Above the falls the trail crosses the stream and follows it upstream to Fifth Debsconeag Lake. You climb a low hill and cross semi-open ledges with views across the lake to the ridge the trail returns on.

The trail drops off the ridge and through the forest toward Sixth Debsconeag Pond. The trail can be hard to follow because it is little used and rarely cleared of blowdowns. You won't get lost, but will surely feel more like an explorer than a day hiker. The regular blue blazes keep you from wandering off the trail. There are many wet areas where you may see moose. This open, mixed forest near several ponds and bogs is good habitat for cows with calves.

For a short stretch the trail follows an old woods road that seems to lead nowhere at either end, a reminder that all of these woods were cut at some point in the past. This section of road must have led from somewhere—likely near where you parked—to somewhere cutting was going on, but now it is just a short section of wide trail—a reminder that wilderness is not a characteristic of the land or forest, but a use pattern.

The trail skirts around the south side of Sixth Debsconeag Pond and passes a side trail that leads 0.6 mile to a campsite on Nahmakanta Lake. That trail continues from there along the lake to its north end. Just past the junction a side trail leads to a rock shelf on the shore of the pond. It's a good place to relax and watch for ducks and moose. On buggy days trout regularly rise to the surface. You can hear—but not see—the outlet stream leave the pond's far side to tumble through the woods and several bogs to Fifth Debsconeag Lake.

Beyond Sixth Debsconeag Pond the trail works around a low hill to Seventh Debsconeag Pond. Here the woods are more open and dry with fewer hardwoods. The trail crosses the outlet stream where bedrock has formed a natural dam that beavers have supplemented. Downstream is an open area of bog that the stream winds through. The pond itself is almost as much a meadow as a pond. If it weren't for the beavers raising the water level, the pond may have already become an open, wet meadow. Just past the stream crossing, there is a large boulder along the shore that you can climb to get a good look at the pond. Watch for beaver and ducks.

The trail circles around the pond and climbs a series of increasingly open ledges with views to the west and south. Near the top of the ridge is an intersection with a trail that leads to the north end of Nahmakanta Lake. The signs at this intersection are confusing at best. Turn right (east) and enter the woods through a glade of ferns, watching for blue blazes. The trail crosses more open ledges with views, including to the north of Katahdin, then drops into the woods.

The trail wanders through the woods and finally climbs a ridge to ledges above Stink Pond with views east and south. From there the trail loops around to the west and descends toward the pond, passing near the pond, but not right to it. When you can see the marshy edge of the pond just to your left, take the small side trail if you want to explore the pond. The marshy rim of Stink Pond is good habitat for plants such as liverwort and other northern bog species. Watch for moose and ducks as well.

The trail drops away from the pond to where the outlet stream falls down a wide shelf of exposed bedrock. The trail loops out across the rock, which can be challenging and slippery when the water is running high. Follow the stream down as it tumbles noisily over boulders and ledges toward Fifth Debesconeag Lake. The trail crosses the stream several times—the last on a wide boulder that the stream crosses in a crack before dropping into a small pool. The trail levels out and passes through a grove of old-growth hemlock. A marked side trail leads out to Fifth Debsconeag Lake. You can see the open ledges on the hills around the lake. Past the side trail you hike across an old dam in the woods and then come to the junction along the stream above the waterfall, completing the loop.

Miles and Directions

0.0   Start from the sign next to the parking area on the north side of Nahmakanta Stream Road. To begin the hike, walk down Nahmakanta Stream Road toward Fourth Debsconeag Lake. (**Note:** There is a sign at the top of the parking lot pointing west up a rough trail to the Debsconeag Backcountry Trail; do not go that way.)

0.4   Pass the Debsconeag Lakes Wilderness Camps dock on Fourth Debsconeag Lake.

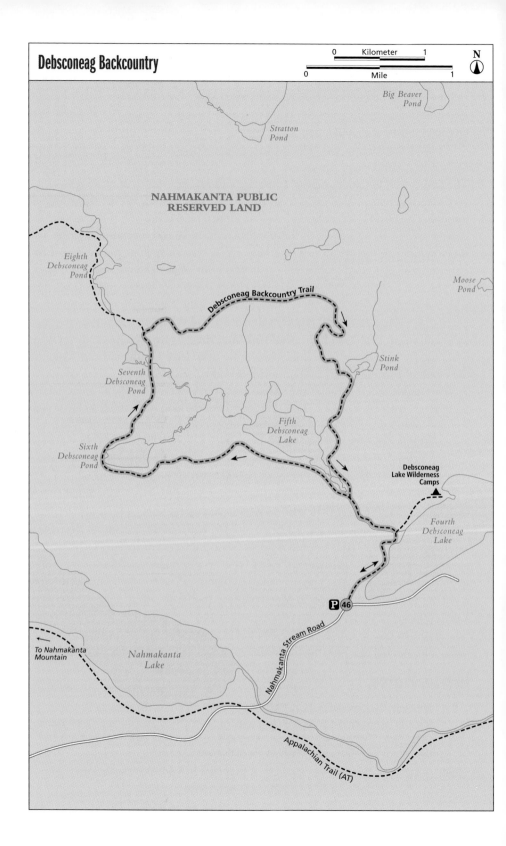

0   Kilometer   1

0   Mile   1

N

Big Beaver
Pond

Stratton
Pond

NAHMAKANTA PUBLIC
RESERVED LAND

Moose
Pond

Eighth
Debsconeag
Pond

Debsconeag Backcountry Trail

Stink
Pond

Seventh
Debsconeag
Pond

Fifth
Debsconeag
Lake

Sixth
Debsconeag
Pond

Debsconeag
Lake Wilderness
Camps

Fourth
Debsconeag
Lake

P 46

To Nahmakanta
Mountain

Nahmakanta
Lake

Nahmakanta Stream Road

Appalachian Trail (AT)

0.7 The road crosses the stream flowing from Fifth to Fourth Debsconeag Lake. Just across the bridge is the Debsconeag Backcountry Trail. Turn left onto the trail.

1.1 The trail follows the stream past increasingly rough water. Above the large waterfall the trail comes to a junction. You will complete the hike by returning from the right. Turn left and cross the stream.

2.2 Continue to follow the stream, coming to a deadwater below Fifth Debsconeag Lake. Just where the trail reaches the lake, it turns away from the water and begins climbing gently, arriving at ledges with views to the north.

3.2 The trail passes a trail that leads to a campsite on Nahmakanta Lake in 0.6 mile and then continues along the lake to its north end. Continue ahead on the Debsconeag Backcountry Trail.

3.4 A short side trail leads out to a shelf of rock on the shore of Sixth Debsconeag Pond.

4.3 The trail passes between a low cliff and the marshy outlet of Seventh Debsconeag Pond, then crosses the outlet stream.

4.4 There is a very large boulder between the trail and the pond that offers a fine view of the marshy pond.

4.7 The trail loops around Seventh Debsconeag Pond, climbing open ledges with views south and west, to a junction. The trail to the left loops past Eighth Debsconeag Pond and on to the north end of Nahmakanta Lake. Turn right, staying on the Debsconeag Backcountry Trail. The signs at this intersection are confusing and wrong. The trail where you need to go is overgrown with ferns, but the blue blazes are clearly visible.

4.9 The trail crosses ledges with views west. You can see Nesuntabunt Mountain, which is across Nahmakanta Lake (which is not visible); to the northeast you can see Katahdin.

5.4 The trail descends gently to a small stream that tumbles down the mountainside.

5.6 The trail crosses a larger stream.

6.4 The trail climbs to the highest point on the hike, an open ledge above Stink Pond with views to the south and east.

7.2 Loop back into the woods and then descend to Stink Pond. The first place you get close to the pond is the only place the trail approaches the pond.

7.3 The trail emerges from the woods onto a steep rock slope that the Stink Pond outlet stream falls over and down. During times of high water, you need to get your feet wet to continue the hike.

7.6 The trail turns back into the woods and descends near the stream, crossing it three times. The last crossing is on a flat boulder that the stream drops across. After this crossing the trail leaves the stream.

7.9 The trail passes through a stand of old-growth hemlock. A short side trail leads out to Fifth Debsconeag Lake.

8.0 The side trail ends at Fifth Debsconeag Lake. Return to the Debsconeag Backcountry Trail to continue the hike.

8.1 Turn right back onto the Debsconeag Backcountry Trail.

8.4 The trail follows along the edge of the deadwater below the lake and then crosses an old dam in the woods, arriving back at the junction with the other end of the Debsconeag Backcountry Trail next to the stream. Turn left to return to the trailhead.

9.6 Arrive back at the trailhead.

IN ADDITION: FINDING MOOSE

I've seen moose in some odd places: High on Sunday River Whitecap a bull moose looked down at me from bog boards across a bulge of granite among stunted spruce trees; looking down from Mount Katahdin's Knife Edge, I saw a cow standing in a shallow pond, perched high on the mountain's shoulder, surrounded by miles of impenetrable spruce; in the middle of the afternoon, a large cow stood in the dooryard of a dairy farm in Bradford, watching the cars go by on ME 221. Some sightings may simply have been a matter of spending a lot of time out and about in Maine. After all, there are nearly 30,000 moose in the state, about 1 per square mile. Eventually I was bound to cross paths with a few.

Most of the moose I've seen were on or near roads, even though hiking trails all around the state show evidence of heavy moose traffic. It often seems moose would rather follow a road or trail than force their way through the underbrush. I would certainly prefer a path. On the other hand, the bull moose I ran into on Sunday River Whitecap had no trouble forcing his way through the tightly packed, stunted spruce to get away from me. Another reason you may see so many moose on roads is that moose seek out salt, especially when aquatic plants aren't available.

Bull moose, in general, spend the summer at higher elevations than cows. Food may be harder to find up on a mountain—especially aquatic vegetation—but it's often cooler and less buggy. Take that bull I ran into on Sunday River Whitecap: It was during an August heat wave. The temperature was in the 90s. The moose was probably more interested in staying cool than in finding something to eat. Or maybe, as a friend of mine who's a registered Maine guide put it: In late summer and fall bull moose go testosterone crazy and don't seem to behave rationally. I prefer to believe that there is some biological reason for moose behavior other than hormone overload.

Cows generally stay lower in the summer because calves can't wander far and cows prefer denser vegetation, both so they can spend less time foraging and as cover. Nearly every baby moose I've seen was standing in water. This may be because in the summer about half a moose's diet consists of aquatic plants. They aren't particularly nutritious, but are the animal's primary source of sodium. Logically, then, the best summer habitat for cows (and their calves) are low elevation areas with good hardwood browse, lots of aquatic vegetation, and dense cover for hiding from predators. This was borne out by the cow I happened upon in the Debsconeag backcountry, lying in a muddy area near Sixth Debsconeag Pond nursing her calf.

Which brings us back to my original question: Why have I hiked and paddled through so much good moose habitat without seeing moose? The logical answer, I suppose, is that it wasn't really such good habitat.

Moose tend to winter on south-facing slopes, especially among regenerating hardwoods. They also like to be near stands of large softwoods—like deer, they use these stands as refuges from deep snow. Also, when nothing else is available, moose eat balsam fir. The fir and hardwood buds and twigs that moose eat in the winter are less nutritious than their summer forage. Even though moose slow their metabolism in the winter, they still rely on fat reserves and lose weight during the winter. As a result, good winter habitat acts like a moose magnet. For example, the Appalachian Trail across Gulf Hagas Mountain winds through brambles and low, bushy hardwoods and is typically several inches deep in moose scat, all of it old and crumbling, left over from winter. Downslope from the trail in the Pleasant River valley are numerous cutover areas with good winter browse. The first moose calf I saw was in the high valley below Whitecap Mountain. The trail—an old logging road—went through shrubby trees, and all had their twig-ends bitten off.

Moose are willing to travel several miles from their core range for salt—both salty roads in the winter and aquatic vegetation in the summer. At the same time, their winter and summer ranges are generally near each other: Moose don't migrate.

One of the moosiest places I've paddled is the south end of Lobster Lake where a small stream flows in, creating a large boggy area crowded with alders. On the shoulder of Big Spencer Mountain, just to the south, I regularly find evidence of moose. On one twilight descent I startled two moose that were coming up the trail as I was coming down. I suspect that Lobster Lake and Big Spencer Mountain are popular with moose because their proximity offers both summer and winter habitats.

It may be that Nollesemic Stream is good summer habitat for cows and their young, but there may be no good winter habitat nearby. Or maybe beaver flowages only look like good habitat. I can't recall ever seeing a moose in one.

On many hiking trips I see moose along the road on the way home, not on the trail. We carry around an iconic image of moose in our heads: the bull moose lifting its head out of a pond, vegetation hanging from his antlers as water drips from his face and ears. There is a pond along the Golden Road, south of Baxter State Park, with a view of Katahdin from its southeast shore. On any summer morning there will be several photographers with their tripods set up, waiting to capture just that image. No photographers rushed out to take a picture of the female I saw in the dairy farm's dooryard.

A moose is no less a moose when wandering down a logging road than when feeding in a pond with a spectacular view of Katahdin. From all my ruminating about moose habitat and where to find moose, I've learned to value each moose for its unique moose-ness. If we spend all our time holding out for the ideal, the iconic, we will miss a great deal that the North Woods has to offer.

47 Turtle Ridge

This fairly long but easy hike explores a granite landscape of cliffs and ponds. There is one of the best views of Katahdin along the Henderson Pond Trail, and fine views of the mountains to the south and west from Turtle Ridge. The remote ponds the hike passes are home to loons and other waterbirds, and are visited by moose. The hike also offers some of the best fall foliage in Maine.

Start: From the Turtle Ridge East trailhead, 275 feet south of the parking area across the bridge

Distance: 8.6-mile lollipop

Hiking time: 5 to 6 hours

Difficulty: Moderate

Best seasons: May to Oct

Trail surface: Woodland path

Land status: Nahmakanta State Reserved Land

Nearest town: Brownville

Other trail users: Hunting allowed on Maine Public Reserved Lands

Water availability: Stream near trailhead and several ponds along the hike

Canine compatibility: Dogs must be under control at all times

Fees and permits: Fee paid at the Jo Mary gatehouse to drive to trailhead

Maps: *DeLorme: The Maine Atlas and Gazetteer:* map 42; USGS Nahmakanta Stream and Wadleigh Mountain

Trail contacts: Nahmakanta Public Reserved Land, (207) 941-4412; www.maine.gov/dacf/parks. KI-Jo Mary Multi-Use Forest, (207) 435-6213; www.northmainewoods.org.

Finding the trailhead: From the bridge over the Pleasant River in Brownville, drive north on ME 11 for 15.7 miles. Turn left onto Jo Mary Road at the Jo Mary Campground sign. The gate where you pay the fee is 0.1 mile from ME 11. From the gate drive 5.9 miles to a fork in the road. Bear right onto Wadleigh Pond Road. At 11.4 miles from the gate you cross a stream and the Appalachian Trail. At 14.1 miles from the gate you pass another gate that is remotely controlled from the gate where you paid your fee. At 15.8 miles from the first gate and 2.7 miles past the second gate, you reach the trailhead parking on the left. The trailhead is 275 feet down the road the way you came in on the same side as the parking lot.

Trailhead GPS: N45 41.028' / W69 06.243'

The Hike

The Turtle Ridge hike skirts several ponds, crosses ridges with fine views, and passes through several different forest and habitat types. But what is constant along the entire 8.6 miles is the granite. Turtle Ridge and the other hills the trails cross are granite mounds with exposed bedrock and cliff faces; the ponds are overlooked by granite cliffs, their shores dotted with boulders. The forest floor is littered with erratics, some as big as a house. Everywhere you step and look there is granite.

The hike begins by winding through a spruce forest with moss-covered boulders of every size. A stream, unseen, tumbles down its rocky course, heading toward Leavitt

Pond. The trail climbs gently to an irregular expanse of granite bedrock. The spruce forest is edged with blueberries and other shrubs that turn fiery red in the fall, contrasting with the rough, gray granite and dark spruce. A cairn holds a trail junction sign pointing to Henderson and Rabbit Ponds. The hike climbs toward Henderson Pond through spruce to a cliff top with one of the best views of Katahdin. The mountain rises in the middle distance across rolling green hills dotted with ponds. At your feet are blueberries and wintergreen edged with moss and gray-green lichen. Beyond the cliffs the trail follows a spine of granite, skirting around the hilltop.

The side trail to an overlook of Henderson Pond goes out a granite ridgetop, but offers only very limited views. There is a granite boulder on the edge that you can climb to stand in the treetops for a somewhat better view. The best way to see Henderson Pond is to continue the hike, dropping down to the north shore of the pond where you can walk out to the rocky shore and look for loons and other waterbirds. Across the pond rises Jo Mary Mountain; at nearly 3,000 feet it is the highest in the region but has no trail to its wooded summit.

Looking southwest across Sing-Sing Pond from Turtle Ridge.

The trail climbs gently away from Henderson Pond on a granite ridge that is drier than the woods so far on the hike. Here scratchy lichen grows on and around the boulders instead of moss. The trail passes Long Pond, although you cannot see the pond or get to it. Long and Henderson Ponds are both outside the Nahmakanta Public Reserved Land in the KI-Jo Mary Forest. As the trail approaches some very mossy cliffs, it winds between boulders and then descends on steps. The trail wanders among granite beneath the cliffs, then ends at the Rabbit Pond Cut-off and Sing-Sing Pond Trail. The Sing-Sing Pond Trail follows a stream past a marshy pond in a low area, then follows an old woods road past Sing-Sing Pond. This section is both moosy and very buggy. There is no access to Sing-Sing Pond along this section; the Turtle Ridge Trail skirts the edge of the pond in the next section.

The Turtle Ridge Trail crosses Sing-Sing Pond's outlet stream, then winds among large fern-covered boulders and pines to the shore of the pond. A shelf of granite sticks out into the pond where you can rest, watch for loons, or swim in the cool water. Just don't sit with your feet hanging in the water for too long or you'll attract leeches.

Turtle Ridge is across Sing-Sing Pond, its three humps visible. The westernmost hump is tree covered; the middle has a large granite cliff; the easternmost is a bare, rounded summit. The trail passes over each hump from west to east. Between the humps the trail drops and crosses behind the ridge with limited views of Katahdin to the north, especially when the trees have no leaves. The view across Sing-Sing Pond and the mixed lowland forest comes alive with color in the fall. In the spring a subtler palate prevails as the maples appear red from their flowers and the new leaves on the beech, birch, and ash appear almost lime green, all contrasting with the dark spruce and fir. On the horizon to the southwest are a line of mountains anchored in the east by Big Boardman Mountain; to the west are the Lily Bay Mountains. In the middle, keeping its snow cover late into the spring, is Whitecap Mountain.

The trail drops down off Turtle Ridge and wanders through the woods past Hedgehog Pond to Rabbit Pond. The trail crosses an exposed granite ledge that acts as a dam, holding back Rabbit Pond. The outlet stream slides across the granite and disappears into the woods. From Rabbit Pond it's a short, rocky climb to the intersection, closing the loop of the hike and ending a day exploring this granite landscape.

Miles and Directions

0.0 Start from the Turtle Ridge East trailhead, 275 feet south on the road from the parking area.

0.5 The trail winds through a boulder-filled forest, then climbs an open granite area where the trail forks. The Turtle Ridge Trail goes to the right; that will be your return trail. Take the Henderson Pond Trail to the left.

1.0 The Henderson Pond Trail climbs through a spruce forest to the top of a cliff with fine views to the north of Mount Katahdin.

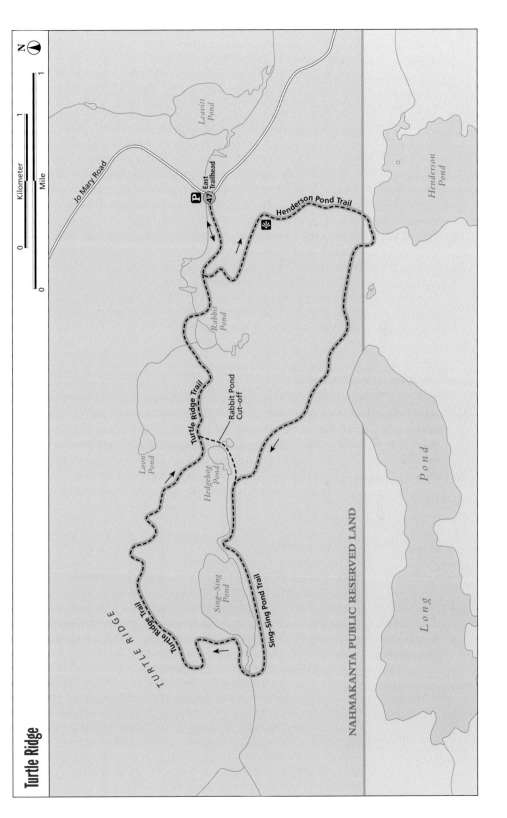

Turtle Ridge

N

Kilometer

0   1

Mile

0   1

Jo Mary Road

Leavitt Pond

East Trailhead

P 47

Henderson Pond Trail

Henderson Pond

Rabbit Pond

Turtle Ridge Trail

Loon Pond

Rabbit Pond Cut-off

Hedgehog Pond

TURTLE RIDGE

Turtle Ridge Trail

Sing-Sing Pond

Sing-Sing Pond Trail

NAHMAKANTA PUBLIC RESERVED LAND

Long   Pond

Henderson Pond

1.4   Beyond the cliffs the trail turns south and follows a granite spine and then woods toward Henderson Pond. There is a marked side trail that goes 0.1 mile to an overlook of the pond, but the views are mostly screened by trees.

1.9   The trail skirts along the west edge of Henderson Pond; an unmarked trail leads to the pond. Across the pond, where you can often see loons, rises Jo Mary Mountain.

3.5   The trail climbs a low, rocky ridge beyond Henderson Pond. Long Pond is to your south, unseen down the steep slope. There is no access to Long Pond on this hike. Past Long Pond the trail drops down the edge of jumbled cliffs and then along their bottom to junction with the Rabbit Pond Cut-off. (**Option:** This short trail skirts the east edge of Hedgehog Pond and ends at the Turtle Ridge Trail. You can use this trail to shorten the hike to 5 miles, but you would miss Turtle Ridge and Sing-Sing Pond.) To continue the hike, turn left onto the Sing-Sing Pond Trail.

3.9   The Sing-Sing Pond Trail passes a small, marshy pond that has an unmarked trail to a large boulder at its edge.

4.6   The Sing-Sing Pond Trail follows a stream, then comes out onto an old woods road. The trail skirts the east side of Sing-Sing Pond, visible through the trees. Access to Sing-Sing Pond is from the Turtle Ridge Trail. This section tends to be very buggy, but offers the possibility of a moose sighting. The Sing-Sing Pond Trail continues 1 mile to the Turtle Ridge West trailhead; the hike turns right onto the Turtle Ridge Trail.

5.0   After crossing the outlet stream of Sing-Sing Pond, the trail winds among large boulders and comes close to Sing-Sing Pond. There is a short, unmarked trail that leads out to the pond where there are boulders at its edge. This is a good spot to rest, swim, and watch for loons and moose. There are fine views across the pond of the three humps of Turtle Ridge.

6.1   The Turtle Ridge Trail climbs up the west end of Turtle Ridge. The first summit hump is wooded with only limited views. The second hump is open, and the trail passes across a high cliff top with views across Sing-Sing Pond to Whitecap and the other mountains to the south.

6.3   The trail turns north from the cliffs and crosses the ridge. From the back of the ridge, there are limited views north of Katahdin. The trail then emerges onto the open summit of the third hump of Turtle Ridge, with unrestricted views in every direction except north.

7.0   The trail descends off Turtle Ridge and skirts below some cliffs, then crosses through the woods to Hedgehog Pond. A short, unmarked side trail leads to the pond where the Turtle Ridge Trail makes a left turn.

7.1   Junction with the Rabbit Pond Cut-off. Continue straight ahead on the Turtle Ridge Trail toward Rabbit Pond to complete the hike.

8.1   The Turtle Ridge Trail crosses a spine of granite, then comes to Rabbit Pond. The trail crosses exposed granite bedrock at the east end of Rabbit Pond. The pond's outlet stream flows over the rock and disappears into the woods. The trail continues across the granite, climbing to the junction with the Henderson Pond Trail. This is a good area for finding blueberries. To return to the trailhead, turn left and descend off the exposed rock.

8.6   Arrive back at the trailhead.

48 Debsconeag Ice Caves

The relatively flat hike to the Debsconeag Ice Caves passes through a mature evergreen forest full of huge boulders. The hike would be worth doing even without the ice caves at its end. The trail splits at the end, leading to a rocky overlook of First Debsconeag Lake, the ice caves, and a steep descent to the lakeshore. Be sure to bring a flashlight to explore the boulders for caves; many have ice in them year-round.

Start: From the Ice Caves parking area at the end of Hurd Pond Road
Distance: 2.5 miles out and back
Hiking time: 2 to 3 hours
Difficulty: Easy
Best seasons: June to Sept
Trail surface: Woodland path
Land status: Debsconeag Lakes Wilderness
Nearest town: Millinocket

Other trail users: None
Water availability: Hurd Brook at the trailhead
Canine compatibility: Dogs not allowed in Debsconeag Lakes Wilderness
Fees and permits: No fees or permits required
Maps: *DeLorme: The Maine Atlas and Gazetteer:* map 50; USGS Abol Pond
Trail contact: The Nature Conservancy, www.nature.org/maine

Finding the trailhead: From exit 244 on I-95, drive west on ME 157 toward Millinocket and Baxter State Park. Drive 11.8 miles into Millinocket where ME 157 ends at a T intersection. Turn right onto Katahdin Avenue, toward Baxter State Park. Drive 8.8 miles to where the road passes between Millinocket and Ambejejus Lakes; there is a store and several lodges at this busy spot. Continue driving 1.3 miles to the left turn for the Golden Road. There are several signs for commercial camps and the Allagash at the turn. Cut across to the Golden Road and turn right, heading north. Drive 9 miles on the Golden Road to Abol Bridge. Just across the bridge turn left onto a wide, unmarked gravel road. A Nature Conservancy information kiosk is 0.1 mile down the road. Drive 3.9 miles to where the road is gated at Hurd Pond Brook. There is a marked parking area on the right. The hike begins by crossing the bridge over the stream.
Trailhead GPS: N45 47.484' / W68 58.703'

The Hike

The Debsconeag Lakes are within The Nature Conservancy's Debsconeag Lakes Wilderness. The eight lakes and ponds are all entirely undeveloped—except for a commercial camp on Fourth Lake. Debsconeag means "carrying place" in the Penobscot language. The first four lakes are connected by short carries, or canoe portages, alongside streams. The lakes are also within carrying distance of Nahmakanta Lake, part of a water highway that connects Maine to the Saint Lawrence River.

First Debsconeag Lake is connected to the Debsconeag Deadwater on the West Branch Penobscot River by a wide, shallow thoroughfare. The long, narrow lake is 140 feet deep at its center. The north shore of the lake is a low ridge of loose boulders covered with a thin veneer of soil. Where large gaps in the boulders exist, there are caves that can hold ice all summer. The caves are not solutional caves where water has dissolved limestone—such as Mammoth Cave or Carlsbad Cavern—but simply gaps in the ill-fitting boulders. There are numerous ice caves in Maine (along the shore of Deboullie Pond on hike 64, for example), but the Debsconeag Ice Caves are the easiest to hike to and among the largest.

The hike begins where Hurd Pond Road is gated at a bridge over Hurd Pond Stream. The trail winds through second growth before entering a forest of mature hemlocks and pines. There is very little growing beneath the tall trees, but the forest floor is littered with boulders. Some of the boulders are as big as houses. These boulders are tightly nestled into the forest floor with few gaps around their edges. But what gaps do exist hint at what awaits you at the end of the trail. The trail wanders from boulder to boulder, gently climbing to the crest of the hill above First Debsconeag Lake. The easy walk would be worth doing even without the ice caves to visit.

Just before the trail begins to descend to the lake, a side trail heads west to the top of a rocky promontory. You can stand on the exposed bedrock alongside two huge boulders and look out across the First Debsconeag Lake. To the east you can see Debsconeag Deadwater and hear Debsconeag Falls on the West Branch. To the west, hidden by the seemingly endless forest, is Second Debsconeag Lake. Directly below this vantage point lies a jumble of boulders dropping away to the lakeshore. The ice caves are hidden in these boulders.

The trail drops down from the overlook trail to another side trail that leads to the ice caves. The ice caves trail ends at a huge boulder that is the roof of the largest ice cave. Iron rungs have been driven into the rock, allowing you to climb down into the cave. Bring a flashlight so you can explore the cave's nooks and crannies. The air in the cave is cool, even on hot days; ice remains on the floor year-round. There are many smaller caves in this boulder field. As you explore the uneven terrain, be careful not to damage the fragile mosses and other ground covers.

The trail continues down to the lake from the ice caves side trail. Along the way it passes a number of smaller caves and a

Looking down the iron rungs into the largest of the ice caves.

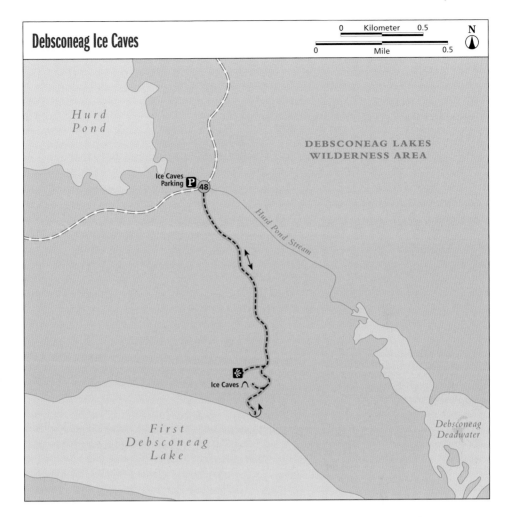

Debsconeag Ice Caves

*Hurd
Pond*

**DEBSCONEAG LAKES
WILDERNESS AREA**

Ice Caves
Parking **P** 48

Hurd Pond Stream

Ice Caves

*First
Debsconeag
Lake*

*Debsconeag
Deadwater*

boulder that overhangs a sandy area that looks like it could have been used as a camping spot for thousands of years. For years the only easy way to visit the ice caves was to paddle up First Debsconeag Lake to where the trail ends on the shore and hike uphill to the caves. Several faded signs hang on trees at the end of the trail, pointing canoeists to the caves. Between the end of the trail and the east end of the pond, there are many more caves in the woods, beneath towering hemlocks and pines, but no trail to them. Looking back uphill the way you came, it's hard to believe that the forest before you overlays so much empty space.

Miles and Directions

0.0   Start by crossing the bridge over Hurd Pond Stream behind the red gate. In 100 feet bear left off the woods road onto a marked hiking trail.

0.8 The trail wanders through the woods, among pines and large boulders, to a junction. Turn right to hike to the overlook.

0.9 Arrive at the overlook. The trail ends atop a cliff with several large boulders sitting on top of it. You have views of First Debsconeag Lake; to the east you can see Debsconeag Deadwater on the Penobscot River and hear Debsconeag Falls. Return back to the trail junction and turn right.

1.1 The trail forks again. Turn right to go to the ice caves.

1.2 The trail ends at the Debsconeag Ice Caves. There is a set of iron rungs down into the largest ice cave. After exploring the jumbled boulders for ice caves, return to the trail junction and turn right to descend to First Debsconeag Lake.

1.4 The trail descends past large boulders to First Debsconeag Lake. To complete the hike, return the way you came.

2.5 Arrive back at the trailhead.

Honorable Mentions

J Whitecap Mountain

Whitecap Mountain is the highest of a group of mountains north of Gulf Hagas. It is not the easiest mountain to get to, but the effort is worth it. The open summit, covered with broken slate, offers fine views in every direction. The hike is an out and back of between 6 and 12 miles—depending how far up the road you can get. The first several miles are relatively flat and pass through good moose habitat. The climb up Whitecap is very steep, but only 1.9 miles. To get to the trailhead, from the bridge over the Pleasant River in Brownville, drive north on ME 11 for 4.8 miles. Turn left onto K-I Road at the sign for Katahdin Iron Works and Gulf Hagas. Drive 6.5 miles to the gate where you pay a fee. Cross the Pleasant River and turn right; drive 3.5 miles to a fork in the road. Take the right fork toward High Bridge. Drive 2.3 miles to a fork and turn left. You will immediately cross High Bridge over White Brook. Take time to explore the small gorge that High Bridge crosses. At 0.1 mile beyond the bridge, the road gets very rough; it is passable for the next 2 miles with 4WD vehicle. If you park at High Bridge, it's 4 miles to the trailhead along the road. You pass several junctions; always stay straight on the main road. The blue-blazed trail begins at the left side of an old logging yard at the end of the road. For more information contact KI-Jo Mary Multi-Use Forest, (207) 435-6213; www.northmainewoods.org; or Maine Appalachian Trail Club, www.matc.org.

K Tumbledown Dick Falls

At 70 feet, Tumbldown Dick Falls is the highest of many waterfalls in the Nahmakanta Public Reserved Land. The waterfall is at the head of a narrow slate gorge, dropping into a large pool. The trail to the falls passes Leavitt and Tumbledown Dick Ponds. After Tumbledown Dick Pond the trail follows Tumbledown Dick Stream. Just before the falls the trail seems to end at a gravel road. Turn left and cross the stream; follow the road for 200 feet to where the trail continues on the other side of the stream to the falls. The falls are 3.7 miles from the trailhead on Jo Mary Road. To find the trailhead, from Brownville drive north on ME 11 for 15.6 miles to Jo Mary Road. There is a large sign at the road for Jo Mary Campground. Turn left onto the road and drive 0.1 mile to the gate where you will need to pay an entrance fee. From the gate drive 6 miles to where the road forks; take the right fork. Drive 8.2 miles to the Henderson gate, which is remotely controlled from the Jo Mary gate. Drive 1.7 miles past the gate to the Turtle Ridge Trail parking on the left. You need to park in this lot and walk 0.1 mile farther up the road to the trailhead for Tumbledown Dick Falls. There is a small sign at the trailhead. For more information contact Nahmakanta Public Reserved Land, (207) 827-6295; www.maine.gov/dacf/parks.

The Moosehead Region

Moosehead Lake is the largest body of fresh water in New England, covering 75,471 acres and containing 4.2 million acre-feet of cold, clear water. It is more than twice as large as Sebego Lake—the second largest in Maine. Moosehead is 40 irregular miles long, stretching from Greenville to Seboomook. At its widest it is 10 miles wide, but is nearly split in two by Mount Kineo. The lake has more than 280 miles of shoreline and eighty islands scattered across it. Thoreau commented in 1853 when he canoed the length of Moosehead Lake that beyond Greenville the lake was almost without evidence of

Two hikers climb the Indian Trail on Mount Kineo with Blue Ridge in the background across Moosehead Lake (hike 52).

THE MOOSEHORN

On the west side of ME 15 just south of the Monson/Abbot town line, a pair of moose antlers is mounted atop a red iron post. In 1853, on his way from Bangor to Greenville, Henry David Thoreau observed: "At a fork in the road between Abbot and Monson, about twenty miles from Moosehead Lake, I saw a guidepost surmounted by a pair of moose horns, spreading four or five feet, with the words 'Monson' painted on one blade, and the name of some other town on the other." The town names once painted on the antlers have disappeared, but they are the same antlers. Even in Thoreau's day the moosehorn had been there for some time and, in fact, was on its second post. No one seemed to know why they were mounted there or by whom. It was suggested that it was to mark the turn to an inn. This seems reasonable as the location is about halfway between Dover-Foxcroft and Greenville. If not for Thoreau's having mentioned seeing them, their history would probably have been lost entirely.

humans. While that hasn't been true for a long time, the Moosehead region is full of wild mountains, remote lakes and ponds, and lots of moose and other wildlife. On a drive from Greenville north to the Golden Road, along the west side of Moosehead Lake, you are almost guaranteed to encounter at least one moose.

The surrounding country is low, endless forest punctuated by isolated mountains. The one exception is the Lily Bay Mountains. This group of mountains east of the lake and south of the Roach Ponds is relatively trailless, with the exception of the old fire warden's trail on Number Four Mountain (hike L). There are several mountains that are more than 3,000 feet high, including Coburn Mountain (hike 55), Boundary Bald (hike 54), Little and Big Spencer Mountains (hike 53), Baker Mountain, and Big Moose Mountain (hike 50). The mountains are arranged around Moosehead Lake is such a way that you cannot see the entire lake from any of the mountains. The closest you can come to seeing the entire lake at once is atop the fire tower on Mount Kineo (hike 52). Driving into Greenville from the south, you first see Moosehead Lake as you top Indian Hill. Amid the bustle of the businesses there, the lake comes into view—an irregular blue mirror set among dark mountains and forest.

There is almost no granite in the Moosehead region, only one mass of it around the ponds on the upper Moose River, south of Jackman. Most of the region's mountains are made of rocks of volcanic origin. It was this hard rock that drew the red-paint people—the first Paleo-Indians to settle in Maine—to Mount Kineo shortly after the glaciers retreated north. Later the Penobscots and other local peoples came to Moosehead Lake to hunt, fish, and collect felsite and rhyolite for tools. By the mid-1800s loggers had begun working the area; soon, rusticators and tourists followed. The number of early fire towers in the region attests to the economic importance of the region's forests. Today Maine is in the middle of a debate on how best to preserve the region and its traditional ways, while maintaining a vigorous economy.

49 Laurie's Ledge

This short, but very steep, hike climbs Indian Mountain to Laurie's Ledge and an overlook just below the mountain's summit. The two overlooks offer fine views of the surrounding mountains and ponds. The hike itself passes through beech forest and then climbs up into the spruce and rock forest atop the mountain, passing several geologically interesting features.

Start: From the Laurie's Ledge trailhead behind the parking area

Distance: 3.0 miles out and back

Hiking time: 2 to 3 hours

Difficulty: Moderate; hike is short, but climbs nearly 1,000 feet

Best seasons: June to Oct

Trail surface: Woodland path

Land status: Appalachian Mountain Club North Woods Recreation and Conservation Area

Nearest towns: Greenville to the west; Brownville to the east

Other trail users: None

Water availability: None

Canine compatibility: Dogs must be under control at all times

Fees and permits: Fee paid at K-I gate (if coming from Brownville) or Hedgehog gate (if coming from Greenville)

Maps: *DeLorme: The Maine Atlas and Gazetteer:* map 41; USGS Number Four Mountain and Hay Mountain

Trail contact: Appalachian Mountain Club, Greenville Office, (207) 695-3085; www .outdoors.org

Finding the trailhead: From Brownville: Drive north on ME 11 for 4.8 miles from the bridge over the Pleasant River. Turn left onto K-I Road at the sign for Katahdin Iron Works. Drive 6.5 miles to the gate where you pay your fee. Cross the Pleasant River and turn right; drive 3.5 miles to a fork in the road. Take the left fork, following the signs to Gulf Hagas. Pass the Gulf Hagas parking 2.9 miles beyond the fork, and the Appalachian Trail 3.5 miles beyond the fork. Turn right onto Little Lyford Ponds Road 7.3 miles past the fork (10.8 miles from the K-I gate). Drive 2.3 miles to the trailhead parking on the left.

From Greenville: From the blinking light in Greenville, drive north on Lily Bay Road. Almost immediately turn right onto Pleasant Street. As you leave Greenville the road becomes East Road. At the airport the pavement ends. At Lower Wilson Pond the road becomes K-I Road. There are numerous side roads—that change from year to year with the needs of the logging companies. The AMC has put up signs directing you to their lodges at most side roads. Follow the signs to the lodges, staying on K-I Road. At 12.1 miles from the blinking light in Greenville, you get to the Hedgehog checkpoint where you pay the fee. Past the checkpoint drive 2.9 miles, then turn left onto Little Lyford Ponds Road. Drive 2.3 miles to the trailhead parking on the left.

Trailhead GPS: N45 31.041' / W69 21.933'

The Hike

The hike to Laurie's Ledge on Indian Mountain begins as a pleasant meander through a beech forest. The trail climbs around exposed bedrock with broken views east of

Looking east from Laurie's Ledge across the Little Lyford Ponds to the Gulf Hagas-Whitecap Range.

the Little Lyford Ponds and Gulf Hagas Mountain across them. Unseen on the south shore of the ponds is the Little Lyford Camps. Built in 1874, this commercial camp was popular with trout enthusiasts, who enjoyed the rustic cabins and isolated setting. In 2003 the Appalachian Mountain Club bought the camps and 60,000 acres of land around them as part of their North Woods Initiative. They have developed more than 80 miles of hiking and skiing trails on their lands that connect to the nearby Appalachian Trail and to Gulf Hagas. The Laurie's Ledge Trail is one of the most scenic the AMC has built.

The trail climbs to an old woods road that it shares with the ski trail that circles around Indian Mountain to Horseshoe Pond. When the yellow-blazed Laurie's Ledge Trail leaves the ski trail, you begin to climb. The trail passes four very large moss- and fern-covered boulders that appear, at one time, to have been one huge piece of bedrock. The trail climbs more steeply to a cliff—perhaps the original home of the boulders below. Take time to study the cliff through the screen of trees. Notice that the rock has cleaved along straight lines and almost forms a box canyon. The bedrock here is clearly not granite, which weathers and breaks apart in a very different way. The trail turns south and follows along the bottom of the cliff, then turns west and climbs very steeply with some views to the south. Across the wide valley rises Barren Mountain.

The trail to Laurie's Ledge passes a huge boulder that has fallen from the cliffs above.

A short side trail, marked with a sign, leads out to a bench atop Laurie's Ledge. From the rocky vantage you can see in every direction except to the west (behind you Indian Mountain, on whose shoulder you stand, blocks that view). To the northeast are the Boardman Mountains and the wooded summits south of the Roach Ponds. Across the Little Lyford Ponds is Gulf Hagas Mountain, behind it you can see the rest of the chain ending with the bare summit of Whitecap Mountain. To the south is the Barren-Chairback Range that the Appalachian Trail crosses before descending to the Pleasant River and then climbing Gulf Hagas Mountain. Spread out in front of you is the famous 100 Mile Wilderness.

Beyond Laurie's Ledge the trail climbs very steeply up Indian Mountain, then slabs to the north around its summit without ever crossing it. The forest is dark and moss-covered. Boulders lie in jumbles beneath the spruce. The trail ends at a rough opening just below the summit with fine views to the west. Below is Horseshoe Pond, and across it rises the almost vertical east face of Elephant Mountain (one of two mountains in Maine with that name—the other is in the Rangeley Lakes region and is crossed by the AT). It got its name because it supposedly looks like an elephant when viewed from a certain angle. This Elephant Mountain is most famous for the remains of a B-52 bomber that lies on its flank after crashing there in 1963. The only trail on the mountain leads to the wreckage, well short of the summit or any views.

Laurie's Ledge

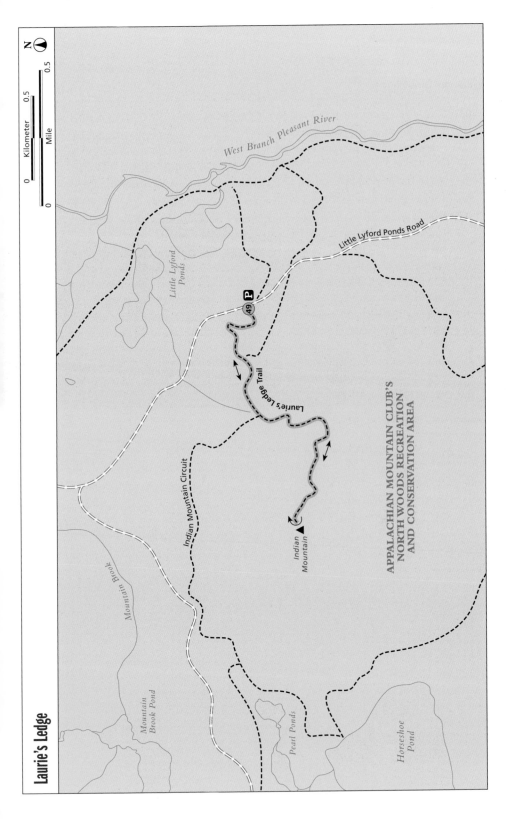

West Branch Pleasant River

Little Lyford Ponds

Little Lyford Ponds Road

Laurie's Ledge Trail

Indian Mountain Circuit

Mountain Brook

Mountain Brook Pond

Pearl Ponds

Horseshoe Pond

Indian Mountain

APPALACHIAN MOUNTAIN CLUB'S NORTH WOODS RECREATION AND CONSERVATION AREA

N

Kilometer
0   0.5

0   0.5
Mile

49 P

To the north rises Baker Mountain, the highest of the Lily Bay Mountains. It is trail-less as well.

Miles and Directions

0.0 Start at the Laurie's Ledge trailhead behind the parking area.

0.3 The yellow-blazed trail climbs gently through the woods with views of the Little Lyford Ponds and Gulf Hagas Mountain where the trail joins the Indian Mountain Circuit ski trail. Stay right on the wide trail. The two trails follow the same route for the next 0.3 mile.

0.6 The ski trail continues straight ahead; the hike follows the Laurie's Ledge Trail to the left.

0.7 The trail climbs gently, passing among a group of very large boulders.

0.8 The trail climbs more steeply to the foot of a cliff. The trail follows along the cliff, then begins climbing in earnest.

1.1 As the trail begins to climb, there is an opening with views to the south. The trail climbs steeply to a side trail that leads 100 feet to an overlook with a bench: Laurie's Ledge. From the overlook there are views east of the Gulf Hagas-Whitecap Range. When the air is especially clear, you can see Katahdin over the low mountains to the northeast.

1.5 Continue climbing past the overlook side trail. Almost immediately there is an opening with views to the south and west. The trail climbs, then slabs around the summit of Indian Mountain, ending at a rough clearing just below the mountain's summit with fine views west. You can see Elephant Mountain looming over Horseshoe Pond and beyond. To complete the hike, retrace your path back to the trailhead.

3.0 Arrive back at the trailhead.

50 Big Moose Mountain

At 3,196 feet, Big Moose Mountain dominates the skyline west of Moosehead Lake. The trail climbs through hardwood forests of beech and maple past the abandoned fire warden's cabin. Beyond the cabin the trail climbs steeply up stone stairs for 0.2 mile. Above the stairs the trail climbs through spruce and fir to the open summit. The summit offers views across Moosehead Lake to Katahdin and the other mountains of Baxter State Park. To the north and west are views of endless wilderness dotted with mountains. More than ten other hikes in this guide are identifiable from the summit.

Start: From the Big Moose Mountain trailhead at the back of the parking lot
Distance: 4.7 miles out and back
Hiking time: About 4 hours
Difficulty: Moderate to strenuous
Best seasons: May to Oct
Trail surface: Woodland trail
Land status: Little Moose Public Reserved Land
Nearest town: Greenville

Other trail users: Hunters use the forest that the first mile of trail passes through
Water availability: Stream crossing at mile 1.5
Canine compatibility: Dogs must be under control at all times
Fees and permits: No fees or permits required
Maps: *DeLorme: The Maine Atlas and Gazetteer:* map 41; USGS Big Moose Pond
Trail contact: Maine Public Reserved Lands, (207) 778-8231; www.maine.gov/dacf/parks

Finding the trailhead: From the blinking light in downtown Greenville, follow ME 6/15 north. Drive 5 miles, then turn left onto North Road at the blue Little Moose Public Reserved Land sign. Drive 1.4 miles on the dirt road. The trailhead parking is on the right, marked by a small brown sign on the road. The trailhead is at the back of the parking lot next to the information kiosk.
Trailhead GPS: N45 28.545' / W69 41.248'

The Hike

The trail up Big Moose Mountain has been in use since at least 1905. That year the first continuously manned fire tower in the country was built on the mountain's summit. Two years earlier more than 200,000 acres of Maine forest land had burned in one dry summer. The M.G. Shaw Lumber Company of Greenville felt the need to protect its forest resources from future fires. They constructed their first tower on Big Moose Mountain, followed by a number of others over the next several years. In 1908, after another bad fire season, the state took over operation of all the fire towers in the state.

In all, the state built and manned 143 towers across the state. By 1950 airplanes had begun to replace towers as the state's preferred method of firespotting. Today most of the towers are gone, either removed or destroyed by the weather. The tower on Big Moose Mountain had been missing its cabin atop the tower for years. The tower itself was removed in 2011. There are plans to rebuild the tower at the Natural Resources Education Center (NREC) on ME 15 south of Greenville.

A mile below the summit, along the trail, the old fire warden's cabin slowly crumbles and falls apart. A tattered blue tarp hangs off its roof, put there by Americorps workers who built the stone stairs on the trail and used the cabin as their base camp. The cabin was built where it was because it sat next to the highest reliable water on the mountain. Each morning the fire warden would climb from the cabin to the summit and sit in the cab atop the tower and scan the surrounding forest for fires. The warden had a phone, later replaced by a radio, to call in fires. They also found ways to entertain themselves with brief conversations with colleagues atop other mountains.

The hike begins next to the kiosk at the rear of the parking area on North Road. The trail climbs gently to an old woods road. The trail coincides with the woods road for nearly a mile, then climbs away from it through open hardwoods—mostly maple and beech. When the trail approaches a stream, it turns right and your climbing begins in earnest. Beyond the fire warden's cabin, the trail climbs nearly 500 feet in less than a quarter mile up stone steps and bare rock.

The level side trail out to a viewpoint after this climb is a welcome break. The vista offers fine views south and west. To the east the rounded summit of Big Moose

Big Moose Mountain from Little Moose Mountain.

Big Moose Mountain

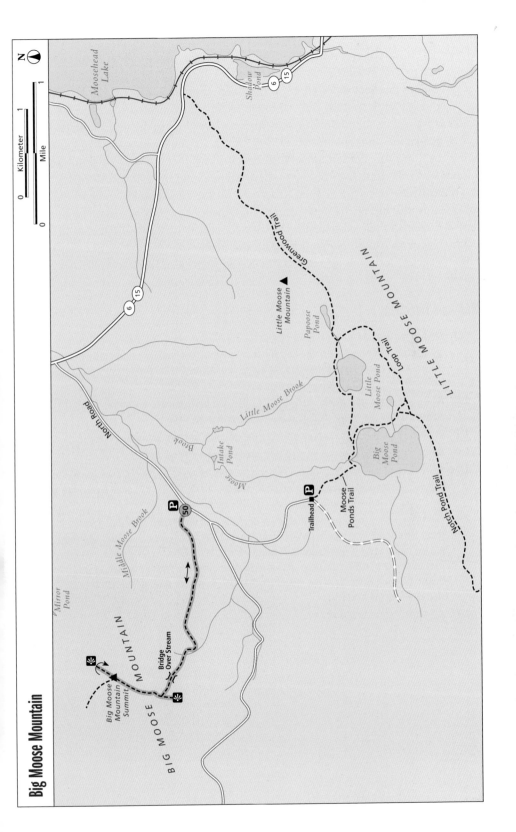

Mountain blocks out everything else. From here to the summit, the trail is through spruce and fir. The mountain has gotten too rocky and steep for maples and beech.

Just before the final rocky climb to the summit, the trail crosses a narrow ridge that falls away sharply on both sides. Through the stunted trees you get glimpses of the views to come. The summit offers views in every direction. To the west the Bigelows and Sugarloaf look surprisingly close. To the north are the widely spaced mountains along the Canadian border and numerous lakes and ponds. The view east, across Moosehead Lake, is partially blocked by a new communications tower. Continue on the trail past the tower to an open rocky area for the view east. The trail continues on down to the top of the now-defunct Big Squaw ski area. You may meet hikers here who came up the ski slope for the view. From here Moosehead Lake is laid out below you, with Mount Kineo jutting up out of the lake. Across the lake Big and Little Spencer Mountains as well as Little Kineo rise out of the woods. Farther out are the Lily Bay Mountains, and beyond them Katahdin and the mountains around it.

Miles and Directions

0.0 Start at the back of the parking lot next to the information kiosk. The trail begins by climbing up to an old woods road. The trail is relatively flat for the first 0.5 mile as it follows the old road, then begins climbing. After 1 mile the trail begins climbing more steeply alongside an unseen stream.

1.5 After passing the abandoned fire warden's cabin, the trail climbs to the bridge over a small stream. Across the bridge the trail climbs steeply up stone stairs.

1.7 The trail reaches a small level area. Follow the overlook trail that leaves to the left.

1.8 The trail ends at a rocky outcropping with good views south and west.

1.9 Arrive back at the main trail. Continue straight ahead, climbing up toward the summit. The trail crosses a narrow ridge that drops sharply on both sides of the trail, then climbs the final rocky bit to the summit.

2.4 The summit used to be the site of the first privately built fire tower in the United States. Today the summit has several communications and scientific towers on it. From the summit the views east are somewhat obscured by the largest of the towers. Continue hiking past the tower and then the helipad to a rocky outcropping with unobstructed views. Below you, on a shoulder of the mountain, is Mirror Pond. Turn around and retrace your steps back to the trailhead.

4.7 Arrive back at the trailhead.

51 Little Moose Mountain

The rocky outcropping on Little Moose Mountain's long ridge offers fine views across the Little and Big Moose Ponds of Big Moose Mountain. To the east is Moosehead Lake and the mountains across it. To get to these views you hike past the two ponds, through woods filled with spring wildflowers. There are three back-country campsites along the hike that are good destinations for young children and first-time backpackers.

Start: From the Moose Ponds trailhead next to the information sign
Distance: 4.0-mile lollipop
Hiking time: 2 to 4 hours
Difficulty: Easy to moderate
Best seasons: May to Oct; late May and early June for wildflowers
Trail surface: Woodland path
Land status: Little Moose Public Reserved Land
Nearest town: Greenville

Other trail users: Hunting allowed on Maine Public Reserved Lands
Water availability: Big and Little Moose Ponds
Canine compatibility: Dogs must be under control at all times
Fees and permits: No fees or permits required
Maps: *DeLorme: The Maine Atlas and Gazetteer:* map 41; USGS Big Moose Pond
Trail contact: Maine Public Reserved Lands, (207) 778-8231; www.maine.gov/dacf/parks

Finding the trailhead: From the blinking light in Greenville, drive north on ME 15. Drive 5 miles and turn left onto North Road at the blue Little Moose Public Reserved Land sign. Drive 1.6 miles, passing the Big Moose Mountain trailhead parking to Little Moose Mountain Road. Turn left and drive 1 mile to the trailhead. The parking is on the left next to the trailhead.
Trailhead GPS: N45 27.740' / W69 41.171'

The Hike

Little Moose Mountain is a long, low ridge that runs southwest from Greenville Junction to the Notch Ponds. The highest point on the ridge is near its eastern end, but the wooded summit has no trail to it. The Greenwood Trail skirts around it. The center of the ridge has several rocky outcroppings overlooking Little and Big Moose Ponds with views of Moosehead Lake and the surrounding mountains. It is these outcroppings that the hike traverses.

The hike begins by descending a low ridge through a hardwood forest dominated by maple and beech. In late spring the forest floor is awash with wildflowers. The hobblebush and wake robin, or blood trillium, bloom first, in early May after the ground has warmed. Hobblebush, a viburnum also known as moosewood, was so named because its long, slender branches intertwine with those of its neighbors and anchor themselves to the ground wherever they touch it, tripping up and grabbing at anyone who tries to bushwhack through them. In Maine hobblebush is found

Looking east across Little Moose Pond to Moosehead Lake. Little and Big Spencer Mountains are visible on the horizon.

growing beneath hardwood forests at mid elevations. They are not particularly dense along the Moose Ponds Trail; rather they add a splash of white to the greening woods.

After the hobblebush and wake robin bloom, the painted trillium, wild lily-of-the-valley, and foamflower bloom as the trees begin to leaf out. By late May the forest is nearly as colorful as it is in October when the leaves change. There are great swaths of wild lily-of-the-valley along the hike. It grows low to the ground, the bell-shaped yellowish-white flowers hanging down inconspicuously. By late June the forest canopy fully shades the forest floor and all is green and brown, except for the lady slipper orchids that bloom along the trail above wet areas in acidic soils.

The trail descends through all these wildflowers to a set of black slate steps down a hillside. The smooth, black stones stand out against the surrounding woods, a reminder that Little and Big Moose Mountains are made of metamorphic rock. You won't see any other slate on the hike, but notice that the rocks along the shore of the ponds and the rocky outcroppings you climb are not granite.

The hike passes three backcountry campsites—one at Big Moose Pond and two on Little Moose Pond. None is more than 1.5 miles from the trailhead. They offer a good place to start kids backpacking. The site on Big Moose Pond is on the north shore with views of the rock outcropping on Little Moose Mountain that offers the best views on the hike. Hardwoods crowd around the pond and dark spruce cap the long mountain ridge, broken by notches where the hardwoods grow. Especially in spring the contrast between the pale green of the new hardwood leaves and the dark spruce is as dramatic as the reds and yellows of fall colors.

Past the junction with the Greenwood Trail, just before the trail climbs the rocky ridge up Little Moose Mountain, is a large vernal pool off the trail to the south. It is

Little Moose Mountain

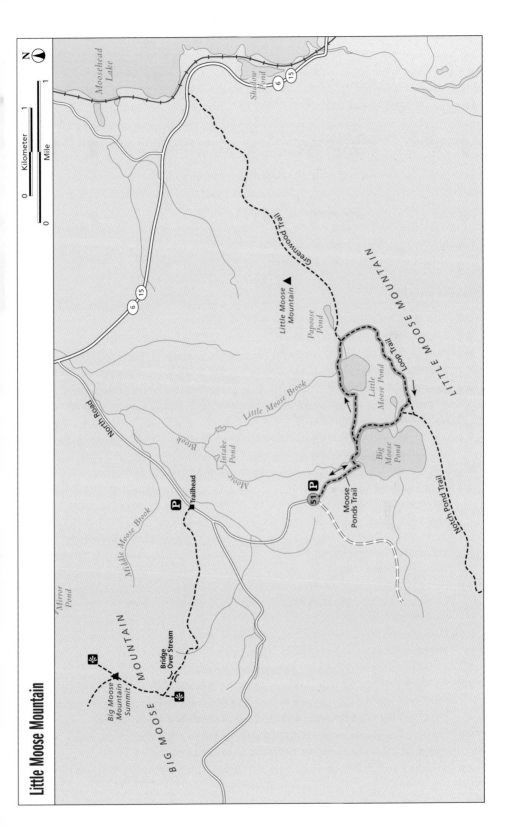

worth checking for frog and salamander eggs in the spring and the growing young later. The trail climbs to the first overlook with fine views across Little Moose Pond of Big Moose Mountain. To the east, partially blocked by the summit of Little Moose Mountain, is Moosehead Lake. Across the lake, from north to south, you can see Mount Kineo, Little Kineo, Little Spencer Mountain, and Big Spencer Mountain.

Beyond the overlook the trail wanders along the ridge with occasional partial views to the side trail out to the large outcropping overlooking Big Moose Pond. From here you can see not only the mountains visible from the first overlook, but also the Lily Bay Mountains across Moosehead Lake south and east of Big Spencer Mountain. South of Little Moose Mountain's summit you can see the mountains in the 100 Mile Wilderness—the Gulf Hagas-Whitecap Range and the Barren-Chairback Range. Away from Moosehead Lake, to the south and west, are endless, rolling forests with occasional mountains.

Miles and Directions

0.0   Start at the Moose Ponds trailhead next to the information sign.

0.4   Junction with the side trail to Big Moose Pond. Turn right and hike to the pond.

0.5   There is a campsite in the woods next to the pond with a view across the pond of Little Moose Mountain.

0.6   Arrive back at the Big Moose Pond Trail. Turn right to continue the hike. The trail passes over an old dam at Big Moose Pond's outlet and then winds through the woods toward Little Moose Pond.

0.8   Junction with the Loop Trail. The trail to the right is where the hike returns. Take the trail to the left toward Little Moose Pond.

1.1   Arrive at Little Moose Pond. There is a campsite here and farther around the pond.

1.7   Junction with the Greenwood Trail. This trail follows the ridge of Little Moose Mountain, skirting around its wooded summit to ME 15. The hike turns right and continues on the Loop Trail.

2.1   The Loop Trail climbs the ridge of Little Moose Mountain to a rocky overlook above Little Moose Pond. There are fine views across the valley of Big Moose Mountain and to the east across Moosehead Lake.

2.5   The trail wanders along Little Moose Mountain, with several partial views, to a side trail to the best view along the entire mountain. Go straight onto the unmarked side trail—the Loop Trail turns left here.

2.55 The overlook is atop a rounded cliff above Big Moose Pond. There are views in every direction except south.

2.6   Arrive back at the Loop Trail. Turn right to continue the hike.

2.7   The trail drops down and goes beneath a mossy cliff, then arrives at the junction with the Notch Pond Trail. This trail goes past the two Notch Ponds and their campsites and ends at a road near Big Indian Pond. Turn right and descend steeply to continue the hike.

3.4   The trail descends steeply then follows along the east shore of Big Moose Pond, arriving back at the Big Moose Ponds Trail. Turn left to return to the trailhead.

4.0   Arrive back at the trailhead.

52 Mount Kineo

Mount Kineo seems to rise out of the middle of Moosehead Lake. It is part of the largest mass of rhyolite known. This hard rock of volcanic origin attracted native peoples for millennia. They used the rock as flint and fashioned it into tools and arrowheads. Later, one of Maine's most famous hotels was at the foot of the mountain. The hike climbs along the edge of the high cliffs that are the mountain's east face. There are fine views from the refurbished fire tower on the summit. The second half of the hike follows the shore of Moosehead Lake around the north and west sides of Mount Kineo.

Start: From the boat dock where the Kineo Shuttle lets you off
Distance: 6.0-mile lollipop
Hiking time: 3 to 5 hours
Difficulty: Moderate
Best seasons: June to Oct
Trail surface: Woodland path
Land status: Mount Kineo State Park
Nearest town: Greenville
Other trail users: None

Water availability: Water and other supplies available from golf course pro shop 0.1 mile east of the trailhead
Canine compatibility: Dogs must be under control at all times
Fees and permits: Fee for the Kineo Shuttle boat ferry from Rockwood to Kineo
Maps: *DeLorme: The Maine Atlas and Gazetteer:* maps 40 and 41; USGS Mount Kineo
Trail contact: Mount Kineo State Park, (207) 941-4014; www.maine.gov/dacf/parks

Finding the trailhead: From the blinking light in Greenville, drive north for 18.8 miles on ME 15. As you enter the town of Rockwood, turn right onto Village Road at the sign for the Kineo Shuttle. Drive 0.4 mile to the town dock's parking area. The shuttle leaves from the town dock. The trailhead is a mile north, across Moosehead Lake, where the shuttle drops you off.
Trailhead GPS: N45 41.433' / W69 44.082'

The Hike

Mount Kineo sits right in the middle of Moosehead Lake, connected to the east shore of the lake by a narrow isthmus. The only way to reach Mount Kineo is by boat from Rockland. The mountain and its near island has a long history of human use. Native Americans made tools, flints, and arrowheads from rock on Mount Kineo. Mount Kineo, like nearby Big Spencer Mountain, is made of rhyolite, a very hard, fine-grained volcanic rock similar to granite. What is now Mount Kineo was formed miles beneath the surface millions of years ago. Since then the softer rock that covered it eroded away, leaving the world's largest rhyolite pluton. The pluton of hard rock is only partly exposed today; much of it remains buried like a rhyolite iceberg floating in Moosehead Lake. In fact, the deepest point in Moosehead Lake—more than 260 feet—is below the cliffs on the northeast side of Mount Kineo.

Mount Kineo from the Kineo Shuttle near the boat dock in Rockwood.

In 1848 the first hotel was built at the foot of Mount Kineo. Over time Kineo became a vacation destination. Visitors would take the stage—later, the train—to Greenville and then a steamer to Kineo. The hotel burned and was rebuilt several times over the years. By the early twentieth century, Kineo was the vacation spot for the rich and famous. The hotel even had its own orchestra that presented daily concerts and a dining room that sat 400. Today the flat part of the peninsula south of the mountain still has numerous private vacation homes and a nine-hole golf course. Hikers can buy drinks and snacks at the pro shop.

The Kineo Shuttle lets hikers off south of Mount Kineo. The sheer east face of the mountain looms over the golf course in front of the boat dock. The hike follows the

MUD SEASON

In spring the limiting factor for hikers isn't snow or high water—it's mud. Logging and forest roads in Maine are generally just graded dirt and often turn soft as the ground thaws. It's easy to get stuck in the mud on your way to a trailhead, so it's best to err on the side of caution when a road looks sketchy. It can be time consuming and expensive to get yourself unstuck. Most of rural Maine has poor cell phone coverage, so you may be walking quite a ways to get help.

Many of the dirt roads in Maine get pretty chewed up by logging trucks and equipment during the winter. If you're traveling before landowners have had a chance to regrade the roads, it's best to avoid areas that were cut during the winter. You also need to watch for washed-out culverts.

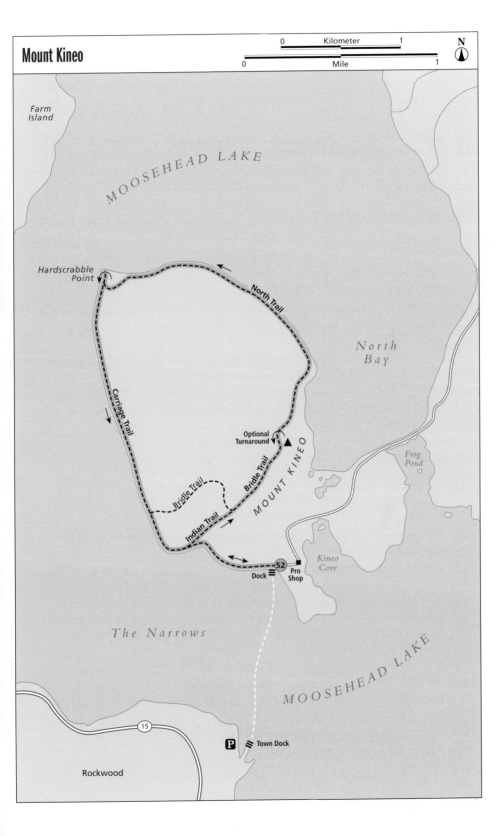

Mount Kineo

0 — Kilometer — 1
0 — Mile — 1

N

Farm
Island

MOOSEHEAD LAKE

Hardscrabble
Point

North Trail

North
Bay

Carriage Trail

Frog
Pond

Optional
Turnaround

Bridle Trail

MOUNT KINEO

Bridle Trail

Indian Trail

52
Dock   Pro
         Shop

Kineo
Cove

The Narrows

MOOSEHEAD LAKE

15

P   Town Dock

Rockwood

old carriage road that runs from the boat dock to Hardscrabble Point at the northwest corner of the peninsula. You pass beneath high cliffs above a scree slope that comes down to the shore of the lake. Notice that unlike granite, the broken rocks and boulders on Kineo are sharp-edged. Many of the small fragments already look sharp enough to be arrowheads or cutting tools.

The hike follows Indian Trail up along the edge of the cliffs with views south and west. As you climb, Moose River, flowing into the lake from the west, appears from behind a group of barrier islands. To the south of the river are Blue and Misery Ridges. Higher still, Brassau Lake comes into view, upstream from Moosehead Lake along the Moose River. Near and far mountains rise out of the forested land: Big Moose to the southwest, Boundary Bald to the northwest, Big and Little Spencer to the southeast, and far to the south the Barren-Chairback Range. The Indian Trail turns away from the cliffs after the best overlook and ends at the Bridle Trail. You follow this trail through the woods to Mount Kineo's summit. There are no views from the wooded summit, but the 64-foot fire tower has been converted to an observation deck with spectacular views in every direction. The first fire tower was built on Mount Kineo in 1910 and twice replaced with a higher tower. The tower was the first in the country to be staffed by a woman.

The descent off the summit on the North Trail is steeper than the climb along the cliffs. The north side of the mountain is thickly forested with spruce, looking and feeling very different from the south and east sides of the mountain. Once down to the lakeshore, you follow the trail along the shore to Hardscrabble Point where there are several campsites. From there you follow the old carriage road back to the trailhead.

Miles and Directions

0.0 Start from the dock where the Kineo Shuttle lets you off. In about 150 feet turn left onto the Carriage Trail; 0.1 mile to the east, across the golf course, is the pro shop where there are bathrooms and you can purchase drinks and snacks.

0.6 The Carriage Trail follows along Moosehead Lake beneath Mount Kineo's cliffs to the junction with the Indian Trail. Turn right onto the Indian Trail.

1.2 The Indian Trail climbs steeply near the cliffs with views out across Moosehead Lake to the junction with the Bridle Trail. Continue straight ahead on the Bridle Trail.

1.7 The Bridle Trail roller-coasters across Mount Kineo's summit ridge to the wooded summit where there is a 64-foot fire tower that has been converted to a viewing platform. (**Option:** To complete the hike as a 3.4-mile out and back, return the way you came to the boat dock.) Continue across the summit onto the North Trail.

2.6 The North Trail descends steeply through a spruce forest to the shore of Moosehead Lake.

3.8 The North Trail follows along the shore of Moosehead Lake to end at the Carriage Trail. Hardscrabble Point is 400 feet to the right. To continue the hike, turn left onto the Carriage Trail.

5.2 The Carriage Trail follows along the shore of Moosehead Lake, passing the Bridle Trail.

5.4 Pass the Indian Trail. Continue straight ahead to return to the boat dock.

6.0 Arrive back at the boat dock.

53 Little Spencer Mountain

Even though Little Spencer Mountain is far from the highest in the state and the distance is short, this is one of the most challenging hikes in this guide. The climb is very steep, crossing several rock slides and climbing a nearly vertical chimney. Leave your dog and small children at home, and come prepared to work hard for the best view of the Moosehead region. From the semi-open summit you can see from the Bigelows to Katahdin, and from the lowlands of the Penobscot Valley to Coburn Mountain and the Allagash Country.

Start: From the Little Spencer trailhead on the north side of Spencer Camps Road
Distance: 2.6 miles out and back
Hiking time: 3 to 4 hours
Difficulty: Strenuous; hike is short, but very steep with some rock scrambling and exposure
Best seasons: June to Oct
Trail surface: Woodland path
Land status: Private timberland
Nearest town: Greenville

Other trail users: Hunting allowed on the timberlands
Water availability: Spring at mile 0.7
Canine compatibility: Not appropriate for dogs
Fees and permits: No fees or permits required
Maps: *DeLorme: The Maine Atlas and Gazetteer:* map 49; USGS Lobster Mountain
Trail contact: Spencer Pond Camps, www .spencerpond.com

Finding the trailhead: From the blinking light in Greenville on ME 15, drive north on Lily Bay Road. The pavement ends at Kokadjo after 18.5 miles. Continue driving for 0.4 mile to a fork. Bear left at the fork onto Sias Hill Road and drive 0.9 mile. Turn left onto Spencer Bay Road; there is a sign for Spencer Pond Camps at the intersection. Drive 0.5 mile to a bridge over Lazy Tom Stream where you have a view of Big and Little Spencer Mountains to the north. Continue driving for another 6.9 miles, then turn right at a 4-way intersection. There is a red sign at the intersection for Spencer Pond Camps. Drive 2.2 miles, with views of Little Spencer Mountain. The trailhead is on the right; there is a small sign for the trail. There is no parking area, but you can park on the south side of the road where it is wide enough to get off the road without getting stuck in the sometimes wet shoulder.
Trailhead GPS: N45 45.282' / W69 32.929'

The Hike

New Hampshire's White Mountains have a long tradition of seasonal residents and visitors building and maintaining trails. In Maine, with a few exceptions, this has never been the case. The Ram Trail up Little Spencer Mountain is one of the exceptions. In the 1960s Dr. Richard A. Manson, who frequented the nearby Spencer Pond Camps, scouted several routes to the summit of Little Spencer Mountain. The easiest and most direct route was developed into the Ram Trail. The trail's name is Manson's initials. The lower portion of the trail—up to the first slide—was originally flagged

Little Spencer Mountain from across Spencer Pond.

by Anne Howe, grandmother of the owners of the camps. The trail is maintained by Spencer Camps to this day.

This is one of the steepest and most challenging hikes in Maine. Little Spencer Mountain is only 3,040 feet, but the hike climbs 1,870 feet in 1.25 miles. The climb includes two rock slides, a steep scree slope, the chimney, and some rock scrambling with some exposure. The trail is well maintained and marked with flagging and cairns at critical places.

The trail begins easy enough, climbing gently through maple and beech along a small stream. The trail steepens up a rocky ridge covered with pine needles from the white pines towering over the trail. You get your first views out across Spencer Pond. The trail climbs steeply to the first rock slide. The slides on Little Spencer Mountain are created by the very hard, weather-resistant rock being fractured by water seeping into cracks and freezing. The freezing water pries the rock apart. Over time squarish hunks of bedrock break off and litter the mountainside beneath the cliff where the rocks originated. The light-colored rocks on the slides seem to radiate light and heat. On a warm day you may feel the need to rush across the slides, but be sure to take time to appreciate the opening views as you get higher on the mountain.

Between the slides the trail climbs a very steep scree slope. Notice that the scree is composed of thin, flat rocks that are orange. Moving up and down the slope generates clouds of dust. These rocks are very different from those on the rest of the mountain. The light-colored rock that makes up the cliffs and slides is metamorphic—sedimentary rock that was transformed by heat and pressure several miles beneath the

Little Spencer Mountain

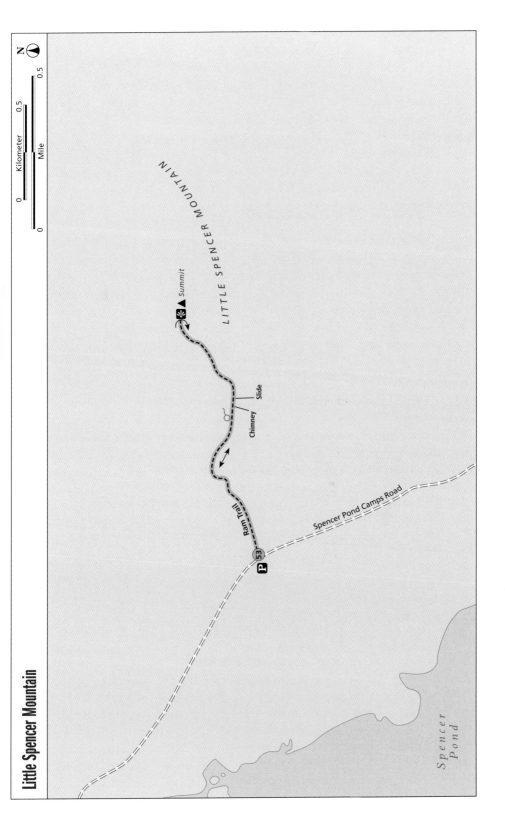

LITTLE SPENCER MOUNTAIN

Summit

Slide

Chimney

Ram Trail

53

Spencer Pond Camps Road

Spencer Pond

N

0   Kilometer   0.5

0   Mile   0.5

surface. The orange rock on the scree slope is sedimentary rock that has not been metamorphosed.

Above the scree slope the trail climbs the chimney, which is a narrow cleft in a cliff that rises 75 almost-vertical feet. There is a rope hanging down that is most useful on the descent. At the top of the chimney, you get an unobstructed view out across Spencer Pond and Moosehead Lake of the endless mountains of the Moosehead region and western Maine. At this point the mountain still blocks the view of Big Spencer Mountain and Katahdin. From the chimney the trail climbs to a good-size slide that seems to drop off a cliff. The trail comes out onto the slide, but does not cross it. Follow the cairns up to the cliffs higher on the mountain. The trail climbs along the base of the cliffs and then you have to scramble up the face to where the slope becomes more gentle. You have fine views all along this section.

The trail climbs through tightly growing spruce to the semi-open summit. From the summit you get partially blocked views east across the mountain's summit ridge to Big Spencer Mountain and Katahdin and the mountains of Baxter State Park beyond. You can also see Lobster Mountain and Lake to the north; beyond them are Chesuncook Lake and the Allagash Country. In the fall the lowland forests around Moosehead Lake are vibrant with color, from lemon-yellow to fire-red and even purple. In early summer the forest is awash with red from maple blossoms and more shades of green than you can name.

Miles and Directions

0.0 Start from the Little Spencer Mountain trailhead on the north side of Spencer Pond Camps Road.

0.5 There are several spots in the next 0.7 mile where you can take the wrong route. Be sure to follow the flagging.

0.7 The trail begins climbing steeply up loose rocks. About 200 feet up the climb the trail bears right; to the left are two very large cedar trees in front of a rock face. If you bushwhack to a cleft in the rock face, you will find the spring. Usually you can hear the water falling down the rock.

0.8 The trail reaches the bottom of the chimney. There is a rope you can use to help you climb. At the top of the chimney, you have fine views to the south and west.

0.9 The trail comes out onto a rock slide that drops off a cliff. Follow the cairns up to the cliffs above you; do not cross the slide.

1.0 The trail climbs along the base of a cliff, then climbs up the rock with some exposure. The top of this climb ends the steepest section of the hike. You have fine views out away from the mountain.

1.3 A very short side trail leads to an overlook with views in every direction. The semi-open summit with spruce-blocked views is 150 feet farther up the trail. The trail ends at the unmarked summit. To complete the hike, retrace your steps back to the trailhead.

2.6 Arrive back at the trailhead.

54 Boundary Bald

Boundary Bald, a mere 6 miles from Quebec, offers fine 360-degree views. You can see well into Quebec and even New Hampshire as well as a large swath of northern Maine. The hike is very steep and rocky in places, but well worth the effort. Boundary Bald is in a geologically complex region where you can find granite and volcanic rocks, as well as slate and other sedimentary rocks. There are two interesting waterfalls between Jackman and the trailhead. The drive in is also a good place to see moose.

Start: From the end of Notch Road where Trail Road continues up the hill
Distance: 5.4 miles out and back
Hiking time: 3 to 5 hours
Difficulty: Strenuous
Best seasons: June to Oct
Trail surface: Woods road and woodland path
Land status: Hilton Timberlands
Nearest town: Jackman
Other trail users: Hunting allowed on the timberlands

Water availability: Stream at mile 1.1
Canine compatibility: Too steep and rough for most dogs
Fees and permits: No fees or permits required
Maps: *DeLorme: The Maine Atlas and Gazetteer:* maps 39 and 47; USGS Boundary Bald Mountain
Trail contact: Hilton Timberlands, (207) 668-9516, thetreeguy@myfairpoint.net

Finding the trailhead: From the junction of US 201 and ME 15 in Jackman, drive north on US 201 for 9 miles to The Falls rest area. There is a waterfall just off the highway here worth checking out. Drive north on US 201 another 0.3 mile and turn right onto Bald Mountain Road. There is both a street sign and a sign for the hike. Drive 4.2 miles on Bald Mountain Road and turn left onto Notch Road. Drive 0.2 mile to the end of Notch Road and park on the left. The hike goes up Trail Road to the right.
Trailhead GPS: N45 45.091'/W70 14.391'

The Hike

Sometimes half the fun of a hike in the remote Maine woods is getting to the trailhead. Boundary Bald—only 6 miles from the Canadian border, is one of those hikes. Before you even reach Bald Mountain Road, you may have seen a moose or two. US 201 is one of the moosiest roads in the state. If you stopped at The Falls rest area, curious to see if there was a falls, you would have found a stream that plummets down an irregularly shaped slate rock face. It's not the biggest waterfall in the state, but worth stopping to see.

A mile from US 201, Boundary Bald Road crosses Heald Stream. Stop along the road at the parking area across the bridge and check out Heald Falls. Again, the stream drops across irregular slate, the bedding turned up on end. Boundary Bald and the two nearby falls are in an area of Devonian slate and mixed volcanic rocks. Boundary

Bald sits right on the fault between these two rock types of about equal age. The mountains around the Moose River and Attean Pond are a granite intrusion. So as you stand on Boundary Bald, you can see geologic chaos.

The first 1.4 miles of the hike are up Trail Road. Once on the actual hiking trail, the geology of the region is right beneath your feet. The trail climbs a deeply eroded trail up crumbled shale, the thin bedding layers stood on end. It makes for awkward footing, but it is interesting how the erosion on the trail has exposed the bedrock in this way. Higher on the mountain the rock is more typically volcanic, almost like granite. As you climb, the areas of different rock types are separated by relatively level shelves that tend to be boggy. On the first shelf the trail goes through a red birch forest. The relatively open woods let in a lot of light, and a profusion of water-tolerant plants abound. This is a good place to startle a moose, especially in the fall. Moose tracks and droppings are more common than boot tracks.

The trail climbs more steeply, up volcanic rock to another shelf. From this shelf, covered with spruce and sphagnum moss, you get a good look at the summit ridge of

The view looking west across Boundary Bald's summit ridge.

Boundary Bald Mountain

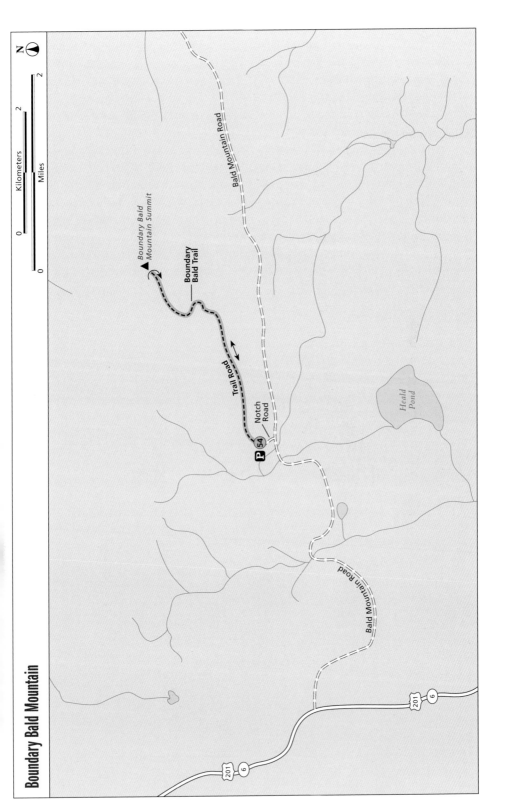

Boundary Bald. The wet trail crosses the shelf and again begins climbing more steeply. The path is narrow and the stunted spruce crowd in, making the trail almost disappear. The rough spruce boughs grab at your clothes and legs. And then you climb out onto the summit ridge. There is a side trail—more obvious than the blue-blazed trail to the summit—that leads out to a rocky outcropping on the south side of the ridge with fine views in every direction.

The trail across the summit ridge to the high point, near the east end of the mountain, can be hard to follow, but there is enough open bedrock that you can make your own trail most of the way. There are two small towers on the summit; in 2013 one was bent in half, testament to the rough winter weather on this mountaintop. You can look out and see Moosehead Lake to the east and the mountains around it. To the southwest the jagged row of mountains are those west of Jackman around Attean Pond and the Moose River. To the northwest is Quebec, and to the north and northeast, the endless North Woods of the headwaters of the Penobscot and St. Johns Rivers.

Miles and Directions

- **0.0** Start at the end of Notch Road, where Trail Road climbs gently.
- **1.1** Trail Road crosses a stream.
- **1.4** Turn left onto the Boundary Bald Trail. There is a sign at the junction.
- **2.2** The trail climbs up loose rocks, levels off through often wet woods, then climbs steeply. It becomes ever more constricted by stunted spruce and fir. The trail is blue blazed, but can be hard to follow. Be sure to pay attention to where to go down on your return as you approach the summit ridge. It can be hard to find the trail. The trail comes to a junction. Turn right to continue to the summit.
- **2.3** A side trail that is more obvious than the blue-blazed trail leads to a rocky outcropping with fine views.
- **2.7** The Boundary Bald Trail crosses the summit ridge to the summit where there are two towers and 360-degree views of endless rows of mountains. To the east you can see Moosehead Lake. To complete the hike, return the way you came.
- **5.4** Arrive back at the trailhead.

55 Coburn Mountain

Coburn Mountain is the highest peak between the high mountains of western Maine and Katahdin. But this remote mountain is rarely visited. The hike up the mountain is steep, but passes over varied and interesting terrain. The semi-open summit has a tower with a viewing platform that offers a 360-degree panorama. You can see all the way from New Hampshire's White Mountains to Quebec and across Moosehead Lake to Katahdin. The drive to the trailhead on US 201 is one of the moosiest stretches of road in Maine.

Start: From the multiuse trail on the left side of the road, climbing west

Distance: 2.5 miles out and back

Hiking time: 2 to 3 hours

Difficulty: Moderate

Best seasons: June to Oct

Trail surface: Multiuse trail and woodland path

Land status: Private timberlands

Nearest town: The Forks

Other trail users: Hunting allowed on the timberlands; ATVs use the road and multiuse trails

Water availability: Stream at mile 0.2

Canine compatibility: Dogs must be under control at all times

Fees and permits: No fees or permits required

Maps: *DeLorme: The Maine Atlas and Gazetteer:* map 40; USGS Enchanted Pond and Johnson Mountain

Trail contact: None

Finding the trailhead: From The Forks drive north on US 201 for 10.7 miles, then turn left onto Enchanted Mountain Road. There is a street sign at the intersection. Drive 2.4 miles to a 4-way intersection in a large clearing. Turn right and drive 0.2 mile, passing a concrete slab that was once the foundation of a ski lodge. The trailhead is on the left where the road bends to the right. **Trailhead GPS:** N45 28.031' / W70 06.599'

The Hike

Between the high mountains in western Maine—Sugarloaf, The Bigelows, Mount Abraham—and Katahdin, Coburn Mountain is the highest peak at 3,718 feet. It is the highest and easternmost of a loose collection of remote mountains between the Canadian border and US 201 south of Jackman, all on private timberlands. These mountains are geologically complex; some are mined for tourmaline and their streams panned for gold. To the north is a granite pluton that encompasses the mountains west of Jackman—all visible from Coburn Mountain's summit. Coburn Mountain is named for the nineteenth-century timber baron and civil servant Abner Coburn. He was one of the founders of the Republican Party in Maine, and after stints in the legislature was governor during the Civil War. In the 1880s there was a move to rename the mountain Enchanted Mountain, but it failed to pass the legislature.

The mountain was once home to the Enchanted Mountain Ski Resort. It's not clear who the developers thought would be willing to drive all the way to Coburn

Looking north from the summit to the ponds and mountains east of Jackman along the Moose River.

Mountain to ski—even with the fine views from the slopes. Near the trailhead you can still find the base lodge's foundation and see the open area of one of the ski runs. The trail used to go up the ski slope before entering the woods high on the mountain's shoulder, but recent logging has obliterated the bottom of the trail. That logging, though, has made access to the hike easier. Before 2013 you had to road walk to the trailhead nearly all the way from US 201. Now you can drive all the way to the new trailhead—an ATV trail that climbs to the top of the ski slope where a small communications tower has been built on the foundation of the old ski lift. The trail climbs to this shoulder on loose orange sedimentary rock. In places the trail feels less like an ATV trail and more like a scree slope.

Above the tower the trail climbs through spruce and fir, getting steeper the higher you climb. There is an open area on the summit with good views; the summit itself is surrounded by dense forest that keeps the view from being a 360-degree panorama. But there is a tower on the summit with a viewing platform. From the tower you get that stunning 360-degree panorama. The view to the north of the granite mountains around Attean Pond and the Moose River is especially fine. To the east are Moosehead Lake and the mountains around it. The lake appears as several gleaming patches that reflect sunlight, separated by dark green forest and mountains. To the

Coburn Mountain

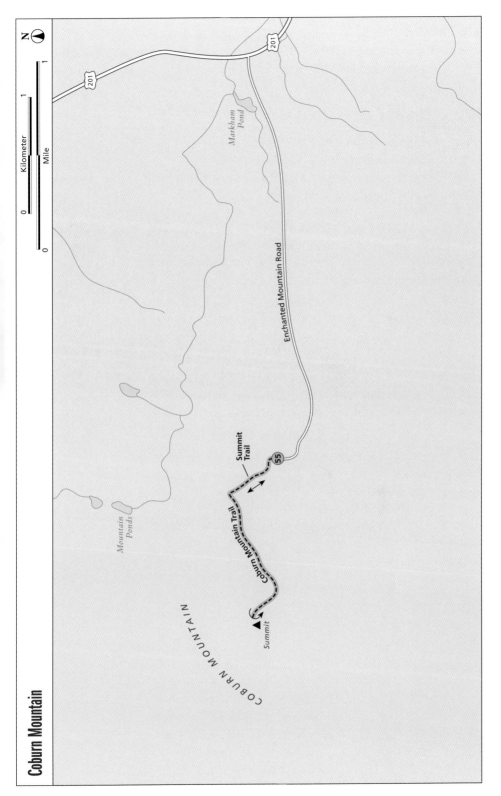

south the high mountains in Oxford County are plainly visible; on clear days you can more than imagine the White Mountains beyond them. To the west, across Kibby Mountain, are Quebec and the Megantic Mountains and the Connecticut Lakes in northernmost New Hampshire.

Miles and Directions

0.0 Start from the multiuse trail on the left side of the road.

0.2 The trail crosses a stream.

0.9 The trail arrives at a clearing with a four-way junction. Turn right, pass a communications tower, and go through the gate.

1.0 Turn right onto the Summit Trail at a cairn.

1.25 The trail climbs steeply to the summit. There is an observation tower on the summit with 360-degree views, from the mountains east of Moosehead Lake to mountains in New Hampshire and Quebec. To complete the hike, return the way you came.

2.5 Arrive back at the trailhead.

Honorable Mention

Number Four Mountain

Number Four Mountain is the only one of the Lily Bay Mountains with a trail to its summit. The 3.3-mile out-and-back hike offers fine views from the summit. The trail begins in an old clear-cut that has regrown with shrubby maples and brambles. The trail is relatively flat for the first 0.4 mile to Lagoon Brook. The trail turns right and begins to gently climb, then more steeply to the rocky old-growth spruce forest. Like most fire warden trails on mountains in Maine, the trail just goes straight up the side of the mountain. It is very steep. At the summit is the old fire tower. The forest on the summit blocks most of the views, but by climbing partway up the tower, you can get spectacular views in every direction. A short trail leads east from the summit to an overlook with views of the Lily Bay Mountains and the forests and mountains to the east. To get to the trailhead, from the blinking light in Greenville, drive north on Lily Bay Road for 17.4 miles, then turn right onto Frenchtown Road. Drive 2.2 miles and turn right onto Lagoon Brook Road. Drive 1.4 miles and turn left onto Meadow Brook Road. Drive 0.9 mile; the trailhead is on the left marked by a small white sign. There is no parking area, but there is room to pull your car off the side of the road.

Baxter State Park

In 1804 Charles Turner, a surveyor from Massachusetts, made the first known assent of Katahdin. For 12,000 years, since emerging from the ice, Katahdin had stood venerated by Native Americans—home to three of their deities. It is visible from Bangor Hill in Orono near the Penobscot village in Old Town, so it's no wonder that Katahdin played an important role in their cosmology. Over time it has come to loom large in the mountain lore of Euro-Americans, too. Not only is Katahdin the highest mountain in Maine, but it dominates the forests it dramatically rises from. It is more than 4,000 feet higher than the country to the south. Around it

Looking up Nesowadnehunk Stream from above Little Niagara Falls (hike 61).

are arrayed numerous other mountains, also among the highest in Maine, that bolster rather than diminish Katahdin's grandeur.

Thoreau was drawn north to climb the mountain in 1846 on his first of three trips to Maine. By then Katahdin had been climbed several times by scientific and surveying parties. Still, Thoreau had to bushwhack from the Penobscot River, roughly following Abol Stream. His party then bushwhacked up Katahdin, aiming for the slide that today is the Abol Trail. The going was so difficult—Thoreau at times walked on top of the stunted spruce trees—that he left his party far behind. As he approached the Tableland, the weather worsened, forcing him to turn back. Thoreau never summitted.

After Thoreau, as logging began in the valleys north of Katahdin, it became the norm to climb the mountain from the east or north. The Appalachian Mountain Club established a camp at Chimney Pond in the Great Basin in 1916. Four years later the soon to be governor of Maine, Percival Baxter, stayed at the newly opened Kidney Pond Camps. He was so impressed by the mountain that he spent the rest of his life working to protect it and the forests around it. He failed as governor to make Katahdin a state park, so he began using his family fortune to buy the land.

In 1930 he purchased 6,000 acres that included Katahdin and donated it to the state. The deed for the land came with specific limitations and expectations. The park was to be kept in its "natural wild state" as a "sanctuary for wild birds and beasts." Of lesser importance was "limited" recreational use. The rules laid out in the deed remain in force today. The park has very limited facilities: no water, no electricity, no phone (or cell service), and only a handful of wilderness campgrounds. To protect the "resource" there are no paved roads and few gravel roads, and dogs are not allowed in the park. Access to many of the popular trails, especially on Katahdin, is limited so they don't get loved to death. You can make camping and trail reservations up to three months ahead.

Between 1930 and 1962, Baxter purchased and donated to the state twenty-nine separate parcels amounting to more than 200,000 acres. Since then several small parcels have been added between the original southern border of the park and the Penobscot River. Then in 2006 a complex purchase and land swap that involved a number of parties added Katahdin Lake to the park. It was the one parcel Baxter had not been able to purchase in his lifetime.

On an average summer day, about half the hikers on trails in Baxter State Park are on Katahdin. Just as it drew Thoreau north, it draws hikers from around the world. But there are more than 200 miles of trails in the park that go over and around spectacular mountains and to wilderness ponds popular with moose. Let this guide help draw you beyond Katahdin into the wilderness that is Baxter State Park.

Baxter State Park has two entrances. The south entrance is reached through Millinocket from exit 264 on I-95. It is 39.2 miles from the interstate to the Togue Pond Gatehouse. The north entrance is reached through Patten from exit 264 on I-95. It is 35.8 miles from the interstate to the Matagamon Gatehouse. Both routes are well marked and easy to follow. Do not try to reach the north end of the park from the south gate. Tote Road is narrow and winding with a speed limit of 20 miles per hour.

56 Katahdin

This is the classic hike. There is no hike more iconic in Maine. The route climbs Keep Ridge with fine views to Pamola Peak. You then descend into—and climb right out of The Chimney. The Knife Edge begins as you cross Chimney Peak. The trail crosses over and around a series of serrated knobs that drop dramatically into the Great Basin. An exhilarating climb brings you to Baxter Peak, the highest point in Maine and the northern terminus of the Appalachian Trail. From there the hike descends into The Saddle with fine views in every direction. The Saddle Trail then drops steeply down a slide, leading toward Chimney Pond. From Chimney Pond it is a little more than a 3-mile descent to the trailhead.

Start: From the Roaring Brook ranger's station at the north end of the parking area
Distance: 9.6-mile loop
Hiking time: 8 to 10 hours
Difficulty: Very strenuous
Best seasons: July to Sept
Trail surface: Woodland path and granite bedrock, more than 4 miles of it above treeline
Land status: Baxter State Park
Nearest town: Millinocket
Other trail users: None
Water availability: Bear Brook at mile 1.4 and a small stream at mile 5.5

Canine compatibility: Dogs not allowed in Baxter State Park
Fees and permits: No fees or permits required for Maine residents; park entrance fee for non-residents. All hikers need a reservation to park at the trailhead. Reservations can be made up to 3 months in advance by calling (207) 723-5140 or online at www.baxterstatepark authority.com.
Maps: *DeLorme: The Maine Atlas and Gazetteer:* map 50 and 51; USGS Mount Katahdin
Trail contact: Baxter State Park, (207) 723-5140; www.baxterstateparkauthority.com

Finding the trailhead: From the Togue Pond Gate at the south entrance, turn right onto Roaring Brook Road. Drive 8 miles to the end of the road. Hiker parking is in the lot to the left. The hike begins at the ranger's station—where you need to sign in before hiking—at the north end of the parking area.
Trailhead GPS: N45 55.180' / W68 51.444'

The Hike

Katahdin creates its own weather and is often capped by a cloud even on clear days. It can snow on any day of the year and is often quite windy above treeline. Hikers should be prepared: Don't wear cotton clothing; bring a hat and coat; pack plenty of water and snacks. Remember that nearly half the hike is above treeline, exposed to the weather. Most importantly, take your time and respect the mountain. The earlier in the day you begin your hike the better; it is not uncommon to see hikers arriving at the trailhead before it is even light. You don't need to start that early, but it is best to be on the trail by 7 or 8 a.m.

The hike begins climbing almost immediately. After all, you begin at an elevation of just over 1,500 feet, and Pamola Peak, the first peak you reach, is at 4,919. That's a lot of climbing in 3.2 miles. As you climb toward the treeline, you have to scale several small rock faces and pass overlooks with views to the east and north. As you climb higher, more of the surrounding country emerges. By the time you reach the treeline, you can see the Turner Mountains to the northeast with The Traveler beyond them. To the east is Katahdin Lake, surrounded by endless forest. To the northwest you can see right into North Basin with its dramatic cliffs that rise to Hamlin and Howe Peaks. The peaks of the North Basin are part of Katahdin. The mountain encompasses not just the peaks around the Great Basin and the Tableland, but the North Peaks and the North and Northwest Basins.

The trail follows the spine of Keep Ridge toward Pamola Peak, steepening as you climb. The north ridge of Pamola begins to block the view northwest, but the arc of the Knife Edge comes into view. Before the final push to the summit, you get a view right through the Chimney. Pamola Peak sits right on the edge of the Great

Two hikers near the summit in a swirling cloud on an otherwise clear summer day.

Basin, with Baxter Peak directly across the great yawning gulf. The jagged arc of the Knife Edge connects the two. To the northwest North Basin has come back into view. Beyond it, across a wide swath of tableland, is the little-visited Northwest Basin. In the distance you can see The Brothers, Mount O-J-I, and behind them Doubletop Mountain. Pamola peak itself seems to be little more than a pile of loose granite mottled with lichen.

> **Katahdin is the northern terminus of the Appalachian Trail. The southern end of the trail is almost 2,200 trail miles away on Springer Mountain, Georgia. There are 281.4 miles of the AT in Maine, from Katahdin to Carlo Col in the Mahoosuc Range. Nine hikes in this guide are either partly or entirely on the AT.**

The descent from Pamola Peak into the Chimney, and then the climb to Chimney Peak, is the most technically difficult section of the entire hike. The trail drops 100 feet of elevation in only 260 feet of trail. The climb up to Chimney Peak is almost as steep. The Knife Edge itself begins as you descend off Chimney Peak. The trail winds over and around a series of serrated ridges that drop dramatically into the Great Basin. More than 1,000 feet below you, Chimney Pond looks like a small puddle.

Baxter Peak is 5,267 feet—13 feet short of a mile. There is a large cairn on the summit that makes the mountain a mile high. Near the cairn is the sign denoting the northern end of the Appalachian Trail. Thru-hikers and day hikers alike queue up to get their picture taken celebrating at the sign. Their whoops can be heard all across Katahdin and even down at Chimney Pond.

The hike follows the Saddle Trail off the summit down into the Saddle. As you descend, you can see the orangish gash of a slide where the Saddle Trail drops down toward Chimney Pond. The trail is extremely steep and descends loose rock. Take your time and enjoy the view of Katahdin as you carefully descend. Even after the trail turns to bedrock and you enter the trees, the trail continues to drop. Then, suddenly, you reach the ranger's station on the shore of Chimney Pond. Roy Dudley was a ranger here for years, entertaining hikers and campers with yarns of Pamola, the mythological creature who lived atop Katahdin and controlled the weather. He was, according to the Penobscots, a giant man with a moose's head and an eagle's legs and wings. It was respect for his power that kept the Penobscots from climbing the mountain.

Before heading down the Chimney Pond Trail to the trailhead, walk out to the shore of Chimney Pond. You can see the jagged line from Pamola Peak across the Knife Edge to Baxter Peak that you just hiked. Even as you hear voices drifting down from above, the scale of the mountain renders the scene almost unreal. But your sore feet and legs know all too well that it was real. You have more than 3 miles to hike back to the trailhead, so don't linger too long.

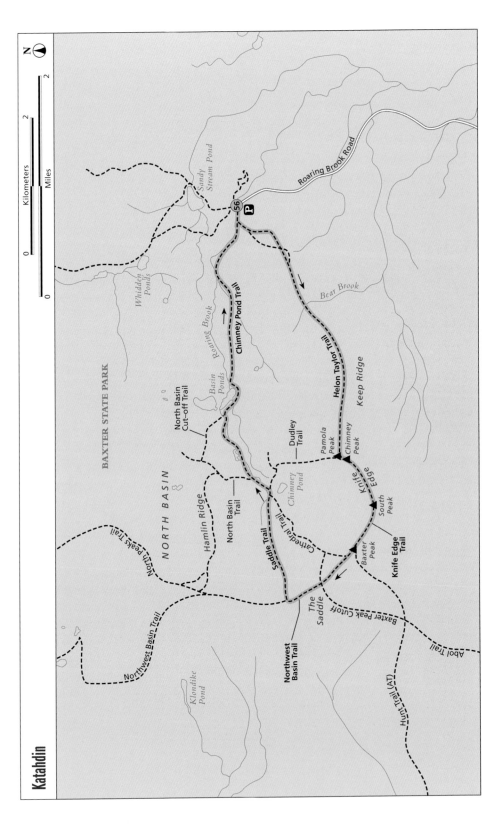

Katahdin

Miles and Directions

0.0 Start from the Roaring Brook ranger's station at the north end of the parking area on the Chimney Pond Trail. Be sure to sign in on the front porch of the ranger's station. In 400 feet pass the Russell Pond Trail, which crosses Roaring Brook within sight of the junction.

0.2 Turn left onto the Helon Taylor Trail.

1.4 The trail crosses Bear Brook.

2.2 The trail reaches the treeline with views ahead to Pamola Peak and into North Basin. As the trail climbs, you get views of the Knife Edge and Chimney Peak.

3.2 Reach Pamola Peak. Turn left onto the Knife Edge Trail.

3.3 The Knife Edge Trail descends very steeply into The Chimney, losing 100 feet of elevation in 260 feet of trail. From The Chimney the trail climbs Chimney Peak, gaining almost 100 feet in less than 500 feet of trail. This is the toughest section of trail on the entire hike.

4.0 The trail crosses the Knife Edge to unmarked South Peak.

4.3 The trail climbs from South Peak to Baxter Peak, the highest point in Maine and the northern terminus of the Appalachian Trail. From the summit descend into The Saddle on the Saddle Trail.

4.5 Pass the Cathedral Trail. This trail descends to Chimney Pond in 1.6 miles, a shorter but more difficult descent.

4.8 Pass the Cathedral Cut-off Trail.

5.2 Junction with the Northwest Basin Trail in The Saddle. The Saddle Trail descends a steep slide to the east from The Saddle. The Northwest Basin Trail climbs out of The Saddle toward Hamlin and Howe Peaks and then on to Northwest Basin.

5.5 The Saddle Trail descends steeply to treeline with views across the Great Basin. Into the trees the trail descends to a small stream.

6.2 Pass the Cathedral Trail.

6.3 Arrive at the Chimney Pond ranger's station. Turn left onto the Chimney Pond Trail and head east toward Roaring Brook. A short side trail leads to the right to Chimney Pond.

6.4 Chimney Pond.

6.7 Pass the North Basin Trail.

7.3 Pass the North Basin Cut-off Trail.

7.7 A short side trail leads 100 feet to Basin Pond, the source of Roaring Brook.

9.4 Turn left onto the Chimney Pond Trail to return to the trailhead.

9.6 Arrive back at the trailhead. Be sure to sign out on the front porch of the ranger's station.

57 The Traveler

The Traveler is as long and difficult a hike as Katahdin—the 10-mile loop climbs nearly 4,100 feet. Because of the difference in geology (Katahdin is granite and The Traveler is rhyolite), the two mountains feel very different. The hiking experience is very different, too. The Traveler is never crowded; most days you have the mountain almost to yourself. Even though all of The Traveler is part of a huge mass of rhyolite, laid down more than 400 million years ago, the four peaks the hike crosses feel and look unique. Much of the hike is spent on open slopes and summits with views in every direction and blueberries everywhere.

Start: From the day-use parking area at the end of South Branch Pond Road
Distance: 10.1-mile loop
Hiking time: 7 to 9 hours
Difficulty: Strenuous
Best seasons: June to Sept
Trail surface: Woodland path with long sections above treeline
Land status: Baxter State Park
Nearest town: Patten
Other trail users: None

Water availability: Lower South Branch Pond near the trailhead and Howe Brook at mile 1.0
Canine compatibility: Dogs not allowed in Baxter State Park
Fees and permits: No fee or permits required for Maine residents; park entrance fee for nonresidents
Maps: *DeLorme: The Maine Atlas and Gazetteer:* map 51; USGS Traveler Mountain and Wassatoquoik Lake
Trail contact: Baxter State Park, (207) 723-5140; www.baxterstateparkauthority.com

Finding the trailhead: From the north entrance of Baxter State Park at the Matagamon Gate, drive 7 miles on Tote Road. Turn left onto South Branch Pond Road at the sign for South Branch Pond. Drive 1.9 miles to the end of the road and the day-use parking area. Begin the hike by walking into the campground past the ranger's station.
Trailhead GPS: N46 06.518' / W68 54.050'

The Hike

Around 400 million years ago, the ancient supercontinent Avalonia collided with North America. During this geologically active period the granites of Maine were laid down. It is also when an ancient volcano erupted; huge ash flows—a mineral called tuff—covered the area north of what is today Katahdin. The heat and pressure of successive layers of ash flow compacted and metamorphosed the older layers. The rock that was created is called rhyolite. It is related to granite, but is harder and finer grained. Like granite, as the rhyolite cooled, it developed shrinkage fractures. Many of the formations you see on The Traveler resulted from the aging and weathering along these fracture lines. Unlike granite, rhyolite tends to break apart and crumble along the fracture lines. As a result much of The Traveler seems to be little more than a giant

The Traveler summit from the Peak of the Ridges.

pile of loose rocks. The Traveler is at the heart of this huge mass of rhyolite that also includes Black Cat and South Branch Mountains to the west and all the mountains north of Traveler in Baxter State Park. The mass of rhyolite is more than 10,000 feet thick and is made of at least 80 cubic miles of bedrock.

The Traveler has four peaks: the Peak of the Ridges, Traveler Peak, Traveler Ridge, and North Traveler. The hike crosses all four. Each is unique in appearance even though they are all part of the same rhyolite formation. This is in large part because of geological forces that have deformed the rock since it was formed, and weathering that has occurred more recently.

The Center Ridge Trail climbs steeply up toward Peak of the Ridges. As you climb, the views open up and the trail becomes almost entirely loose rocks. The peaks that stick up out of the ridge are rhyolite masses with abundant shrinkage fractures, which tended to create hexagonal columns of rock packed together. The varying size of the hexagons is a function of how quickly the rock cooled. Among the rocks, in protected pockets where soil has accumulated, blueberries and mountain ash flourish.

The hexagons are very obvious on the summit of Peak of the Ridges—that is if you can tear yourself away from the view to look at them. Beyond Turner and Wassataquoik Mountains, Katahdin looms. The North Peaks block a clear view of the Great Basin, but the Knife Edge stands out against the horizon. Farther west is the jumble of mountains that include Doubletop, The Brothers, and Mullen Mountain. To the east the scree-covered slopes of Traveler Peak rise to its long and irregular summit ridge. To the north, across Howe Brook Valley, the long ridge of North Traveler blocks everything beyond it.

From the Peak of the Ridges, the trail descends a rocky ridge that drops steeply on both sides—especially the south. The ridge is called the Little Knife Edge for its resemblance to the larger, more famous formation on Katahdin, visible on the horizon. The shrinkage fractures are very noticeable where the trail crosses atop the ridge.

The trail drops down into a wooded saddle, passing through a forest of smallish fir—a cool, shady respite from the open ridges of the last several miles. The ascent up Traveler Peak is on mostly loose rocks that are football-size and larger. The summit offers the same views as Peak of the Ridges with the addition of the East Branch Penobscot River winding through the woods below you to the east. It is the view of The Traveler from the East Branch that gave the mountain its name. Because The Traveler is such a large, irregularly shaped mountain, and because the East Branch takes such a sinuous course beneath it, early river drivers felt the mountain was moving, traveling along with them. Beyond the river are Sugarloaf and Mount Chase—two isolated mountains that are not part of the Traveler Rhyolite.

The descent off Traveler Peak is steep, but mostly not on loose rocks. There are abundant blueberries as well as numerous alpine plants, including mountain cranberry. After dropping into the woods to a noticeable notch, the trail climbs gently to cross Traveler Ridge. The ridge is generally open with views north around North Traveler to the mountains of the Five Ponds area. After crossing the unmarked high point on the ridge, the trail again drops steeply down into a forest of birch to a noticeable notch.

The climb up to the summit of North Traveler is surprisingly short and easy. The summit seems to be nothing more than a large pile of loose rocks. The rhyolite here has broken into smaller, flatter pieces that have weathered to a dusty orange due to iron in the rock.

The long descent to Lower South Branch Pond alternates between birch forest, grassy meadows, exposed bedrock cliff tops, and loose rock slides. Take your time and enjoy the varied and many views. Far below you, canoes and kayaks move around the pond. You may even see a moose swimming across the pond. Just before the trail drops into the woods for good, you get one last view of Katahdin on the horizon through Pogy Notch.

Miles and Directions

0.0 Start from the day-use area by walking past the ranger's station and through the campground.

0.2 Turn right off the campground road onto the Pogy Notch Trail.

0.3 Pass the North Traveler Trail.

1.0 The Pogy Notch Trail follows the shore of Lower South Branch Pond in the woods 100 yards back from the pond. Just past the south end of the pond, pass the Howe Brook Trail and cross Howe Brook. In the spring and after a rain, you will have to wade across the stream.

2.1 The trail crosses the woods between the Lower and Upper South Branch Ponds. Just when Upper South Branch Pond becomes visible through the trees, the trail bears left and climbs a rock face to the junction with the Center Ridge Trail. The junction is in a grove of

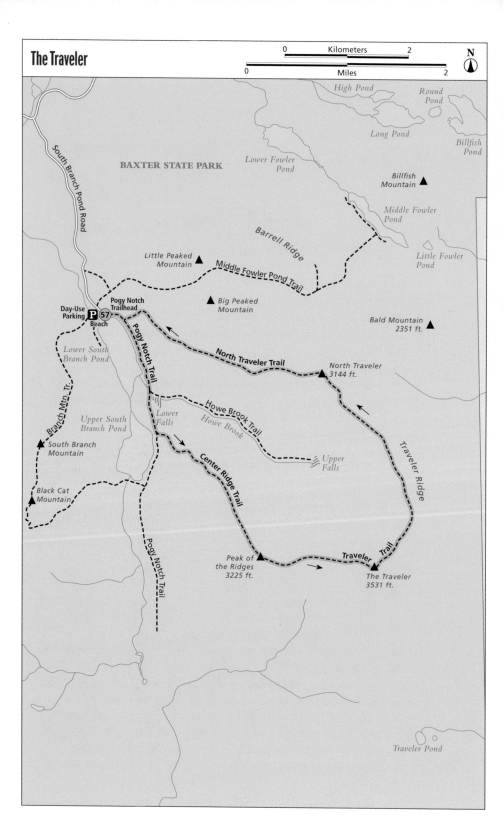

The Traveler

0 Kilometers 2
0 Miles 2

N

High Pond
Round Pond
Long Pond
Billfish Pond

BAXTER STATE PARK

Lower Fowler Pond

Billfish Mountain ▲

Middle Fowler Pond

South Branch Pond Road

Barrell Ridge

Little Fowler Pond

Little Peaked Mountain ▲

Middle Fowler Pond Trail

Pogy Notch Trailhead

Big Peaked Mountain ▲

Bald Mountain 2351 ft. ▲

Day-Use Parking P 57
Beach

Lower South Branch Pond

Pogy Notch Trail

North Traveler Trail

North Traveler 3144 ft. ▲

Branch Mtn. Tr.

Upper South Branch Pond

Lower Falls

Howe Brook Trail

Howe Brook

Traveler Ridge

South Branch Mountain ▲

Upper Falls

Black Cat Mountain ▲

Center Ridge Trail

Pogy Notch Trail

Peak of the Ridges 3225 ft. ▲

Traveler Trail

The Traveler 3531 ft. ▲

Traveler Pond

Peak of the Ridges from the trail ascending Traveler Peak.

red pines atop a high cliff that drops straight down into Upper South Branch Pond. Turn left onto the Center Ridge Trail.

2.8 The trail climbs very steeply, then switchbacks up the rocky ridge to the first peak on the ridge with views in every direction.

3.4 The trail climbs steadily over two other peaks to Peak of the Ridges. The "trail" is often over loose rocks and boulders among blueberries and mountain ash. The Center Ridge Trail ends on Peak of the Ridges; the trail continues as the Traveler Trail.

4.0 The trail descends steeply down a rock spine into the wooded saddle between Peak of the Ridges and Traveler Peak.

4.7 The trail climbs steadily up loose rocks and small groves of stunted trees to Traveler Peak.

5.4 The trail descends steeply to a wooded notch between Traveler Peak and Traveler Ridge.

6.3 The trail climbs gently to the long, open summit of Traveler Ridge. The unmarked high point of Traveler Ridge is at its far north end.

6.7 The trail descends steeply through birch to the notch between Traveler Ridge and North Traveler.

7.4 The trail climbs steadily along rock spines to North Traveler's summit, which is little more than a pile of small, broken rocks. The Traveler Trail ends on the summit; the trail continues as the North Traveler Trail.

9.8 The North Traveler Trail descends steadily, passing in and out of wooded areas and across open cliff tops. On the steepest sections the trail is covered with small, loose rocks. After a particularly steep section with a fine view of Katahdin to the south through Pogy Notch, the trail drops into the woods and descends steadily to the Pogy Notch Trail. Turn right to head back to the trailhead.

10.1 Arrive back at the day-use parking area.

58 Howe Brook Falls

The Howe Brook Trail follows Howe Brook from near where it flows into Lower South Branch Pond, upstream past a lower falls, and on to an upper falls. The lower falls is a long series of drops, pools, and sluices over and around exposed bedrock. You'll find several large swimming holes and sunny, flat rocks to dry out on. The upper falls is a single drop off a cliff that arcs across the valley. Just below the upper falls, you can explore Howe Brook. The section of the brook just below the upper falls is much like the lower falls, except even more vertical.

Start: From the day-use parking area at the end of South Branch Pond Road
Distance: 6.2 miles out and back
Hiking time: 3 to 4 hours
Difficulty: Moderate
Best seasons: June to Oct
Trail surface: Woodland path
Land status: Baxter State Park
Nearest town: Patten
Other trail users: None
Water availability: Lower South Branch Pond near the trailhead and Howe Brook

Canine compatibility: Dogs not allowed in Baxter State Park
Fees and permits: No fee or permits required for Maine residents; park entrance fee for nonresidents
Maps: *DeLorme: The Maine Atlas and Gazetteer:* map 51; USGS Traveler Mountain and Wassatoquoik Lake
Trail contact: Baxter State Park, (207) 723-5140; www.baxterstateparkauthority.com

Finding the trailhead: From the north entrance of Baxter State Park at the Matagamon Gate, drive 7 miles on Tote Road. Turn left onto South Branch Pond Road at the sign for South Branch Pond. Drive 1.9 miles to the end of the road and the day-use parking area. Begin the hike by walking into the campground past the ranger's station.
Trailhead GPS: N46 06.518' / W68 54.050'

The Hike

The landscape of Baxter State Park is one shaped by water. Most famously, the glaciers of the last ice age scraped the mountains down to granite bedrock and left the nearly vertical-sided bowls of the basins of Katahdin. But, in fact, as the earth warmed and the ice retreated, water continued shaping the land. You can see this process being played out along the hike to Howe Brook Falls.

The first you see of Howe Brook, near where it flows into Lower South Branch Pond, it has a wide bed of football-size rocks, all worn round over time as the flowing water jostled them against one another. Most of the summer the stream almost disappears beneath the rocks, making for an easy, dry crossing. In the spring, overflowing with snowmelt, Howe Brook rages between its banks. Even after a hard summer rain, the water rises over the rocks, making a crossing a cold, wet prospect. The sound of

The first falls you come to on the Howe Brook Trail.

the stream rushing over the rocks fills the whole valley between The Traveler and South Branch Mountain.

The lower falls is not one waterfall but several hundred yards of drops, pools, and sluices. The water backs up behind exposed masses of bedrock and either slides in thin sheets over the rock or finds a weakness in the rock and creates a crack that it widens year by year. The pools collect rounded rocks visible through the crystal clear water. In places the stream has undercut overhanging rock faces, creating shaded pools overhung by cedars. Mostly, though, the lower falls is a sunny place with expanses of bare bedrock. The rock is kept smooth and clear by annual scourings of spring runoff. During the summer they make for great places to sit and sun after a dip in one of the cool pools.

The trail beyond the lower falls is washed out in several places, forcing you to either step from stone to stone in the streambed or struggle on the steep slopes above Howe Brook, improvising a trail. These washouts occur on the outside of bends in the stream, where the water beats on the streambank, trying to go straight rather than bend with the streambed. Over time the stream gets wider and rockier. The hardwood trees of the surrounding forest hold the bank in place with their roots. Roots and rocks stick out of the undercut banks, as the smaller, lighter soil and rocks fall away.

The upper falls is a single drop off a 20-foot cliff that arcs from bank to bank. You can see the bedding in the rock and its uneven weathering, which is very different from the smooth, hard rock at the lower falls. Just downstream from the upper falls the bedrock is more like that around the lower falls. If you explore downstream, you'll see where the stream flows through a series of cracks in the bedrock. Some are

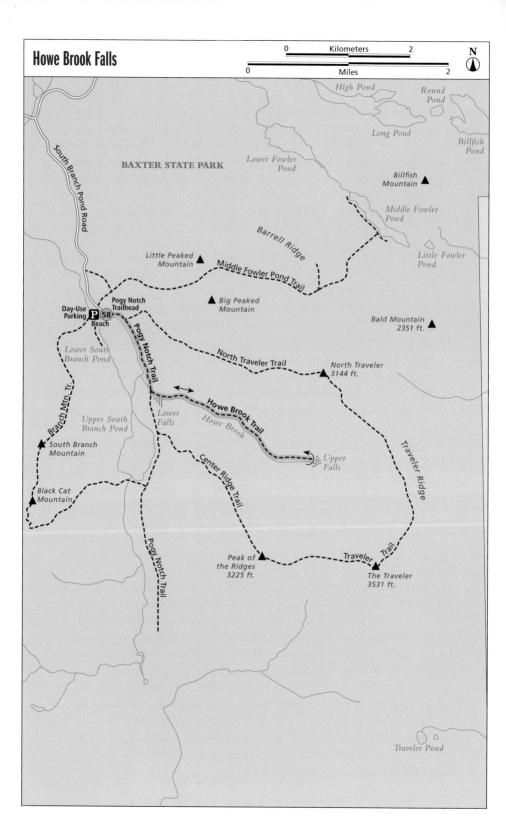

Kilometers

Miles

N

BAXTER STATE PARK

South Branch Pond Road

High Pond

Round Pond

Long Pond

Billfish Pond

Lower Fowler Pond

Billfish Mountain ▲

Middle Fowler Pond

Little Peaked Mountain ▲

Middle Fowler Pond Trail

Little Fowler Pond

Barrell Ridge

Pogy Notch Trailhead

Big Peaked Mountain ▲

Bald Mountain 2351 ft. ▲

Day-Use Parking P 58

Beach

Lower South Branch Pond

Pogy Notch Trail

North Traveler Trail

North Traveler 3144 ft. ▲

Branch Mtn. Tr.

Upper South Branch Pond

Lower Falls

Howe Brook Trail

Howe Brook

Upper Falls

Traveler Ridge

South Branch Mountain ▲

Center Ridge Trail

Black Cat Mountain ▲

Pogy Notch Trail

Peak of the Ridges 3225 ft. ▲

Traveler Trail

The Traveler 3531 ft. ▲

Traveler Pond

very narrow still; others have widened to where you would not call them cracks any longer.

High above Howe Brook, unseen through the hardwood forest, rise the several peaks of The Traveler. The mountain makes a half circle around Howe Brook's valley. The bare summits of the mountain are rhyolite in various stages of weathering. The hard, volcanic rhyolite originated in the same volcanic activity as the smooth bedrock of the lower falls and below the upper falls. Glaciers scoured out the valley that Howe Brook flows down to Lower South Branch Pond, and now the stream continues to eat into the bedrock. Year by year the water subtly alters the course of the stream, carrying more and more of the mountain down to the pond. In our lifetimes, these changes are small and seen only in the rearranging of rock in the streambed and the undercutting of the stream's banks.

Miles and Directions

0.0 Start by walking past the ranger's station and through the campground.

0.2 Turn right onto the Pogy Notch Trail. Remember to sign in at the trailhead.

0.3 Pass the North Traveler Trail.

0.9 The trail circles around Lower South Branch Pond to a small beach where canoeists leave their boats to continue on foot.

1.0 Turn left onto the Howe Brook Trail.

1.2 The trail follows the stream to the beginning of the lower falls—a series of drops, pools, and sluices that continue for more than 0.1 mile.

3.1 The trail follows Howe Brook, turning away from the stream to make the last climb to the upper falls where the trail ends. Be sure to explore Howe Brook downstream from the falls where it drops through a series of sluices. To complete the hike, return the way you came.

6.2 Arrive back at the trailhead.

59 Doubletop Mountain

Doubletop Mountain rises west of Nesowadnehunk Stream. The two peaks offer fine views across the valley as well as of Katahdin. Situated on the western boundary of Baxter State Park, you can see most of the park from the summit. If you turn away from Katahdin, you can see across the lakes country south and west of the park. The middle section of the climb is very steep, but involves only a little rock scrambling. The easiest and safest route is to hike out and back from Nesowadnehunk Field; the trail from Kidney Pond is steeper and longer.

Start: From the Doubletop Mountain trailhead west of the parking area at the sign-in box next to the bridge over Nesowadnehunk Stream
Distance: 7.6 miles out and back
Hiking time: 5 to 6 hours
Difficulty: Strenuous
Best seasons: June to Sept
Trail surface: Woodland path
Land status: Baxter State Park
Nearest town: Millinocket
Other trail users: None

Water availability: Nesowadnehunk Stream at the trailhead and Doubletop Stream at mile 1.8
Canine compatibility: Dogs not allowed in Baxter State Park
Fees and permits: No fee or permits required for Maine residents; park entrance fee for nonresidents
Maps: DeLorme: The Maine Atlas and Gazetteer: map 50; USGS Doubletop Mountain
Trail contact: Baxter State Park, (207) 723-5140; www.baxterstateparkauthority.com

Finding the trailhead: From the south entrance of Baxter State Park at the Togue Pond Gate, drive 16.7 miles on Tote Road. Turn left into the Nesowadnehunk Field camground. The day-use parking is 0.2 mile farther next to the ranger's station, before the end of the road. The trailhead is at the sign-in box next to the bridge over Nesowadnehunk Stream.
Trailhead GPS: N45 58.570' / W69 04.696'

The Hike

Doubletop Mountain is a narrow ridge that rises sharply above Nesowadnehunk Stream west of Katahdin. Its relative isolation makes it stand out even more, visible off and on from Tote Road from Daicey Pond north all the way to Nesowadnehunk Lake. The mountain's east face, the one you see from the road, is so steep that huge areas of it are bare rock. The Doubletop Mountain Trail goes over the mountain from Nesowadnehunk Field to Kidney Pond. But because the south face of the mountain is much steeper than the north ridge, it's easiest to climb the mountain from Nesowadnehunk Field and return the same way. You could hike the mountain as a shuttle, but be warned that the descent off South Peak toward Kidney Pond is among the steepest trails in the state, with several rock faces that need to be negotiated.

Starting from Nesowadnehunk Field the trail crosses Nesowadnehunk Stream and passes through the campground. The trail leaves the south end of the campground and follows along the stream. The first mile is an easy climb through hardwoods. After a short, steep descent the trail crosses Doubletop Stream. This is where the climb begins. At first the trail climbs through hardwoods, the trail composed of dirt and rocks. Soon the forest transitions to evergreens, and the trail becomes rockier with some slabs of bedrock to scale. You begin to get partial views through the trees to the north.

After gaining more than 1,200 feet in 0.7 mile, the trail levels out. Just in case you thought you might be on the summit ridge, there is an old sign nailed to a tree letting you know that the summit is still a mile away. The trail weaves through evergreens and moss, not climbing for much of that mile. After a steep climb that is as much rock scrambling as hiking, you reach the North Summit. This is the higher of the two summits; it is a large square boulder that sits on the ridgetop, rising above the stunted spruce. The sign marking the summit is 20 feet below you in a small clearing

Doubletop Mountain from the south, along Nesowadnehunk Stream.

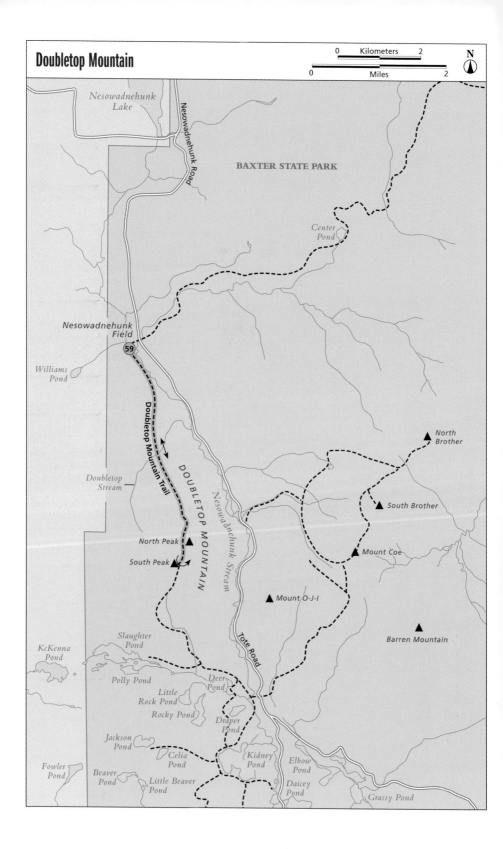

Doubletop Mountain

0 — Kilometers — 2
0 — Miles — 2

N

Nesowadnehunk Lake

Nesowadnehunk Road

BAXTER STATE PARK

Center Pond

Nesowadnehunk Field

59

Williams Pond

Doubletop Mountain Trail

Doubletop Stream

DOUBLETOP MOUNTAIN

Nesowadnehunk Stream

North Peak

South Peak

North Brother

South Brother

Mount Coe

Mount O-J-I

Barren Mountain

Tote Road

Slaughter Pond

KcKenna Pond

Polly Pond

Little Rock Pond

Rocky Pond

Deer Pond

Draper Pond

Jackson Pond

Celia Pond

Kidney Pond

Elbow Pond

Fowler Pond

Beaver Pond

Little Beaver Pond

Daicey Pond

Grassy Pond

where the trail continues. From the summit you have fine views of the mountains across Nesowadnehunk Valley: Mount O-J-I, the North and South Brothers, and Mount Coe. Behind them looms the granite mass of Katahdin.

The trail drops down from the peak to the north and loops around, dropping slightly, to the narrow saddle between the two peaks. Especially to the east, the ridge drops off nearly vertically. The trail crosses the uneven granite atop the cliffs. South Peak rises slightly, a large boulder sitting on a sheet of bedrock surrounded by cliffs on three sides. Below you are a string of ponds that Nesowadnehunk Stream winds between.

▶ *Nesowadnehunk* is a Penobscot word meaning "stream flowing between mountains." The name has also been spelled *sowadnehunk* or *souadnehunk*—both of which are closer to the pronunciation. It is pronounced "sourd-knee-hunk."

The Doubletop Mountain Trail tumbles down the west face of the mountain, trending south toward Kidney Pond. The steepest sections are invisible in trees that don't quite reach the summit ridge. From below, near Kidney Pond, Doubletop Mountain looks like a nearly perfect triangle, capped with bare granite. This view is looking end-on at the mountain to South Peak. From Ledge Falls, along Tote Road between Kidney Pond and Nesowadnehunk Field, you get a better view of the whole east face of the mountain with its two peaks. Doubletop is one of those picture perfect mountains that demand to be climbed. And the view from the peaks rewards the work and fulfills all expectations.

Miles and Directions

0.0 Start from the sign-in box next to the bridge over Nesowadnehunk Stream.

0.3 The trail crosses the bridge and turns left, following the stream through the campground. At the end of the campground, the woods road becomes a trail.

1.8 The trail climbs gently, then descends to ford Doubletop Stream.

2.5 The trail begins climbing steeply immediately across Doubletop Stream. When the trail begins to level out, you pass an old sign informing hikers that it is another 1 mile to the North Peak.

3.4 The trail climbs gently along the summit ridge, then steeply to North Peak. The sign for the peak is 20 feet below the rock summit.

3.8 The trail drops off North Peak and crosses the mostly open saddle between the two peaks along cliff tops with views across Nesowadnehunk Valley. South Peak is a rocky projection that hangs off the south end of the summit ridge. To complete the hike, return the way you came. (*Option:* The Doubletop Mountain Trail continues by dropping very steeply off the west side of the summit ridge, reaching Kidney Pond in 4.3 miles. You could use this trail to cross over the mountain and make the hike an 8.1-mile shuttle hike.)

7.6 Arrive back at the trailhead.

60 South Turner Mountain

The summit of South Turner Mountain offers the best view of Katahdin there is. The hike up the mountain is relatively flat to and around Sandy Stream Pond. There are three side trails of bog boards to the pond that give you a chance to look for moose and ducks. Beyond the pond the trail is very steep up South Turner Mountain; the final push to the summit is up a slide of loose rocks. From the summit you not only have the best view of Katahdin, but also can see almost all of Baxter State Park and the North Woods beyond.

Start: From the Roaring Brook ranger's station at the north end of the parking area

Distance: 4.0 miles out and back

Hiking time: 3 to 4 hours

Difficulty: Strenuous; second mile of the hike climbs more than 1,500 feet

Best seasons: June to Sept

Trail surface: Woodland path and rock slide to the summit

Land status: Baxter State Park

Nearest town: Millinocket

Other trail users: None

Water availability: Roaring Brook near the trailhead, Sandy Stream at mile 0.8, and a spring at mile 1.6

Canine compatibility: Dogs not allowed in Baxter State Park

Fees and permits: No fees or permits required for Maine residents; park entrance fee for non-residents. All hikers need a reservation to park at the trailhead. Reservations can be made up to 3 months in advance by calling (207) 723-5140 or online at www.baxterstatepark authority.com.

Maps: *DeLorme: The Maine Atlas and Gazetteer:* map 51; USGS Katahdin Lake

Trail contact: Baxter State Park, (207) 723-5140; www.baxterstateparkauthority.com

Finding the trailhead: From the Togue Pond Gate at the south entrance, turn right onto Roaring Brook Road and drive 8 miles to the end of the road. Hiker parking is in the lot to the left. The hike begins at the ranger's station—where you need to sign in before hiking—at the north end of the parking area.

Trailhead GPS: N45 55.180' / W68 51.444'

The Hike

Every morning throughout the summer, dozens of cars pull into the parking lot at the end of Roaring Brook Road. Hikers get out and mill around, readying themselves. In dribbles and drams they head into the woods. Almost all of them are hiking up Katahdin to look out across the seemingly endless North Woods. Very few of them head to other trails to explore those endless woods or to climb other mountains and gaze at Katahdin. The hike from Roaring Brook to South Turner Mountain offers the chance to do both.

The hike begins at the often crowded Roaring Brook ranger's station, crosses Roaring Brook, and disappears into the solitude of the woods. The trail skirts around

Looking up to the summit from the base of the slide on South Turner Mountain.

Sandy Stream Pond where there are three short side trails of bog boards that go to the pond's edge. In the morning or evening, this is one of the best places in Baxter State Park to find moose. Often fingers of mist drift over the pond as ducks quietly bob on the water. South Turner Mountain rises steeply to the north.

The trail loops around the pond, crosses Sandy Stream, then heads toward South Turner Mountain. The trail becomes a boulder hop for a few hundred yards, then begins to climb relentlessly through a mixed hardwood forest. A little less than halfway up the mountain, a side trail leads to a spring at the head of a small brook. The stream tumbles noisily down the mountain toward Sandy Stream. Above the spring the trail becomes rockier and the woods transition to evergreens.

The trail arrives at a level spot at the bottom of a slide. To the west you can see Katahdin. Baxter Peak is hidden behind Pamola Peak, but you can look directly into North Basin and see the arc of Katahdin around Great Basin. The bottom of the slide is mostly small, orangish rocks. As you look up the slide, the rocks get larger and grayer, ending at a bare bedrock dome. You can see, 175 feet almost straight above you, the wooden sign on the summit. There are blazes on the rocks up the slide, but the easiest way to the summit is to pick a likely route and make your own way. As you near the summit, the loose rock gives way to bedrock and easier climbing.

The view from the summit is unparalleled. Not only do you have the best view of Katahdin there is, but you can also see almost all of Baxter State Park. To the north, across North Turner Mountain, is The Traveler, and to its west, Black Cat Mountain. Closer, you can see the mountains around Russell Pond and, amazingly, Wassataquoik Lake nestled among them. Below you to the east is Katahdin Lake and the hazy,

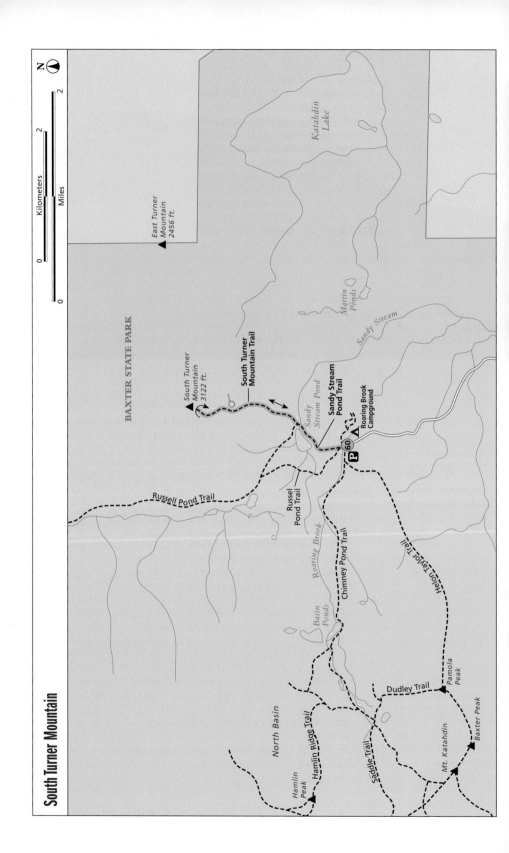

South Turner Mountain

BAXTER STATE PARK

East Turner Mountain 2456 ft.

South Turner Mountain 3122 ft.

South Turner Mountain Trail

Sandy Stream Pond Trail

Sandy Stream Pond

Roaring Brook Campground

Russell Pond Trail

Russel Pond Trail

Roaring Brook

Basin Ponds

Chimney Pond Trail

Helon Taylor Trail

Pamola Peak

Dudley Trail

North Basin

Hamlin Peak

Hamlin Ridge Trail

Saddle Trail

Mt. Katahdin

Baxter Peak

Katahdin Lake

Martin Ponds

Sandy Stream

N

Kilometers

Miles

P 60

South Turner Mountain from across Sandy Stream Pond on the hike to the mountain.

endless woods. As you stand on the summit, turning from view to view, remember that less than 3 miles away nearly a hundred hikers crowd Katahdin's summits and flanks. You have South Turner Mountain all to yourself, except for maybe a scolding junco or two.

Miles and Directions

0.0 Start from the Roaring Brook ranger's station at the north end of the parking area. Be sure to sign in for the hike on the porch of the ranger's station. In 400 feet turn right onto the Russell Pond Trail and cross Roaring Brook.

0.1 Turn right onto the Sandy Stream Pond Trail.

0.5 A side trail leads to Sandy Stream Pond. This side trail loops back to the main trail.

0.6 The Big Rock Viewpoint Trail leads 100 feet to Sandy Stream Pond.

0.7 The trail crosses Sandy Stream.

0.8 A side trail leads 100 feet to Sandy Stream Pond.

0.9 Turn right onto the South Turner Mountain Trail.

1.6 The South Turner Mountain Trail is flat, winding among and over boulders for 0.1 mile, then climbs steadily to the side trail that leads 200 feet to a spring.

1.9 Past the spring the trail steepens, coming out at the bottom of a slide.

2.1 The trail climbs the slide to the open summit with 360-degree views. To complete the hike, return the way you came.

4.0 Arrive back at the trailhead. Remember to sign out at the ranger's station.

61 Niagara Falls

Big and Little Niagara Falls on Nesowadnehunk Stream are two of Baxter State Park's wilder waterfalls. They are also among the most accessible. The short hike along the southbound Appalachian Trail is an easy walk on a wide, flat trail through an evergreen forest full of rocks and moss. The hike first visits the Toll Dam, a remnant of Nesowadnehunk Stream's history of log drives. Below the dam are the two falls and the rapids above and below them. At each falls are large areas of granite that you can climb on and explore, offering different views of each falls.

Start: From the day-use parking area where the Appalachian Trail crosses Daicey Pond Road

Distance: 3.0 miles out and back

Hiking time: 2 to 3 hours

Difficulty: Easy

Best seasons: June to Sept

Trail surface: Woodland path

Land status: Baxter State Park

Nearest town: Millinocket

Other trail users: None

Water availability: Nesowadnehunk Stream at the Toll Dam

Canine compatibility: Dogs not allowed in Baxter State Park

Fees and permits: No fee or permits required for Maine residents; park entrance fee for nonresidents

Maps: *DeLorme: The Maine Atlas and Gazetteer:* map 50; USGS Doubletop Mountain and Rainbow Lake East

Trail contact: Baxter State Park, (207) 723-5140; www.baxterstateparkauthority.com

Finding the trailhead: From the south entrance of Baxter State Park at Togue Pond Gate, drive 10.1 miles on Tote Road. Turn left onto Daicey Pond Road at the sign for Daicey Pond. Drive 1.5 miles; the day-use parking is on the right where the Appalachian Trail crosses the road. The hike follows the southbound AT.

Trailhead GPS: N45 52.940' / W69 01.909'

The Hike

Nesowadnehunk Stream runs for 17 miles from Little Nesowadnehunk Lake just west of Baxter State Park south to the Penobscot River. The first 5 miles from the lake to Nesowadnehunk Field drops very little. Between Nesowadnehunk Field and Kidney Pond Road, the stream is much wilder, dropping in a series of falls and rapids, including Ledge Falls along Tote Road. Between Kidney Pond and Daicey Pond, Nesowadnehunk Stream is relatively flat again, winding among ponds and marshy areas choked with alder. Below Daicey Pond the stream begins a wild descent to the Penobscot River. The two largest waterfalls in this section of Nesowadnehunk Stream are Little and Big Niagara Falls.

Beginning in the mid-1800s, Nesowadnehunk Stream was the waterway used to float logs from what is now western Baxter State Park to the Penobscot River—and on to Bangor or Old Town to be milled. Nesowadnehunk Field was created as a farm to raise grain and food for the animals used in the logging operations as well as the loggers themselves. Along Tote Road between Kidney Pond and Ledge Falls, there is a memorial cross to the unknown river driver—a testament to the dangers and wildness of Nesowadnehunk Stream. The hike, which follows the Appalachian Trail to the falls, first passes the old Toll Dam. Most of the dam has been washed away over the years, but part of it still clings to the far shore of the stream. This dam was used to regulate the waterflow down Nesowadnehunk Stream during the log drives. From the site of the Toll Dam, you can look upstream and see Mount O-J-I framed by the stream.

A short distance farther southbound on the AT, you come to a side trail to Little Niagara Falls. The trail leads out onto a flat expanse of granite that Nesowadnehunk Stream veers around before plunging into a deep pool. Rumor has it that this pool offers some of the region's best wild trout fishing. You can climb around on the rock here and get several different perspectives on Little Niagara Falls. When the stream is

Little Niagara Falls.

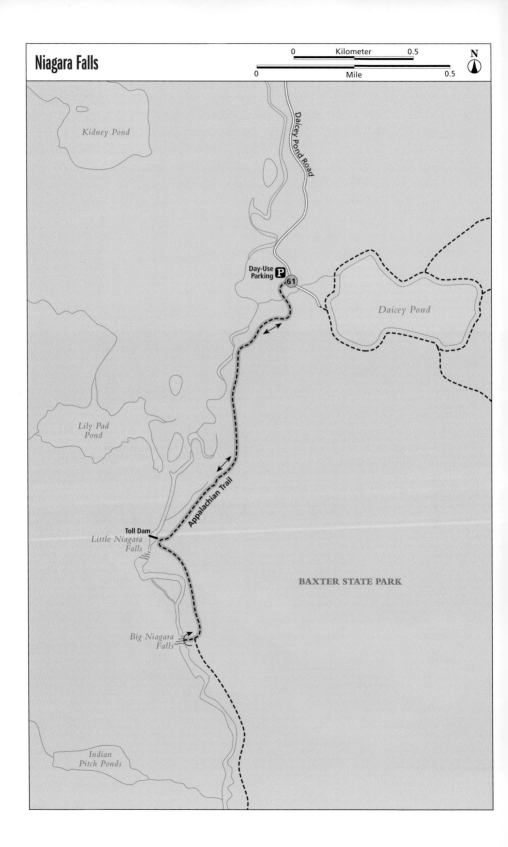

Niagara Falls

0   Kilometer   0.5
0   Mile   0.5

N

Kidney Pond

Daicey Pond Road

Day-Use
Parking **P**
61

Daicey Pond

Lily Pad
Pond

Appalachian Trail

Toll Dam
*Little Niagara
Falls*

BAXTER STATE PARK

*Big Niagara
Falls*

*Indian
Pitch Ponds*

running low, a large sandy beach along the pool is exposed and is a good swimming spot.

Big Niagara Falls is about half a mile farther downstream. The falls are somewhat higher and more of a plunge than Little Niagara Falls. Rather than a pool below the falls, there is a jumble of huge boulders—many with trees growing on top—that Nesowadnehunk Stream makes its way around. Looking downstream from Big Niagara Falls gives you a good idea of what Nesowadnehunk Stream looks like the rest of the way to the Penobscot River.

After exploring both falls, enjoy the easy hike back to the trailhead through the evergreen forest full of rocks and moss.

Miles and Directions

0.0   Start from the southbound Appalachian Trail at the south end of the parking area.

0.1   Junction with the Daicey Pond Trail. Turn right and continue on the southbound AT.

0.8   A marked side trail leads 200 feet to the Toll Dam site on Nesowadnehunk Stream.

0.9   A marked side trail leads 300 feet to the top of Little Niagara Falls.

1.4   A marked side trail leads 500 feet to the top of Big Niagara Falls. To complete the hike, return the way you came.

3.0   Arrive back at the trailhead.

Options

You can lengthen the hike as much as you want by following the AT as it follows the stream past several named and unnamed falls and rapids, the last within sight of the Penobscot River. If you're feeling very adventurous, you can cross Nesowadnehunk Stream below Little Niagara Falls to find a trail on the other side of the stream that runs north to Lily Pad Pond and south to Windy Pitch Pond. This 0.9-mile-long trail between these two small ponds is not connected to any other trails or to a trailhead.

Honorable Mentions

M Barrell Ridge

Barrell Ridge is a narrow mountain north of The Traveler and southwest of the Fowler Ponds. From the ridge's open summit, The Traveler looms to the south. If you can tear your eyes away from its high, rocky summit, you can see Little and Big Peaked Mountains to the west and the Fowler Ponds and Billfish Mountain to the east. The 6.6-mile out-and-back hike begins at the Ledges trailhead along South Branch Pond Road, 0.1 mile north of the day-use parking at the end of the road. Follow the Middle Fowler Pond Trail east, climbing steadily between Little and Big Peaked Mountains. The trail crosses Dry Brook just below a waterfall, then climbs to a notch. Just below the notch a 0.3-mile side trail leads steeply up to Barrell Ridge's open summit. Even on sunny summer days, you are likely to have the whole mountain to yourself. To find the trailhead, enter Baxter State Park through the north entrance. On Tote Road drive 7.3 miles past the Matagamon Gate to South Branch Pond Road. Turn left onto South Branch Pond Road and drive 2.3 miles to the day-use parking at the end of the road. The trailhead is 0.1 mile back up the road on the right. For more information contact Baxter State Park, (207) 723-5140; baxterstate parkauthority.com.

N The Sentinel

The Sentinel is so named because it appears like a guard from the Penobscot River, protecting the higher mountains to its north. The mountain, in the southwest corner of Baxter State Park, is only 1,837 feet high, but rises more than 1,000 feet above Nesowadnehunk Deadwater on the Penobscot River. The 5.6-mile out-and-back hike begins at Kidney Pond. There is a 0.6-mile loop trail around the semi-open summit with fine views of the Penobscot River valley to the south and Katahdin and the surrounding mountains to the north. Along the way, blueberries grow in great quantities. To find the trailhead, enter Baxter State Park's south entrance. On Tote Road drive 10.6 miles past the Togue Pond Gate to Kidney Pond Road. Turn left onto Kidney Pond Road and drive 0.9 mile to the end of the road. The trailhead is at the south end of the parking area. For more information contact Baxter State Park, (207) 723-5140; www.baxterstateparkauthority.com.

The North Country

Maine's North Country is within Aroostook County, which is the largest county east of the Mississippi River, larger than Connecticut and Rhode Island combined. Mainers simply refer to it as "The County." This part of Maine was contested between France and Britain and later between the United States and Britain. The boundary between Canada and Maine was not agreed upon until after Maine became a state in 1820. Many of the

Two hikers cross the base of the slide on Deboullie Mountain, moving west along the shore of Deboullie Pond (hike 64).

people who settled in The County were French speaking. Even today their French culture and accent are part of the region's charm.

Aroostook County is divided into two distinct areas, roughly along the line that ME 11 follows north from Patten to Fort Kent. East of ME 11 is rolling farm country, famous for its potatoes. Almost all the people who live in The County live in the towns along the Aroostook and St. John Rivers near the New Brunswick border in the eastern part of the county. Geologically, this area is a northern extension of the Central Highlands. You can see this in the mountains of the region that seem to be randomly strewn across the land. The hikes in this part of Aroostook County offer stunning views of distant mountains, especially those in Baxter State Park, and a patchwork of dark spruce forest and potato fields.

West of ME 11 the country is very different. The land is almost entirely forested, owned mostly by multi-national timber and paper companies. There are no incorporated towns except right along the St. John River. There are virtually no paved or public roads in this part of Maine. The woods are broken by a spider's web of gravel logging roads; there are more miles of logging roads in Maine than public roads. These roads are generally open to traffic, but are regulated by a series of staffed gates where visitors need to register and pay a fee.

This was the last part of the state covered with glacial ice. The land is overlain by a thick layer of glacial debris, hiding the bedrock and smoothing out the topography. The hidden bedrock is not the altered and metamorphosed rock that is typical of the rest of Maine. Here the bedrock is mostly undisturbed shale and sandstone. Where bedrock is exposed, you can often find fossils in the rock.

The North Country region contains the headwaters of several of Maine's major rivers: the Penobscot, and the St. John's and its tributaries. This is the famous Allagash Country. The best way to see this wild land is by canoe. A hiker has to be content with gazing out across this country from one of the mountains near its edges.

62 Mount Chase

The hike up Mount Chase, named for a man who started a forest fire at the behest of a Bangor timber baron, follows the old fire warden's trail. The trail begins in hardwood forest and climbs through mixed forest to a spruce forest near the summit. The small open area on the summit offers fine 360-degree views, most notably of the mountains of Baxter State Park to the southwest.

Start: From the trailhead 100 feet west on the two-track past the parking area
Distance: 3.6 miles out and back
Hiking time: 2 to 3 hours
Difficulty: Moderate
Best seasons: June to Oct
Trail surface: Woodland path
Land status: Private timberlands
Nearest town: Patten

Other trail users: Hunting allowed on the timberlands; lower section of the trail used by ATVs
Water availability: None
Canine compatibility: Dogs must be under control at all times
Fees and permits: No fees or permits required
Maps: *DeLorme: The Maine Atlas and Gazetteer:* map 52; USGS Island Falls
Trail contact: None

Finding the trailhead: From I-95 exit 264 drive north on ME 158, which changes to ME 11, for 9.5 miles to Patten. Drive north through Patten on ME 11, passing ME 159, which leads to the north entrance of Baxter State Park. Drive north on ME 11 past ME 159 for 6.4 miles and turn left onto the gravel Mountain Road. There is a street sign at the corner. Drive 2.1 miles west on Mountain Road to a clearing where you can park on the right. Beyond the clearing the road becomes a narrow two-track. The trailhead is 100 feet down this two-track on the right. There are two signs for the hike at the trailhead. The last 0.5 mile of the road is narrow and fairly rough. Many people park in a small clearing past the borrow pit and walk the last road section.
Trailhead GPS: N46 05.650' / W68 28.131'

The Hike

According to local legend one of Bangor's timber barons wanted to chase the Canadian loggers from the area around Patten so he could log the area. He hired a man named Chase to come north and burn the hay fields where the Canadians grew feed for their animals. The timber baron figured if the Canadians couldn't feed their animals they would leave the area, opening the resources for him. Mr. Chase started the fire as directed, except it grew out of control and burned several townships of forest. To escape the fire, Chase climbed the mountain that now bears his name and was forced to stay there for more than a week, surviving on blueberries. He stayed on the mountain and dreamed of the cool, clear water of the Shin Ponds below him, unable to come down off the mountain because of the heat in the burning woods.

No one seems to know what year this fire took place, if indeed it really happened. It had to have been before 1864 when the town of Mount Chase was incorporated.

The mountains of Baxter State Park from the summit of Mount Chase.

It is true that fires were common in and around timber operations in the nineteenth century. For example, in 1903 a huge fire burned 132 square miles of forest in what is now Baxter State Park. The fires started west of Mount Chase, near The Traveler. Many of these fires burned so hot they sterilized the land for years. It has even been suggested that most of Maine's bare mountaintops—including Mount Chase—resulted from fires that burned off the trees and the soils. Without soil, trees were not able to regrow on these mountaintops. Whatever the truth is behind the story of Mount Chase's name and the origin of its bald summit, that summit offers one of Maine's best views.

The hike climbs the old woods road to the fire warden's cabin, which still stands. ATVs also use this trail so it is wide and not particularly steep. Beyond the cabin the trail becomes a footpath that climbs the rocky mountain. High on the shoulder of the mountain, a rough side trail leads to a rocky dome known locally as Eagle Point. The views from it are the same as from the summit—plus a view of Mount Chase's summit. Past this side trail the trail climbs steeply through increasingly stunted spruce and fir to the open summit. From below—and Mount Chase is visible from a fair distance in every direction because the surrounding country is relatively flat—Mount Chase appears to have a tree-covered summit. The open area on the summit is not large, but it is enough to offer fine views in every direction. The most dramatic view is of the mountains in Baxter State Park, all visible to the southwest. To the north you can see, it seems, all the way to Canada, across endless rolling forest lands dotted with lakes and low mountains. But the eye is drawn back to pick out Katahdin and Turner Mountain in the south of Baxter State Park and The Traveler in the north of the park.

Miles and Directions

0.0   Start from the trailhead 100 feet down the two-track west of the parking area. The trail is on the right marked with two homemade signs.

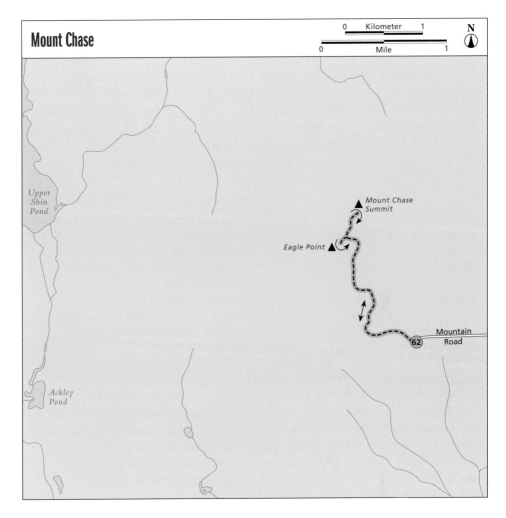

0.8 The trail crosses a skidder trail. Continue straight ahead on the trail.

1.1 The trail passes the abandoned fire warden's cabin. The trail bends to the left and reenters the woods. Just into the woods is a sign to the summit.

1.5 The trail climbs more steeply to a saddle between the summit and Eagle Point. A rough side trail leads to Eagle Point. The rock dome offers 360-degree views, including all the mountains of Baxter State Park and the forested summit of Mount Chase. To continue the hike, return back to the main trail.

1.7 Arrive back at the main trail; turn left and climb to the summit.

1.9 The trail climbs out of the forest to the open rock summit with 360-degree views. To complete the hike, return the way you came.

3.6 Arrive back at the trailhead.

63 Shin Brook Falls

Shin Brook Falls is one of Maine's highest and most scenic waterfalls. The hike to the falls is short and easy. The descent to the base of the falls can be challenging, but the view is worth the work. The pool below the falls is a fine swimming hole. Like so many waterfalls in Maine, Shin Brook Falls drops over dark slate. Nearby, where Shin Brook empties into the Seboeis River is Grand Pitch—a falls not as impressive as Shin Brook Falls, but worth hiking to. This falls is surrounded by a forest of towering pines. The 1.1-mile hike to it is relatively flat.

Start: From the trailhead west of the parking area where the road makes a turn to the right
Distance: 0.9 mile out and back
Hiking time: About 1 hour
Difficulty: Easy
Best seasons: June to Oct
Trail surface: Woodland path
Land status: Private woodlands
Nearest town: Patten

Other trail users: Hunting allowed on the private woodlands
Water availability: Shin Brook below the falls
Canine compatibility: Dogs must be under control at all times
Fees and permits: No fees or permits required
Maps: *DeLorme: The Maine Atlas and Gazetteer:* map 51; USGS Hay Brook Mountain
Trail contact: None

Finding the trailhead: From I-95 exit 264 drive north on ME 158, which becomes ME 11, for 10 miles to Patten. Turn left onto ME 159 (Shin Pond Road) at the sign for the north entrance to Baxter State Park. Drive 14.7 miles west, passing Shin Pond. (At Shin Pond the state route ends and the road name changes to Grand Lake Road, although there are no signs.) Turn left onto a gravel logging road; there is a wooden sign on a tree pointing to Shin Brook Falls. The turn is 0.9 mile east of where Grand Lake Road crosses the Seboeis River. Drive 0.3 mile south on the logging road (Shin Brook Falls Road, not signed). Park on the left where the road makes a sharp right turn. The trailhead is just west of the parking area on the south side of the road.
Trailhead GPS: N46 08.532' / W68 36.956'

The Hike

Sometimes in Maine you can find the most extraordinary things where you least expect. Shin Brook Falls is like that. Shin Brook is a short stream that runs from Shin Pond around Sugarloaf Mountain to the Seboeis River, a total distance of 5 miles. The falls is about halfway between Shin Pond and the Seboeis River. The stream bends around some slate bedrock, dropping twice over ledges that block the stream. Each drop is about 8 feet. Then the stream plunges 40 feet over a cleft in the slate. Huge, broken boulders lie in the falls and at its base. Mist hangs in the air above the pool beneath the falls and along the rock face next to the drop. It is one of Maine's highest and most scenic waterfalls.

The hike is relatively flat, passing through a mixed forest that has some wet spots—a good hike for a variety of spring wildflowers. The trail to the bottom of the falls

Shin Brook Falls.

is more like a scramble down a slide than a hike. But the view from the base of the falls is worth the effort. The pool at the bottom of the falls is ideal for swimming on a warm day. Because the stream flows roughly west at the falls, the falls and the pool tend to be in full sun during the summer. The dark slate rock warms up in the sun. After a swim in the cool stream, the warmth of the rocks is especially welcome. All this light and contrast also makes for great photographs.

The main trail leads out to the rocks at the top of the falls. You can stand on the edge of the stream right where it plunges off the drop. The trail loops upstream past the two smaller drops. The stream appears dark and calm in the pool below the falls. Then it wiggles out and winds away toward the Seboeis River. A few miles downstream, Shin Brook empties into the Seboeis River just below that river's Grand Pitch.

Miles and Directions

0.0   Start from the trailhead west of the parking area. There is a sign on a tree next to the trail.

0.1   The trail comes to a blocked-off ATV spur on the right. Turn left.

0.2   Turn right onto a trail that is marked with faded red flagging.

0.3   The trail descends steeply down to Shin Brook at the pool below the falls. To continue the hike, climb back up to the main trail.

0.4   Turn right onto the main trail.

0.5   Turn right onto a side trail marked with blue flagging. Past the blue-flagged trail the main trail is too wet to hike.

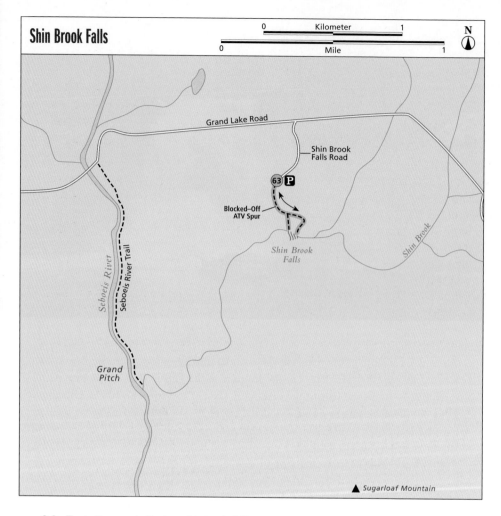

Shin Brook Falls

Kilometer

Mile

N

Grand Lake Road

Shin Brook
Falls Road

63 P

Blocked–Off
ATV Spur

Shin Brook
Falls

Shin Brook

Seboeis River

Seboeis River Trail

Grand
Pitch

▲ Sugarloaf Mountain

0.6 The trail comes to the top of the main falls and loops around upstream past the two upper falls. To complete the hike, return the way you came, passing the path to the bottom of the falls.

0.9 Arrive back at the trailhead.

Option

On Grand Lake Road, 1 mile west of the logging road that leads to the Shin Brook Falls trailhead, there is a parking area for the Seboeis River Trail. This trail follows the Seboeis River south for 1.1 miles from Grand Lake Road to Grand Pitch. You can climb up to the top of a rock face above the river to see the falls. Although not as impressive as Shin Brook Falls, Grand Pitch was too much for log drivers to boat down. The area around Grand Pitch is a forest of towering pines growing on irregular rock ledges, everything covered with moss and orange needles.

64 Deboullie Mountain

This hike in the Deboullie Public Reserved Land is among the most remote in the state. In a region of gentle rolling hills, these rocky mountains surrounded by ponds attract hikers and lots of anglers. The hike passes several ponds, climbs through mature hardwoods, crosses a large rock slide, offers expansive views of the North Woods, and goes by an ice cave. The hike is well worth the 28 miles of logging roads you have to drive to get to it.

Start: From the Black Pond trailhead at the north end of the parking lot
Distance: 6.1-mile loop
Hiking time: 3 to 5 hours
Difficulty: Moderate
Best seasons: June to Oct
Trail surface: Woodland path
Land status: Deboullie Public Reserved Land
Nearest town: Portage
Other trail users: Hunting allowed on Maine Public Reserved Lands; trails used by anglers to get to various ponds in the area

Water availability: Streams at miles 1.1 and 4.5
Canine compatibility: Dogs must be under control at all times
Fees and permits: Fee paid at the Fish River Gate
Maps: *DeLorme: The Maine Atlas and Gazetteer:* maps 62 and 63; USGS Deboullie Pond
Trail contact: Deboullie Public Reserved Land, (207) 435-7963; www.maine.gov/dacf/parks

Finding the trailhead: From the junction of ME 11 and ME 163 in Ashland, drive north on ME 11 for 10.9 miles to Portage. Turn left onto West Road. Drive 1 mile around the south shore of Portage Lake and turn left onto gravel Fish Lake Road. There is no street sign at the intersection, but there are numerous advertisements for commercial camps. Drive 4.3 miles on Fish Lake Road, passing through an active mill yard in the first mile, to the Fish River Gate. Stop and pay your entrance fee. Beyond the gate drive 1.8 miles, then turn right onto Hewes Brook Road; there is a road sign at this intersection. Drive 12.6 miles on Hewes Brook Road. Turn left onto an unmarked road; at the junction is a small blue sign for Deboullie Public Reserved Land and Red River Camps. Drive 7.8 miles, using the signs to Red River Camps as a guide, staying on the main road at each intersection. At a junction where a road comes downhill from the left, there is a brown state sign. Go straight toward Deboullie Pond for 0.2 mile to a fork. The left fork goes to Red River Camps; take the right fork to Deboullie Pond. Drive 0.6 mile to the end of the road, crossing the Red River where it flows out of Pushineer Pond and passing several marked campsites, a boat landing, and finally a privy. The trailhead is at the north end of the parking area at the sign.
Trailhead GPS: N46 57.860' / W68 50.226'

The Hike

The trek to Deboullie Mountain is one of the most remote hikes in Maine. The trailhead is more than 27 miles from a paved road. But the campsites in the Deboullie

Looking west from Deboullie Mountain across Gardner Mountain.

Public Reserved Land are generally full on weekends. Mainers are drawn to the natural beauty of the chain of ponds and the mountains that surround them. It doesn't hurt that the fishing is good. In fact, most of the people you are likely to see on the trails are carrying fly rods. Most of the trails in the reserved land lead to or circle around ponds. Two of the three trails this hike uses are exceptions to that.

The word *deboullie* is from a French word meaning "tumbledown" and refers to the south face of Deboullie Mountain. This face, which the hike descends, is very steep and rocky; the hike also crosses a large rock slide on the lower slopes of the mountain on the shore of Deboullie Pond. These mountains are more rugged than the gently rolling land around them. They are part of the divide between the Aroostook and Allagash watersheds. Farther southwest this same line of mountains divides the St. John and Penobscot watersheds. The bedrock in this part of Maine is the least altered by mountain building or volcanism. It is one of the only areas in the state where you can find fossil-bearing rock. Most of the region is covered by a thick layer of glacial bedrock, and where there is exposed bedrock you can often find scratches caused by moving glaciers. In most of Maine the scratches run from north to south. In theDeboullie Mountain area, they run southeast to northwest. This reversed ice flow is because this was the last part of the state covered with ice during the last ice age; as this last remnant of glacial ice melted, it drifted northwest, toward the St. Lawrence River.

The hike first passes Black and Little Black Ponds. A side trip to the Little Black Ponds offers a fine view of the mountains and the possibility of seeing moose, especially early in the day. The trail crosses the stream that runs between the ponds and then begins climbing Black Mountain through mature hardwoods. The very large trees allow enough light to reach the forest floor for ferns and wildflowers to grow. The trail loops up to the first overlook on the hike. Like most of the overlooks, the view here of Black Pond was enhanced by the trailbuilders removing some trees.

The trail then climbs to the long summit ridge of Black Mountain. As you are roller-coasting along through the mature hardwoods, be on the lookout for ruffed grouse—"partridge" as they're called in Maine. In early summer the hens will come right at you, head down, like they mean to attack. Then, when just a few feet away, they'll turn and move off, acting injured and mewing like a cat. They are trying to draw your attention away from their young. If you look in low branches near where the mother grouse began her display, you will often see several brown, robin-size, immature grouse sitting quietly.

There is one marked overlook on Black Mountain's summit ridge: The Pond Overlook has a broken view of Deboullie Pond and several of the smaller ponds to the south of Black Mountain. The trail then crosses over the unmarked summit and descends on the north side of the mountain through spruce. The hike to this point has been entirely through hardwoods. Generally you would expect to find a spruce forest higher on a mountain than the hardwoods, but Black Mountain's relatively low, flat summit ridge is ideal for hardwoods, and the steep sides of the mountain are better suited to spruce and other evergreens. On the north slope is the Fifth Pelletier Lake Overlook. Interestingly, the small horseshoe-shaped lake at the foot of the mountain is much smaller than the ponds on the south side of Black Mountain, demonstrating the arbitrariness of the use of "pond" and "lake" in Maine. The Pelletier Lakes drain north into the St. John River.

The descent into the saddle between Black and Deboullie Mountains is steep, dropping you back into a hardwood forest, but the climb up Deboullie Mountian is surprisingly gentle. As you come around the north side of Deboullie Mountain, you pass Gardner Slide Overlook. This slide is very similar to the one on the south slope

BUNCHBERRY

As you're walking through the woods, take a moment to examine a carpet of bunchberries. The leaves are oval with pointed ends and parallel veins. The white flowers have four large petals shaped much like the leaves and a green center made up of several small beads. Each of these beads later becomes a red berry. You may be thinking that the bunchberry's leaves and flowers look an awful lot like the leaves and flowers of a dogwood tree. In fact, bunchberry is a dogwood, one that has adapted to the northern woodlands. The carpet of individual bunchberry plants are actually all connected underground. You could say that bunchberry is a dogwood tree that has adapted to the cold winters of the northern woodlands by having the entire tree live underground except the leaves and flowers.

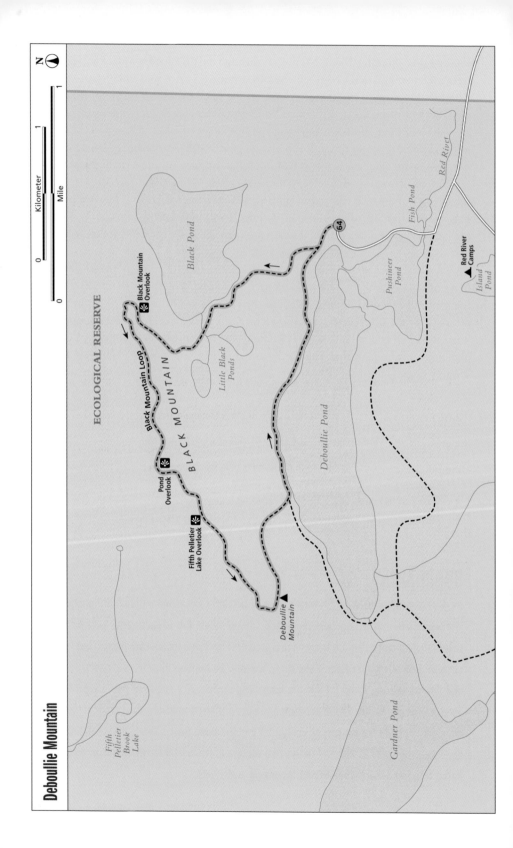

Deboullie Mountain

ECOLOGICAL RESERVE

Black Mountain Loop

Black Mountain Overlook

Pond Overlook

Fifth Pelletier Lake Overlook

BLACK MOUNTAIN

Black Pond

Little Black Ponds

Deboullie Mountain

Deboullie Pond

Fifth Pelletier Brook Lake

Gardner Pond

Pushineer Pond

Fish Pond

Red River

Red River Camps

Island Pond

64

N

Kilometer

Mile

0   1

0   1

of Deboullie Mountain that the trail crosses. You can see across Gardner Mountain to the Allagash Country beyond.

The summit of Deboullie Mountain, where the fire tower and fire warden's cabin occupy a small clearing, offers no views. But if you climb even partway up the fire tower, you get fine views in every direction. This is one of the tallest fire towers still standing in the state. The hike then descends on the old fire warden's trail. Not surprisingly, it is very steep. Once off the mountain the hike returns to the trailhead along the shore of Deboullie Pond, crossing a large rock slide and passing an ice cave. The small cave, marked with a sign, is a small hole in the ground that shows you have been walking on glacial debris, with space between the rocks covered with soil and trees. Water that filters down into the spaces between the rocks remains frozen year-round.

Miles and Directions

0.0 Start from the Black Pond trailhead at the north end of the parking area.

0.2 Junction of the Deboullie and Black Mountain Loop Trails. Turn right onto the Black Mountain Loop Trail toward Black Pond.

0.8 The trail skirts around Black Pond, passing a side trail to the Little Black Ponds.

1.1 The trail crosses the stream that runs from the Little Black Ponds to Black Pond.

1.6 The trail climbs through a mature hardwood forest to the Black Mountain Overlook with views south and east across Black Pond.

2.0 The trail climbs to the long summit ridge of Black Mountain, reaching the Pond Overlook with views south.

2.5 The trail roller-coasters along the summit ridge, crossing the unmarked summit.

2.6 The trail descends steeply down the north face of Black Mountain to the Fifth Pelletier Lake Overlook with views north.

3.1 Come to an unmarked overlook with views north and west.

3.3 The trail descends into the saddle between Deboullie and Black Mountains.

3.8 The trail ascends Deboullie Mountain gradually to the Gardner Slide Overlook with views west.

3.9 Reach the Deboullie Mountain summit where there is an abandoned fire warden's cabin and a tall tower that still has its cabin on top. The only unobstructed views from the summit are gained by climbing partway up the tower. To continue the hike, descend the Deboullie Mountain Trail down the south face of the mountain.

4.5 The trail descends, steeply at times, to a small stream.

4.6 The Deboullie Mountain Trail ends at the Deboullie Loop Trail. Deboullie Pond is 100 feet straight ahead. Turn left onto the Deboullie Loop Trail.

4.7 The trail crosses a rock slide.

5.5 The trail passes a marked ice cave. Even in summer ice is visible among the rocks under the thin layer of soil.

5.9 Arrive back at the junction with the Black Mountain Loop Trail. Go straight to return to the trailhead.

6.1 Arrive back at the trailhead.

65 Quaggy Joe Mountain

Quaggy Joe Mountain rises from the rolling hills of Aroostook County southwest of Presque Isle. The mountain is made of erosion-resistant rhyolite, a volcanic rock found in several parts of Maine. The mountain was formed when the softer sedimentary rock around Quaggy Joe Mountain eroded away, leaving a small, steep-sided mountain. The trails on the mountain reflect this geologic history: They are steep and rocky. North Peak offers fine views in every direction.

Start: From the trailhead on the east side of the parking area, away from the lake
Distance: 2.3-mile loop
Hiking time: 2 to 3 hours
Difficulty: Moderate
Best seasons: May to Oct; park open in winter for skiing and snowshoeing
Trail surface: Woodland path and park road
Land status: Aroostook State Park
Nearest town: Presque Isle
Other trail users: None

Water availability: Spigots 200 feet up the trail from the trailhead and in the campground
Canine compatibility: Dogs must be on a leash at all times. A section of the South Peak Trail is too steep with loose rocks to be safe for dogs.
Fees and permits: State park entrance fee
Maps: DeLorme: The Maine Atlas and Gazetteer: map 65; USGS Echo Lake
Trail contact: Aroostook State Park, (207) 768-8341; www.maine.gov/dacf/parks

Finding the trailhead: From Presque Isle drive south on US 1 for 3.8 miles. Turn right onto Spragueville Road at the sign for Aroostook State Park and drive 1.1 miles. Turn left onto State Park Road at the sign for the park and drive 0.9 mile to the entrance gate. After paying your fee, drive 0.1 mile to a fork. The campground is to the right; day-use parking is down to the left. The trailhead is on the west side of the parking area, uphill away from the lake. **Trailhead GPS:** N46 36.775' / W68 00.336'

The Hike

Aroostook County is best known for its potato farms in the river valleys and endless forested hills crisscrossed by logging roads and trout streams. Quaggy Joe Mountain rises from farmland near Presque Isle. The mountain is made of very dense and fine-grained rhyolite. This volcanic rock is found in a number of places around Maine, most notably Mount Kineo, The Traveler, and the Bold Coast. Rhyolite can be several different colors; Quaggy Joe Mountain rhyolite is orange or buff in color. It almost looks like the sedimentary rock that underlays most of Aroostook County.

Quaggy Joe Mountain was formed when, over time, the softer rock around the mountain eroded or was ground away by glaciers, but the harder rhyolite remained. The result is a mountain with very steep, rocky slopes. The trails up and down the mountain on the hike reflect that geologic history. But the first thing you'll probably notice is the spelling of Quaggy Joe on the sign near the trailhead. *Quaquajo* is the name given the mountain by local Indians. Depending on who you listen to, it either means "boundary mountain" or "twin-peaked."

The hike climbs the higher South Peak first. After walking from the parking area to the campground along a wide trail, you reach the South Peak Trail. The trail begins climbing steeply almost immediately. There are two places on the climb that have as much to do with rock climbing as hiking. For this reason, Aroostook State Park recommends not descending this trail or taking dogs or small children up it. The second climb is up a nearly vertical face of crumbling rhyolite. From the top of this climb you have views to the east.

There are no views from the south summit of Quaggy Joe Mountain, only a small clearing with a tower. Follow the Ridge Trail east off the summit toward North

Looking north toward Presque Isle from atop a steep section of trail. Yes, the trail comes up that rock face.

Peak. The trail descends through hardwoods. Notice the absence of boulders in the relatively open forest. Most mountains in Maine are littered with boulders, left behind by glaciers during the last ice age. The hard rhyolite may crumble, but it doesn't break into boulders. The glaciers scrubbed the mountain clean, leaving all the boulders and rubble in the valleys.

As the trail begins to climb North Peak, you'll notice the trail is often dusty with powdered rhyolite that looks a lot like sand. The trail passes a backcountry campsite with fine views to the east. Watch for hawks or even eagles soaring on the air currents that rise up the mountain from Echo Lake. Eagles are rare in Maine away from the coast, but not unheard of in Aroostook State Park.

From the north summit you get fine views in every direction. Mostly you can see endless rolling hills either darkly forested or planted with potatoes. To the northeast, about 6 miles away, the rocky knob of Haystack Mountain is visible. Like Quaggy

▶ There are 123 species of butterflies that breed in Maine. Many are small, inconspicuous, and easily confused with moths. Some species, such as cabbage whites, are widespread and fly all summer; others, like the brown elfin, are restricted both by specific habitat needs and a short flying season. Still, you are likely to see at least a few butterflies on almost any hike. Don't just look for butterflies in flowery meadows; many species that live in Maine visit animal scat, mud puddles, open hilltops, and even shady spruce forests.

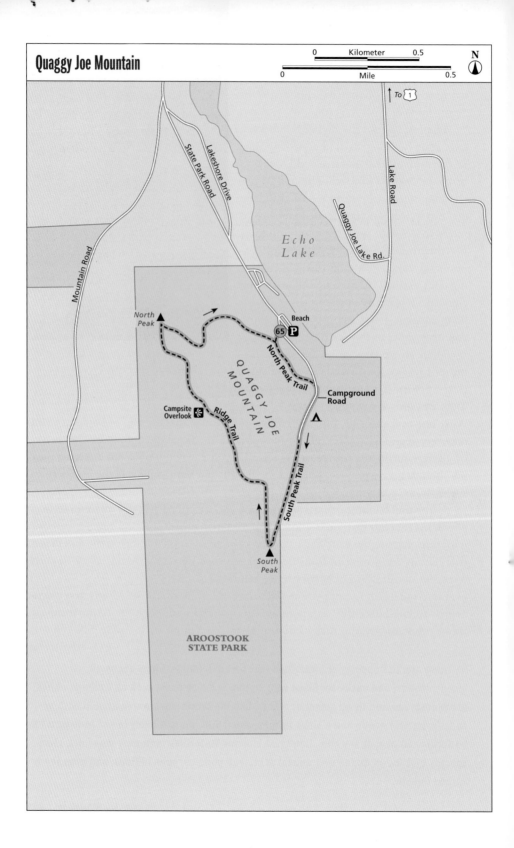

Quaggy Joe Mountain

0   Kilometer   0.5
0   Mile   0.5

N

To ①

State Park Road

Lakeshore Drive

Lake Road

Echo Lake

Quaggy Joe Lake Rd.

Mountain Road

North Peak

Beach

65 **P**

North Peak Trail

QUAGGY JOE MOUNTAIN

Campground Road

Campsite Overlook

Ridge Trail

South Peak Trail

South Peak

AROOSTOOK STATE PARK

Joe Mountain, Haystack is rhyolite. (There is a short, very steep trail to its summit, accessed from a small roadside park along ME 163.) To the west you can see the loose line of mountains in the Allagash Country. On a clear day it seems as if you could see all the way to Montreal. On the semi-open summit, between the overlooks, watch for butterflies hilltopping on sunny days. Often you'll see several different kinds of male butterflies bouncing around on the air above the rocks, all trying to attract females.

Miles and Directions

0.0 Start from the trailhead with the information sign at the west end of the parking area, away from the lake. In 200 feet cross the campground road where there is a water spigot. Climb to a junction with the North Peak Trail. Turn left toward the campground and playground.

0.2 The North Peak Trail ends at the campground road. To continue the hike, turn right and walk through the campground.

0.3 The South Peak Trail begins at campsite 18. Leave the campground on this trail.

0.6 The South Peak trail ascends very steeply to an open climb up crumbling rock. There are fine views east from the top of the climb.

0.7 Junction with the Ridge Trail. The South Ridge Trail continues another 100 feet to the wooded South Peak. Turn right onto the Ridge Trail toward North Peak.

1.3 The Ridge Trail descends to the saddle between Quaggy Joe Mountain's two summits. A ski trail comes in from the west. Continue straight ahead on the Ridge Trail.

1.5 The Ridge Trail passes a backcountry campsite at an overlook with views to the east.

1.6 The Ridge Trail ends at the North Peak Trail. Continue straight to reach North Peak.

1.7 On North Peak there are overlooks with views in each direction. To continue the hike, return to the junction with the Ridge Trail.

1.8 Arrive back at the junction. Turn left and descend on the North Peak Trail.

2.2 The North Peak Trail descends steeply at first, then more gradually to the junction with the trailhead trail. Turn left to return to the trailhead.

2.3 Arrive back at the trailhead.

Honorable Mention

○ Mattawamkeag Wilderness Park

The Mattawamkeag River drains a large area in southeastern Aroostook County; it is one of the Penobscot River's larger tributaries. A few miles upstream from the Penobscot River, the Mattawamkeag drops through Sleugundy Heater Gorge. Along this stretch of river is the Mattawamkeag Wilderness Park. There are 15 miles of hiking trails along the river, through wetlands, and in 1,000 acres of old-growth forest to the east of the river. You can visit Lower and Upper Gordon Falls or follow a moose through a boggy forest. The park, operated by the town of Mattawamkeag, has a campground and backcountry lean-tos so you can spend more than one day exploring. To get to Mattawamkeag Wilderness Park, take I-95 exit 227 (Lincoln) River Road to Lincoln. Turn left onto US 2 and drive through Lincoln. Continue north on US 2 for 12 miles to Mattawamkeag. In town turn right at the wilderness park sign onto Mattawamkeag Wilderness Park Road. The park is at the end of the road. Park facilities are open from May through September. For more information contact Mattawamkeag Wilderness Park, (207) 290-0205; www.mwpark.com.

Appendix A: Clubs and Organizations

Appalachian Mountain Club (AMC)
www.amcmaine.org
(207) 655-9097

Friends of Acadia
www.friendsofacadia.org
(207) 288-3340

Friends of Baxter State Park
www.friendsofbaxter.org

Maine Appalachian Trail Club (MATC)
www.matc.org

Maine Audubon
maineaudubon.org
(207) 781-2330

Maine Outdoor Adventure Club
(MOAC)
www.moac.org
(207) 775-6622

Appendix B: Maine Land Trusts

Bangor Land Trust
www.bangorlandtrust.org
(207) 942-1010

Blue Hill Heritage Trust
bluehillheritagetrust.org
(207) 374-5118

Boothbay Region Land Trust
www.bbrlt.org
(207) 633-4818

Downeast Coastal Conservancy
www.downeastcoastalconservancy.org
(207) 255-4500

Great Pond Mountain Conservation
Trust
greatpondtrust.org
(207) 469-7190

Harpswell Heritage Land Trust
http://hhltmaine.org
(207) 721-1121

Mahoosuc Land Trust
www.mahoosuc.org
(207) 824-3806

Maine Coast Heritage Trust
www.mcht.org
(207) 729-7366

Orono Land Trust
www.oronolandtrust.org
(207) 866-3104

Rangeley Lakes Heritage Trust
www.rlht.org
(207) 864-7311

The Nature Conservancy in Maine
www.nature.org/ouriniatives/maine
(207) 729-5181

For a comprehensive list of the land trusts in Maine with links to their websites, visit the Maine Land Trust Network, (207) 729-7366; http://mltn.org.

Hike Index

About the Author

Greg and his wife, Ann, live in Glenburn, Maine, with their two children, Henry and Emma. Greg grew up in Cincinnati and cut his hiking teeth in the Smoky Mountains and Kentucky's Red River Gorge. His family traveled all around the United States, exploring our country's national parks and wildlands. He's had the hiking bug ever since. Greg has worked as a carpenter, sous chef, college instructor, newspaper carrier, bookstore manager, and in a salmon cannery in Alaska. He has visited every state except Hawaii and most of the Canadian provinces.

Greg is a freelance writer and editor. He has published more than forty articles in newspapers and magazines. His work regularly appears in the *Bangor Daily News*'s "The Weekly." Mostly Greg writes about natural history, hiking, and other outdoor activities, but he has written stories on many subjects.

He is currently writing a book about backpacking with Henry from one end of Baxter State Park to the other. They completed the backpacking in six trips, walking out to Abol Bridge in the rain in July 2013. Greg is also completing his MFA from the University of Southern Maine.

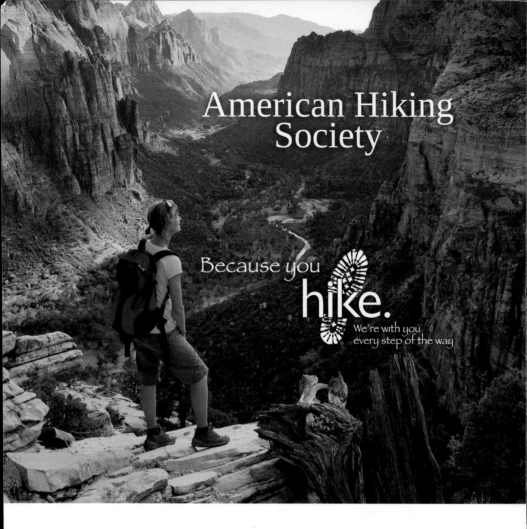

American Hiking Society

Because you **hike.**
We're with you every step of the way

As a national voice for hikers, **American Hiking Society** works every day:

- Building and maintaining hiking trails
- Educating and supporting hikers by providing information and resources
- Supporting hiking and trail organizations nationwide
- Speaking for hikers in the halls of Congress and with federal land managers

Whether you're a casual hiker or a seasoned backpacker, become a member of American Hiking Society and join the national hiking community! You'll enjoy great member benefits and help preserve the nation's hiking trails, so tomorrow's hike is even better than today's. We invite you to join us now!

American Hiking Society

www.AmericanHiking.org • info@AmericanHiking.org